CW01650332

Yorkshire's own kitchen

A guide to the best food and drink from Yorkshire and Humber

deliciouslyorkshire®

Acknowledgements

Our passionate Yorkshire chefs Rosemary Shrager, James Martin, Brian Turner, Andrew Pern, Stephanie Moon, James Mackenzie, Frances Atkins, Steve Smith; Yorkshire champion Alan Titchmarsh and all members and staff of the Regional Food Group.

Editor Jane Chamberlain; text Kindred; design and images Words&Pictures.

Published by the Regional Food Group for Yorkshire and Humber, Tadcaster, Yorkshire.

Printed and bound by Pindar on FSC stock using environmentally-friendly inks. A CIP catalogue record for this book is available from the British Library.

ISBN: 978-0-9556344-2-0

Contents

Foreword

Alan Titchmarsh

I was born in the farming country of the Yorkshire Dales and consider myself blessed to have grown up in a county rich and diverse in so many things: its people, places, sport, culture, heritage – and of course its glorious food and drink.

From Yorkshire puddings with roast beef and gravy to Whitby fish and chips, or tea with a fancy cake, the region is teeming with the very best produce served up by hard-working, ingenious folk, passionate about what they do.

The post-war years when I was a kid were not a time of plenty, but my mum always baked wonderful breads, buns and pies (I'm a bit of a pie man) and you could always tell what time of year it was by the fresh food on your plate – roots and cabbage in winter and blackcurrants, raspberries and strawberries in summer. The fresher the food, the better the flavour.

Throughout my career, I've always championed the benefits of local seasonal produce, whether its wearing my gardening hat and encouraging people how to 'grow your own', or bestowing my National Treasure awards on unsung food and drink heroes who bring us fantastic produce in traditional and sustainable ways that benefit the local economy.

I don't have a lot of time to cook myself, but I thoroughly enjoy it when I do. I also seem to be constantly surrounded by delicious dishes produced by the marvellous Rosemary Shrager – resident chef on my TV show – and my numerous other talented guests. One of my favourite recipes though is still my wife's clever fish pie made using cod, hard-boiled eggs, prawns and cheese sauce.

There's something really satisfying about growing, buying, cooking and eating out locally and I think it is partly to do with getting back in touch with yourself and your environment in a fast world where we often don't have time to catch our breath.

So put the kettle on, sit back and enjoy browsing this deliciouslyorkshire guide to food and drink in Yorkshire and Humber – there's passion in every page...

Find out more – and discover some mouth-watering recipes on pages 12-42 and at www.deliciouslyorkshire.co.uk

"There's something really satisfying about growing, buying, cooking and eating out locally"
Alan Titchmarsh
Buy local, think deliciouslyyorkshire

deliciouslyorkshire food

deliciouslyorkshire really is the name on everyone's lips! As more and more people turn to food with proven provenance, the Regional Food Group's campaigning brand is fast becoming the equivalent of a food and drink industry quality 'hallmark'.

You'll find the instantly recognisable black and green logo on the finest quality regional food in every supermarket, independent store, farm shop and delicatessen across the county that's worth its salt. You'll see it emblazoned on food marquees and cookery theatres at all the leading food events, festivals and agricultural shows.

It's our way of championing and celebrating delicious locally-sourced, lovingly-made food and our promise to you the customer that what you are buying is the authentic, pukka product with full traceability.

By buying deliciouslyorkshire food and drink, you can not only be confident that you are getting the finest produce on the market, you can also congratulate yourself on supporting the local economy, protecting the livelihoods of hardworking, dedicated producers and safeguarding the countryside and rural way of life that's such a valued part of our UK heritage. deliciouslyorkshire – lower case 'd', capital taste!

deliciouslyorkshire menu club

New for 2010 is the deliciouslyorkshire menu club which highlights places where you can be sure to be served great tasting food by members committed to using local produce and passionate about providing you with the freshest, tastiest ingredients.

It's an extension of the highly successful deliciouslyorkshire breakfast club, run in conjunction with Welcome to Yorkshire. A truly distinctive Yorkshire experience isn't complete without a full 'Yorkshire'.

The club has proved so popular that it has now been expanded to cover all menus, not just breakfast and allow especially distinguished cafes, tearooms and B&Bs to join the club.

Participating members' websites are highlighted on both the Welcome to Yorkshire website at www.yorkshire.com and the deliciouslyorkshire website at www.deliciouslyorkshire.co.uk – so you can eat the best of Yorkshire as well as visit it!

See deliciouslyorkshire menu members on p220.

deliciouslyorkshire awards

The annual deliciouslyorkshire awards, now in their sixth year, celebrate the very pinnacle of the food and drink sector in Yorkshire and Humber.

They beat the drum for outstanding local produce and driven deliciouslyorkshire members who continue to push the envelope of food and drink quality, value and innovation in the region.

Each year the number of entries goes up and the bar is raised even higher by passionate newcomers and their ingeniously delicious products. Winners of the coveted awards – traditionally held in November – consequently achieve considerable publicity: watch out for stories about them and their awards in your local and regional media.

You can also read about the winners of the 2009-2010 deliciouslyorkshire awards in this guide – they are each identified by the special awards logo.

www.deliciouslyorkshire.co.uk

"You can eat the best of Yorkshire as well as visit it!"

Uniquelyorkshire

This guide is packed with information about the very best food and drink to be had in a county renowned for the exceptional quality and diversity of its culinary offering. But some foods in Yorkshire and Humber are so distinctive that they warrant special protection. They have such a strong regional identity, produced using age old methods or ingredients exclusive to their place of origin, that they cannot be matched anywhere else in the world. These truly authentic foods are not only deliciouslyorkshire, they are uniquelyorkshire.

Four incomparable Yorkshire foods have now been awarded Protected Food Name (PFN) status by the European Union, which means they are legally registered and protected from imitation anywhere in Europe. Two more are going through the lengthy and robust application process as we go to print and may also be protected food names by the time you read this.

Traditional Grimsby Smoked Fish – Protected Geographical Indication (PGI)

In the 1930s when Grimsby was the biggest fishing port in the world, there were 80 companies smoking fish. Now only a small group of dedicated fish smokers – The Traditional Grimsby Fish Smokers Group – smoke cod and haddock in the authentic way, overnight in 100-year-old 10-metre high chimneys. The product of their labours has no artificial flavours or colourings and is a cream to beige colour with a distinctive flavour, a dry texture and a very appealing aroma.

Yorkshire Forced Rhubarb – Protected Designation of Origin (PDO)

There were once 200 growers of forced rhubarb in the famous Yorkshire rhubarb triangle between Wakefield, Leeds and Bradford. Now there are just 12 producing the sweet pink vegetable often thought of as a fruit. The roots live outside for two years before being lifted from the ground and taken into the dark

forcing sheds where heat is applied. The rhubarb grows quickly as it looks for light, and by the time it is harvested by candlelight it is tender, sweeter, more delicately flavoured and more brightly coloured than rhubarb grown outside.

Swaledale Cheese – Protected Designation of Origin (PDO)

The Swaledale Cheese Company was the first Yorkshire food producer to be accredited with a PFN for cheese made in the Dale that bears its name. Swaledale Cheese has been made in the area for centuries, with the recipe handed down from generation to generation but known only by a select few. It's a cylindrical shaped full-fat hard cheese, creamy off-white in colour and coated with a greeny blue-greyish mould. Hand-crumbed curds give a soft crumbly texture with a clean zesty flavour and nutty finish.

Swaledale Ewe's Cheese – Protected Designation of Origin (PDO)

Swaledale cheese was originally made with the milk of Swaledale sheep before dairy cows were introduced into the dale in the 17th century. It's a handmade, cylindrical, full-fat hard cheese like its cows' milk cousin, but has a slightly more 'gamey' flavour and a character of its own.

Yorkshire's PFN (Protected Food Name) foods-in-waiting are:

Real Yorkshire Wensleydale Cheese

The Wensleydale Creamery at Hawes has applied for a PFN to protect its creamy-white cheese which derives its distinctive flavour and texture from the skill and labour involved in the cheesemaking process, the unique bulk starter culture used at the creamery, and the character of the local milk due to the geology, flora and protected environmental status of the area.

Yorkshire Beer

Yorkshire is home to more than 80 breweries producing hundreds of varieties of real ale. The Society of Independent Brewers (SIBA) has now applied for a PFN for Yorkshire Beer to safeguard our rich brewing heritage.

Seasonality chart

Spring

Rhubarb...the vegetable that thinks it's a fruit...grown in Yorkshire's very own rhubarb triangle

Lamb...tender and flavoursome... great for roasting

Crab...very versatile... scrumptious seafood

Trout

Broccoli...steam or boil...look out for the purple sprouting variety

Spinach...at its most tenderest... a must for spring

Asparagus...only in season a short while...superior quality – especially from Yorkshire!

Summer

Strawberries...you can't beat in-season British strawberries

Raspberries...another summer treat...delicious

Courgettes...young and tender... low in calories

Radishes...crisp and crunchy... great in salads

Venison

Lettuce

Tomatoes

Herbs

Sloes

Apples/pears

Beetroot...best when fresh for its sweet, slightly earthy flavour

Autumn

Leeks...sophisticated flavour... great in soups and stews

Pears...a treat for autumn... plenty of variety

Apples...lots of varieties... spoilt for choice

Rabbit...best time to buy... subtle gamey flavour

Blackberries...pick your own... great for cold or hot puds

Outdoor pork

Pumpkins/squashes

Dover Sole

Mushrooms

Winter

Brussels Sprouts...synonymous with winter... and versatile

Venison... superior in quality... from deer naturally reared

Goose...rich, dark and flavoursome...a winner at Christmas

Turkey

Pheasant

Kale...fresh and green...and plentiful in winter

Recipes

Alan was born on the very edge of Ilkley Moor, Wharfedale. He's a passionate supporter of local seasonal produce – as he says, "there's something really satisfying about growing, buying, cooking and eating out locally."

Alan Titchmarsh

Lamb Cutlets Ilkley

INGREDIENTS

8 lamb cutlets
½ oz vegetable fat
4 ozs button mushrooms
4 tbsp redcurrant jelly
2 tbsp Worcester sauce
Juice of 1 lemon
1 level tbsp plain flour
¼ - ½ pt stock
Salt and freshly ground pepper
Pinch ground nutmeg
Chopped parsley

Serves 4

METHOD

1. Trim excess fat from cutlets. Heat fat in frying pan, brown cutlets on both sides in hot fat. Trim and slice mushrooms.
2. Remove cutlets from pan and place in casserole dish with mushrooms.
3. Measure redcurrant jelly and together with Worcester sauce and lemon juice add to a saucepan. Stir over low heat until jelly has melted and ingredients are blended. (Stirring with a whisk often helps redcurrant jelly to soften) Draw off the heat.
4. Add flour to hot fat remaining in frying pan and if necessary, add extra to help absorb the flour. Stir over low heat for about 10 minutes until a golden brown. Stir in jelly mix and then sufficient stock to make a thick gravy. Bring to boil stirring all the time to get smooth. Season with salt, pepper and nutmeg. Strain over cutlets.
5. Cover and place in a moderate to slow oven (325°f/170°c or gas 3) and cook for 1½ hours.
6. Sprinkle with parsley and serve.

"One of the many prides of Yorkshire has to be the wonderful cheeses, which is why I've picked this marvellously adaptable recipe for this year's guide. It uses Judy Bell's award-winning Yorkshire Blue which is perfect for a panna cotta because it's not too strong and is beautifully soft and creamy."

Rosemary Shrager

Yorkshire Blue Panna Cotta with Walnuts

INGREDIENTS

1 gelatine leaf
(or agar agar if vegetarian)
Juice of ½ lemon
125g Yorkshire Blue cheese
125g cream cheese
150ml whipping cream, whipped
Salt and pepper

For the dressing

4 tbsp walnut oil
2 tbsp extra virgin olive oil
2 tbsp red wine vinegar

For the garnish

Large handful mixed young salad leaves
20 walnut halves
Micro herbs

Serves 4

METHOD

1. Soak the gelatine for 15 minutes. In a small saucepan, heat the lemon juice and add the gelatine to the pan. Stir until melted.
2. Mash the cheeses with a fork till smooth, then fold in the whipped cream. Season with pepper and a little salt, then fold in the melted gelatine. Divide between 4 ramekins or dariole moulds and refrigerate for about 3 hours, or until set.
3. Whisk together the oils and vinegar until emulsified. Toast the walnuts in a dry pan. Just before serving, toss the salad in the dressing.
4. To serve, arrange the salad, herbs and walnuts on individual plates and turn out the panna cotta onto it.

"I've picked this lamb recipe because it's not at all difficult but it's a real pleaser. I always buy my lamb from the same butcher in Grassington because he's never let me down and I know that area of the Yorkshire Dales around Bolton Abbey has wonderfully rich pasture that produces really flavoursome lamb."

James Martin

Roast Cannon of Lamb with Braised White Bean and Herb Cassoulet

INGREDIENTS

4 cannons of lamb trimmed
300g soaked white beans
3 shallots peeled and diced
2 cloves garlic crushed
150ml white wine
1 litre vegetable stock
2 sticks of rosemary
1 leek, diced & washed
4 tomatoes, blanched, de-seeded & diced
600ml lamb stock reduced
2 dsp chopped chives
200g butter diced
salt & pepper
2 dsp olive oil

Pomme Puree

900g (2lb) large Maris Piper potatoes, peeled and quartered
100g (4oz) unsalted butter
120ml (4 fl oz) double cream
salt & pepper and freshly grated nutmeg

Serves 4

METHOD

1. Pre-heat the oven to 200°c.
2. In a thick based pan add a little oil and sweat off the shallots. Add the soaked beans and garlic and cook for 3-4 minutes. Add the wine, then the stock and cook over a gentle heat until the beans are tender. Remove from the heat, add the rosemary and allow to cool.
3. In a non-stick pan drizzle a little oil and place the seasoned lamb. Colour until golden brown. Add a few cubes of butter and baste the lamb. Place into the oven for 3-4 minutes or until medium rare.
4. Place the leeks into a pan with a little butter and fry, not allowing to colour, then add the beans and the reduced lamb jus. Gently bring to the boil, add the tomato and chives, season and set to one side.
5. Pipe the pomme puree (see recipe below) on one side of the plate, spoon some of the bean mix next to the mash, then slice the lamb and arrange on top of the bean mix. Spoon over the sauce and serve.

Pomme Puree

1. Boil the potatoes in salted water until cooked, approximately 20–25 minutes depending on size.
2. Drain off all the water, replace the lid and shake the pan vigorously to start to break up the boiled potatoes. Add the butter and single cream, a little at time, while mashing the potatoes.
3. Season with salt, pepper and some freshly grated nutmeg according to taste. The potatoes will now be light, fluffy, creamy and ready to eat.

"Yorkshire produce gets better and better as every year goes by. Just like rhubarb, Yorkshire products will soon be known as the best in the world."

Brian Turner

Rhubarb and Ginger Fool

INGREDIENTS

450g (1lb) Yorkshire forced rhubarb
55g (2oz) unsalted butter
55g (2oz) caster sugar
1 x 5cm (2in) piece fresh root ginger, peeled and cut in half
300ml (10fl oz) double cream
Icing sugar to taste

Serves 4

METHOD

1. Trim the rhubarb and cut it into 2.5cm (1 in) strips. Put into a pan, and add about 2 tbsp water. Add the butter, sugar and ginger, and slowly simmer away until cooked, about 10 minutes. Remove and discard the ginger, and allow the rhubarb to cool.
2. Take out a third of the rhubarb and drain through a sieve or colander, keeping the resulting juice. Put the juice on to the heat to reduce by about two-thirds, then cool.
3. Meanwhile, divide the drained rhubarb between four glasses.
4. Take the remaining rhubarb and purée in a blender or processor; do not make a fine purée, leave some texture.
5. Whip the cream to soft peaks – do not over-whip – then sweeten with icing sugar to taste. Fold in the rhubarb purée. Using a piping bag with a 1cm (½ in) nozzle, pipe the fool mixture in a circular fashion into each glass. Chill for 2 hours only.
6. Pour the reduced juice over the top of each glass, and serve.

The Pipe and Glass, South Dalton

"I developed the recipe when we first came to The Pipe & Glass, and I think it encompasses what we are all about I think this is a very northern inspired dish that looks fantastic on the plate. A lot of people are reluctant to order offal these days, but these devilled kidneys in an English mustard and breadcrumbs never return to the kitchen." **www.pipeandglass.co.uk**

James Mackenzie

Grilled Barnsley Chop with Devilled Kidneys, Nettle and Mint Sauce

INGREDIENTS

4 Barnsley Chops
A little chopped thyme
4 lamb kidneys
200ml whipping cream
2 tbsp strong English mustard
4 tbsp white breadcrumbs
Dash of brandy
1 tsp cayenne pepper
1 tsp chopped parsley
50g butter
4 tbsp nettles, picked, blanched and rough chopped
4 tbsp mint, roughly chopped
4 tbsp white wine vinegar
4 tbsp olive oil

Serves 4

METHOD

1. Season the lamb chops with salt, pepper and a little chopped thyme and place on a greased tray under a hot grill for about 10 minutes. Turn after 5 minutes and rest in a warm place.
2. For the devilled kidneys, slice the kidneys in half and cut out the fatty sinew. Heat a little oil in a frying pan and fry the kidneys for about 2 minutes until golden brown and just cooked. Take the kidneys out of the pan and on to an ovenproof dish. Deglaze the pan with a little brandy, add cream and mustard and reduce to sauce consistency and pour over the kidneys. Mix the crumbs, butter, parsley and cayenne together in a bowl and then sprinkle over the kidneys and grill until crumbs are golden brown.
3. To make the sauce, place the nettles, mint, white wine vinegar and olive oil in to a liquidiser and puree. Check the seasoning.
4. To serve place the chop on your plate with two half kidneys and serve with nettle sauce and boulangere potatoes.

The Yorke Arms, Ramsgill

Frances Atkins, chef proprietor of The Yorke Arms, is one of only six female Michelin-starred chefs in the UK and is a fellow of the Masterchefs of Great Britain. She uses fresh, seasonal, organic, local produce creating a real sensual pleasure with her ingredients. **www.yorke-arms.co.uk**

Frances Atkins

Bramley Apple & Olive Oil Cake

Serve with Spiced Apple Puree, Clotted Cream & Farmhouse Wensleydale Cheese

INGREDIENTS

120g (4 oz) sultanas
150ml olive oil
200g caster sugar
2 free range eggs
350g (12 oz) 00 flour
1tsp cinnamon
1½ tsp bicarbonate of soda
½ tsp cream of tartar
½ tsp sea salt
500g Bramley apples - grated
Grated rind of 1 organic lemon
200g walnuts
60g demerara sugar

Serves 4

METHOD

1. Soak the sultanas in warm water for 20 minutes or so.
2. Heat the oven to 180°c, gas 4.
3. Pour the oil into a bowl, add the sugar and beat until the sugar and oil become homogenised. Add the eggs, one at a time and beat until the mixture has grown in volume and looks like a thin mayonnaise.
4. Sieve the flour, cinnamon, bicarbonate of soda, cream of tartar and salt.
5. Add gradually to the oil and sugar mixture, folding them in with a metal spoon.
6. Mix thoroughly and then add the apples and the lemon rind.
7. Drain and dry the sultanas and add to mixture. Mix very thoroughly.
8. The mixture will be stiff, with the appearance of apple and sultanas coated in cake mixture.
9. Butter and flour a 20cm (8 inch) spring clip tin. Spoon the mixture into the tin. Chop the walnuts and mix with demerara sugar – sprinkle over the top of the cake. Bake for at least 1 hour, until spongy & light.
10. Remove the cake from the tin and cool on a wire rack.

Apple puree

1. Wash a couple of Bramley apples thoroughly and core. Add 200g of sugar and a little grated nutmeg. Add 1 tbsp of water and cook. Put through a food processor, sieve, cool and serve while still warm with the cake and Wensleydale Cheese.

The Star Inn, Harome

Michelin-starred chef Andrew Pern says of his Yorkshire recipe: "A plate of six separate components, from Paul Talling's ducks, reared just outside Harome, all that is except the foie gras which comes from further afield, and some of the eggs from Sim and Josie Barker's farm, Aby Green, round the corner from the pub, down past the duck pond.

Andrew Pern

A Plate of Harome-reared 'Loose Birds' Duck with Garden Lemon Thyme Mash and Traditional Yorkshire Sauce

INGREDIENTS

4 duck legs
1 ltr duck fat
2 duck breasts
200ml red wine
4 duck eggs
100g redcurrant jelly
300g duck foie gras
150g sugar
4 duck chipolatas
500g mashed potato
10g lemon thyme
100g butter
1 orange
100ml cream
1 bay leaf
A little white wine vinegar
1 star anise
100ml duck jus

Serves 4

METHOD

1. Confit the duck legs in the duck fat with the star anise and bay leaf in an oven for 2½ hours at 140°c. For the Yorkshire sauce - peel the orange and cut the peel into julienne strips removing all the white. Place in a pan with the red wine, sugar and redcurrant jelly. Juice the left-over orange and add to the pan as well. Reduce until it becomes syrup, and add the duck jus.
2. Once the duck legs have cooled down, split the thigh and the drumstick, then put onto a baking tray. Boil the potatoes, drain and mash. Reduce 100g of butter and 100ml cream by half and add to the mash. Season. Add the lemon thyme leaves and keep warm. Grill the chipolatas until just cooked and put on the baking tray with the leg and thigh.
3. Pan-fry the duck breasts until the skin is crispy but still there. Place on the tray and then in a preheated oven at 190°c for 5 minutes.
4. Meanwhile, reheat the mash and put into a piping bag, poach the duck eggs in simmering water with a little white wine vinegar for about 3 minutes, keep warm. Pan-fry the foie gras until it becomes spongy. Pipe 5 turrets of mash around the outside of the plate and 1 in the centre. Place each ingredient on one of the mashed potato turrets, slice and save the duck breast for the centre of the plate, drizzle the Yorkshire sauce around and over the dish ingredients.
Serve immediately.

The Devonshire Arms, Bolton Abbey
Steve Smith is head chef at the Devonshire Arms, overseeing the Michelin-starred Burlington Restaurant. Steve says: "I have a great line-up of talented chefs who have been very responsive to my demands and the Michelin star is just reward for their commitment. We are also very fortunate to have wonderful local produce and suppliers right on our doorstep." **www.thedevonshirearms.co.uk**

Steve Smith

Apple Pie Mousse, Blackberry Jelly and Apple Sorbet

INGREDIENTS

Apple Pie Mousse
400ml double cream
4 egg yolks
80g caster sugar
90g apple puree
3 gelatine leaves
400ml double cream (semi-whipped)

Blackberry Jelly
1ltr blackberry puree
400ml water
14g agar agar

Granny Smith Apple Jelly
250ml apple puree
250ml apple juice
5g agar agar

Apple Sorbet
1ltr apple boiron puree
1ltr apple juice
600g caster sugar
200g trimoline
10 drops granny smith flavouring
3 drops lime green food colouring
Serves 4

METHOD

Apple Pie Mousse
1. Whisk eggs and sugar, bring cream to the boil, pour over eggs
2. Cook through
3. Add gelatine and puree, allow to cool but not set
4. Fold in cream
5. Allow to set
6. Pipe into cylinders and tie.

Blackberry Jelly
1. Whisk ingredients into a pan, allow to stand for 10 minutes
2. Bring to a boil
3. Pour equal amounts into trays and allow to set.

Granny Smith Apple Jelly
1. Warm apple puree and apple juice, pass
2. Allow to cool, add agar agar
3. Bring to the boil, add flavouring and colouring
4. Set in bread loaf tin
5. Cut into 1cm cubes.

Apple Sorbet
1. Bring apple juice, sugar and trimoline to a boil
2. Pour over boiron, whisk, pass
3. Allow to completely cool, add drops
4. Churn.

Renowned chef Stephanie Moon is deliciouslyorkshire's food and drink champion and works closely with us to encourage more use of the fantastic range of delicious home grown goodies on offer from the region. You can see Stephanie at many of the county's shows and festivals taking part in cookery demonstrations and hosting workshops, as well as helping to judge our annual awards which showcase the very best from the region. Practising what she preaches in this recipe, Stephanie uses fruit from Spillman's farm near York in her tribute to Yorkshire strawberries.

Assiette of Strawberries

INGREDIENTS

Strawberry Shortcake
2 punnets of local strawberries washed, hulled and sliced
250g plain flour
250g unsalted butter
125g corn flour
125g sugar

Chantilly Cream
1 pint double cream
Seeds scraped out from 1 large vanilla pod
100g caster sugar

Serves 4

METHOD

Strawberry Shortcake

1. Sieve the plain flour. Add the remainder of the dry ingredients and then add the butter. Mix together until it forms a paste, do not over mix.
2. Roll out on a dusted floured work surface and cut out into discs. You will need 3 discs for each dessert.
3. Chill for 10 minutes then bake at 170°c for approximately 10 minutes until cooked.

Chantilly Cream

1. Whip the cream, caster sugar and vanilla in a bowl until stiff and then place the mixture in a piping bag,

To assemble the dish

1. Place a blob of cream in the centre of each plate and place a disc of shortbread on top.
2. Swirl the Chantilly cream over the disc and then placed the sliced strawberries on the top and repeat this process for the next layer.
3. Finally place a disc of shortbread on the top with a final swirl of cream and half a strawberry and a sprig of mint to garnish.
4. Serve with vanilla ice-cream.

Stephanie Moon

Strawberry Soup

600g of Sessay strawberries, washed, hulled and pureed
250ml of water
250ml caster sugar
150ml local natural yoghurt (I use yoghurt from Whixley near York)
A few mint leaves for garnishing

Strawberry, Gooseberry and Elderflower Syllabub

80g fresh gooseberries
40g strawberries
50ml gooseberry and elderflower jam (I use local company, Rosebud Preserves)
½ pint double cream, softly whipped
200ml sweet white wine
80g plus 80g caster sugar
Zest of one lemon
1 vanilla pod

Strawberry Soup

1. Put 250 ml of water and 250 ml caster sugar in a pan and boil until all the sugar has dissolved. Pour over the strawberries immediately.
2. Blend together with the yoghurt using a small stick blender and pass through a sieve.
3. Serve chilled with a mint leaf to garnish.

Syllabub

1. Place the fruit in a small pan with 80g caster sugar and cook until stewed and soft.
2. Place most of this in the base of four martini glasses and allow to cool, reserve a little to put in the syllabub.
3. Add 200 ml white wine to the other 80 g caster sugar, split the vanilla pod and add the seeds (if the vanilla pod is large only use ½ and put the rest in a jar of sugar to make vanilla sugar).
4. Add the gooseberry and elderflower jam, double cream, lemon zest and the remainder of the fresh gooseberry mix. Whisk this until stiff and pipe into the glasses.
5. Set in the fridge for ½ hour and serve with some shortbread biscuits or cookies.

As Yorkshire Life Magazine's Food & Drink consultant, Annie gets out and about across Yorkshire picking up ideas for great recipes and food features. Whitby is one of her favourite coastal spots and the inspiration for this classic recipe. "A classic way to serve crab – simple and delicious," says Annie. **www.yorkshire.greatbritishlife.co.uk** for more recipes and restaurant reviews.

Annie Stirk

Annie Stirk's Dressed Whitby Crab

Allow 1 dressed crab per 2 people

INGREDIENTS

1-2 cooked crabs will give sufficient white and brown crab meat for this recipe
150ml mayonnaise
50g brown breadcrumbs
1 tsp Dijon mustard
Salt & freshly ground black pepper
2 hard boiled eggs – yolks and white separated and chopped finely
2 tbsp freshly chopped parsley

Serves 2

METHOD

1. Mix the prepared flaked white crab meat with the mayonnaise and season.
2. Mix the dark crab meat with the breadcrumbs and mustard.
3. Separate the cooked egg white from the yolk.
4. Finely chop the egg white and the yolk, keeping them both separate.
5. Spread the dark crab meat into the base of the cleaned crab shells.
6. Spread the flaked white crab meat onto the top of the dark meat.
7. Sprinkle the chopped egg white on one side of the crab shell and the chopped egg yolk at the other side.
8. Finish off with plenty of chopped parsley in the centre.
9. Serve with crusty bread and wedges of lemon or lime.

I cooked this dish for my Radio 2 piece on the Simon Mayo show as I wanted to highlight great British ingredients as used by a very talented Yorkshire chef. Andy Barber is creating great things in the kitchen at The Forge, Covent Garden, but started out as a pot washer at Uncle Sam's in Sheffield. The key thing is to make sure that the skate is sustainable (or ray, as most of it actually is - same family), so therefore try to use spotted, cuckoo and starry.

Nigel Barden

Nigel Barden's Skate Wing & Razor Clams baked in a paper bag

INGREDIENTS

1 filleted skate wing 400-500g (cut into 2 pieces)
4 razor clams medium size
1 shallot chopped finely
½ clove crushed garlic
1 tsp chopped chilli
100ml white wine
100g butter
1 tbsp chopped flat leaf parsley
2 wedges of lemon
100g baby mixed leaf salad
Salt & pepper
50ml vegetable oil
2 pieces of silicone baking parchment 50cm x 25cm (silicone is easily available and doesn't char)
1 tbsp of whisked egg white

Serves 4

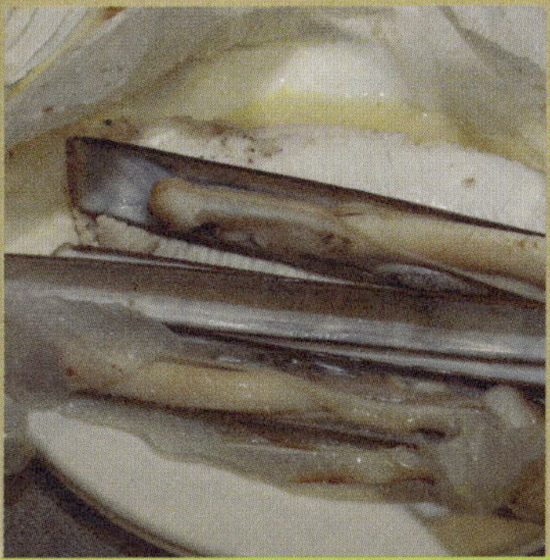

METHOD

To create one paper bag parcel per person:

1. Fold the piece of baking parchment in half lengthways.
2. Unfold it and on the left hand side in the centre rub with butter and a drizzle of olive oil, sprinkle half of the shallots, chilli, garlic & parsley onto the butter.
3. Place a piece of skate on top of the butter, season with salt and pepper.
4. Distribute the clams equally.
5. Drizzle 50ml of white wine and the juice of one lemon wedge.
6. Brush the outer edges of the parcel with egg white and fold over to create a parcel, then twist and press the edges down until a seal is formed.
7. Place in the fridge until required.

To serve

1. Preheat oven to 180°c.
2. Place a frying pan or skillet onto a medium heat and drizzle a teaspoon of vegetable oil into the pan.
3. Place the parcel into the pan and wait until it puffs up (approx 1 min).
4. Then remove from heat and place in the oven for 8 minutes.
5. While cooking assemble your salad and dress with a light herb vinaigrette of your choice (tarragon is great).
6. Remove the parcel from the oven and serve immediately on a warm plate.

Serve with a glass of chilled Riesling.

Nigel Barden, deliciouslyorkshire awards judge and compère

Artisan, Hessle

This is a simple dessert recipe that can be prepared well in advance for dinner party entertaining, says chef Richard Johns who runs **Artisan** with his wife Lindsay. The restaurant is North East of England Restaurant of the Year in the Which? Good Food Guide 2011 **www.artisanrestaurant.com**

White Chocolate Pot with Raspberry Jelly and Raspberry Sorbet

INGREDIENTS

400g best quality white chocolate
450ml whipping cream
Zest of one orange
I vanilla pod
2 egg yolks
700g fresh raspberries
Squeeze of lemon juice
50ml raspberry liquor (optional)
1 leaf gelatine
400ml cold stock syrup (300g of caster sugar, 25g glucose, 400ml water, boiled together for five minutes)

Serves 6

METHOD

For the pots

1. Place the cream, zest and vanilla pod (deseeded) into a pan. Bring to boil and infuse for 30 minutes. Melt white chocolate and then add yolks. Bring cream back to simmer, add to chocolate, mixing well. Pass through a sieve into a jug. Pour into six shot style glasses and fill, stopping around 6mm from the top of glass. Cool to room temperature, then place in fridge.

Raspberry sorbet

1. Puree raspberries and pass through sieve. Measure out 600g of puree, reserving the rest. Add around 300mls of stock syrup to puree. Add raspberry liquor to taste, along with a squeeze of lemon. Rest in fridge for a couple of hours, then churn in ice cream maker. Place in freezer.

Raspberry jelly

1. Soften gelatine in a little cold water. Heat up remaining puree with around 50ml of stock syrup. Squeeze out gelatine, add to raspberry puree. Leave to cool, mixing regularly. When nearly setting, top chocolate pots with jelly, return to fridge to set.
2. To serve, place chocolate pot on plate and decorate with raspberry sauce, optional caramel springs (practice required!) and fresh raspberries. Place sorbet on plate and serve.

Richard Johns

The Black Swan at Oldstead, York
Named a Michelin 'Rising Star' for 2010, The Black Swan is owned by the Banks family who have farmed at Oldstead for generations. Celebrating Yorkshire's finest meat and seafood, this dish tastes as good as it looks!
www.blackswanoldstead.co.uk

Belly of Old Spot Pork with Seared King Scallops, Dressed Baby Fennel and French Onion Puree

INGREDIENTS

2 pints of chicken stock
½ a pork belly (deboned)
4 onions
2 carrots
2 sticks of celery
1 bulb of garlic
1 bunch of thyme
2 bulbs of baby fennel
12 hand-dived King Scallops (shells & corals removed)
Selection of herbs for garnish
Wharfe Valley rapeseed oil

Serves 4

METHOD

1. The day before, place the belly pork in a large oven-proof tray with a sprig of thyme, half a bulb of garlic (peeled), one onion and roughly chopped carrots and celery. Add chicken stock, bring to the boil on stove top, cover with foil and place in a medium oven for 4 hours.
2. Once cooked, place on a flat tray topped with another flat tray and place a heavy weight on top before leaving in a fridge overnight.
3. When chilled, remove skin, keeping as much of the fat as possible. Cut into 4 portions and return to the fridge.
4. Slice the onions, crush garlic and chop the thyme. Cook together slowly in a heavy-based pan until golden brown and the liquid has evaporated. Blend until smooth and pass through a fine sieve.
5. Blanch the fennel in boiling water for 2 minutes then refresh in ice-cold water. Cut into small pieces and dress in rapeseed oil, lemon juice, salt and pepper.
6. Pick the garnishing herbs from their stalks and leave them in iced water.
7. Heat a non-stick frying pan with rapeseed oil until smoking hot and place the belly pork in skin side down. Put in the oven for 8-10 minutes.
8. Gently warm the onion puree in one saucepan and the fennel and dressing in another.
9. Sear scallops in hot frying pan with foaming butter for 1½ minutes on each side. Remove and rest on absorbent cloth.
10. Spoon the onion puree onto the plate, place the belly pork skin side up and garnish with warm fennel, scallops, chopped tomato and herbs – serve immediately.

Adam Jackson

Lakeside Restaurant at Chevin Country Park Hotel & Spa, Otley
Chef Debbie Rhodes says of this dish: "Beautifully tender and always impressive, the saddle is made up of two loins, it's the ultimate lamb roast easy to cook and elegant to present. With a fruity apricot and fragrant rosemary stuffing it is a taste of the Far East as well as traditionally British all at the same time."
www.crerarhotels.com

CHEVIN COUNTRY PARK HOTEL
& SPA, OTLEY
Lakeside Restaurant

Oven roasted saddle of lamb with rosemary & apricot farce served with roasted honey parsnip, minted sweet potato mash and redcurrant sauce

INGREDIENTS

For the lamb
1kg saddle of lamb, skinned and boned
2 tbsp cumin seeds
Sea salt & freshly ground black pepper
Olive oil for cooking

For the farce
150g dried apricots, soaked in warm water overnight
30g pine nuts
25g fresh breadcrumbs
3g fresh rosemary
1tbsp olive oil

Serves 4

METHOD

1. Trim off the excess fillets at both ends of the saddle so that you can roll the lamb into a neat log.Toast the cumin seeds, then, coarsely grind with salt and pepper and rub half of it over the lamb.
2. For the farce, finely chop apricots and pine nuts, tip into a bowl, stir in breadcrumbs and rosemary, olive oil and the rest of cumin, salt and pepper.
3. Lay the lamb on a large sheet of cling film and open out like a butterfly. Season and pile the farce in a neat row along the centre. Fold the sides over the stuffing and wrap the parcel to form a tight log and chill for an hour to slightly set the shape.
4. Heat the oven to 180°c/gas 4. Remove the cling film from the lamb and tie the log with kitchen string at 2-3cm intervals. Heat a little olive oil in an ovenproof frying pan until hot, seal the saddle for 3-4 minutes on each side until browned, transfer to the oven, roast for 35-40 minutes turning and basting the lamb halfway through cooking. It should feel slightly springy when pressed and the meat should be pink in the centre – rest for 10-15 minutes.
5. Slice the lamb thickly and serve with honey roasted parsnips, minted sweet potato mash and redcurrant sauce.

The Coach House, Flamingoland
This recipe from head chef Mark Stanley at Flamingoland's Coach House restaurant is a tribute to the region's finest pork: wonderfully moist, tender pork loin, fillet and terrine, served with crisp Yorkshire apples and a sherry vinegar and port jus. **www.flamingoland.co.uk**

A Show of Yorkshire Pork

INGREDIENTS

800g pork loin
2 x 200g pork fillets
100g flour
100g polenta
1 egg
Handful of basil

150g apples, peeled, cored and cut into cubes
Juice of half of lime

For the terrine
250g diced pork
200g belly pork minced or chopped
250g diced black pudding
1 egg
10 sage leaves, chopped
5g flat-leafed parsley, chopped

For the sauce
7ml sherry vinegar
50ml port
500ml veal or chicken stock
2 shallots & 100ml red wine

Serves 6

METHOD

1. Preheat your oven (250°c, gas 9) and put in an oiled baking tray to get hot. Season the loin with salt and pepper and place onto your heated tray and roast for 15-20 minutes. Then, turn the heat down to 180°c and roast for approx 25 minutes per 450g until cooked through.
2. Cut your fillets in half crossways and season well. Roll in flour, egg and polenta. Heat one tbsp of oil in a frying pan and fry the meat for 2-3 minutes until browned. Then roast for 15 minutes until cooked through.
3. Make the terrine filling by dicing up the pork, add the egg. Place in a food processor and purée. Place in a bowl and add the belly pork, black pudding, button onions, sage and parsley. Gently fold in and season well.
4. Roll in cling film and tin foil. Place the terrine in a large deep roasting pan and place in the oven. Carefully pour in hot water around the terrine until half way up the terrine. Bake for 50 minutes-1 hour until cooked through.
5. Melt butter and sauté the apples. Add a touch of lime juice and warm for another few minutes.

For the sauce

1. Sauté the shallots, add the vinegar until it's almost evaporated. Add the port, reduce to half, add red wine and reduce by half again. Add the chicken stock and simmer for 1 hour, strain and adjust the seasoning.
2. Best served with butternut squash purée, seasonal Yorkshire vegetables and creamed potatoes.

Mark Stanley

The General Tarleton Inn, Ferrensby
Menus at the General Tarleton, run by John and Claire Topham, change daily to reflect the seasons and the pick of the catch or crop that day. They strive to obtain the very best seasonable produce, supporting a network of excellent regional suppliers. The classic combination of pork and apple make this dish a celebration of the region's finest ingredients.
www.generaltarleton.co.uk

Pot Roast Belly Pork Braised in Ampleforth Abbey Cider

INGREDIENTS

1.2 kilo belly pork stripped of skin and bones
1 heaped tbsp fennel seeds toasted
Zest 1 lemon
Bunch of sage
Bunch of thyme
1 pint Ampleforth Cider

2 red onions
2 white onions
1 bulb garlic
4 large carrots
1 butternut squash
½ of a celeriac
Sprinkling of thyme
Sprinkling of sage
3 tbsp local rapeseed oil
salt, pepper and pinch sugar

Serves 6

METHOD

1. Lie the belly pork (meat side up) on a chopping board, spread the fennel seeds, zest of a lemon, thyme and sage evenly over the meat, season with salt and pepper, roll up tightly and tie with string.
2. Place in a roasting pan and cook in a pre-heated oven at 190°c for 30 minutes.
3. Turn the oven down to 160°c and pour the cider into the roasting pan.
4. Roast for a further 2 hours. Remove from oven and keep in a warm place to rest for 10 minutes before carving.
5. While the pork is cooking, prepare the roast roots – peel and chop the vegetables into similar sized chunks.
6. Place in a roasting tin, toss with the rapeseed oil, season with the salt, pepper and sugar and roast for 45 minutes until tender and lightly caramelised.
7. Portion the vegetables placing the carved pork on top and drizzle with the braising juices.

Lightwater Shopping Village, Ripon
With a great range of locally-sourced meals and snacks, including a mouth-watering Sunday carvery and a sinful range of homemade cakes, why not take a fresh look at The Granary Restaurant at Lightwater Shopping Village.
www.lightwatervalley.co.uk

the granary
Restaurant and Coffee Shop

Beef and Black Sheep Ale Pie

INGREDIENTS

2.5kg diced chuck steak
2 onions
1.5 pints Black Sheep ale
Splash Worcestershire sauce
Mixed herbs and
salt & pepper to taste
Gravy thickener, water

For the puff pastry top

250g plain flour
1 tsp salt
250g butter (room temp)
150ml cold water

Serves 12

METHOD

For the pastry

1. Sift the flour and salt into a large bowl, roughly break the butter into small chunks, add to the bowl and rub in loosely. Make a well in the bowl, pour in 2/3 of the cold water and mix until you have a firm dough (add extra water if needed). Cover with cling film and leave to rest in the fridge for 20 minutes.
2. Turn out onto a lightly floured board, knead gently and form into a smooth rectangle. Roll the dough in one direction only until about 20 x 50cm, then fold one half over the other and roll out again. Fold again and cover with clingfilm for 20 minutes before rolling out.

For the filling

1. Marinate the chuck steak in Black Sheep ale (preferably overnight).
2. Fry off the onions and meat (to seal).
3. Add enough water to just cover the meat.
4. Add the Worcestershire sauce, herbs and seasoning.
5. Bring to boil then reduce heat and simmer for approx one hour (or until meat is tender).
6. Add gravy thickener (plus more seasoning if required) and bring back to the boil.
7. Place in individual dishes, add a puff pastry top and cook in the oven at 190°c for 20-25 minutes or until golden brown.

Clocktower Restaurant, Rudding Park, Harrogate
These burgers appear on the menu at Clocktower accompanied by real chips, onion rings in Black Sheep beer batter, red onion marmalade and a side salad – a real Yorkshire winner! **www.ruddingpark.co.uk**

Rudding Park

Clocktower Burger With Beer Battered Onion Rings and Chunky Chips

INGREDIENTS

600g organic minced beef (Rudding Park use Adrian Procter, Far Cappleside Farm)
1 tsp Worcestershire sauce
2 shallots, peeled and finely chopped
4 mini gherkins (or ½ a large one), finely chopped
2 tsp capers
1 heaped tbsp tomato ketchup
4 x sesame bread bun
Mixed salad leaves
4 rashers bacon (Rudding uses Sykes House Farm)
400g Wensleydale cheese

For the onion rings

1 x onion, cut into rings, use approximately three large rings per person
200g self raising flour
1 x bottle Black Sheep Beer
Pinch of salt

For the marmalade

3 large red onions, peeled and sliced into thin half moon pieces
½ bottle of red wine
3 tbsp soft brown sugar
2 tbsp red wine vinegar
4 sprigs finely chopped thyme (leaves only)
2 tbsp olive oil for frying

Serves 4

METHOD

1. To make the marmalade, fry the onions until they start to soften. Add the red wine vinegar, red wine, sugar and thyme. Continue to boil until the onions have a rich sheen and are deep red in colour. Season with a little salt and pepper.
2. For the onion rings, mix the flour with enough Black Sheep beer to form a thick batter consistency and add a pinch of salt. Dust the rings of onion with flour before putting them into the batter. Plunge the onion rings into the deep fat fryer and cook until golden and crispy.
3. To make the burgers, mix all the ingredients in a bowl and season well. Form four burgers, and heat some vegetable oil in a frying pan. Place the burgers in the pan and cook for approximately 2 minutes on each side over a moderate heat until golden brown. Once brown on both sides, place in the oven at 180°c for 6 minutes.
4. Cook the bacon under a grill until cooked but not crispy, then melt the Wensleydale cheese on top of the burger under the grill.

Serve with Maris Piper chunky chips and enjoy!

Jerome Gaudre

The Bull, Broughton
Comfort food at its best, this signature dish from The Bull is sure to be a family favourite.
www.thebullatbroughton.co.uk

The Bull Fish Pie, Baked with Mashed Potato, sprinkled with Wensleydale Cheese

INGREDIENTS

240g salmon – diced
120g coley – diced
120g haddock - diced
120g raw prawns
1 leek – halved and sliced thinly

For the sauce

50g butter
55g plain flour
250ml milk
250ml cream
5 drops lemon juice
Salt & pepper to taste
Chopped parsley

For the mash

1 kg potatoes
100ml milk
20g butter
Handful of grated Wensleydale cheese

Serves 4

METHOD

1. Warm the milk and cream together.
2. Make a roux with the flour and the butter.
3. Slowly add the warm milk and keep whisking so there are no lumps, season to taste and add the lemon and parsley then remove from the heat.
4. At the pub we lightly steam the diced fish first and then place into the dish. If you don't have a steamer place the fish in an earthenware dish and add a splash of white wine, cover in tinfoil and bake for 6 minutes in a hot oven.
5. Sweat off the leeks in butter.
6. Add all the juice from the fish and leeks to the veloute and season.
7. Cut the potatoes into equal pieces then place into a pan of salted water.
8. Bring to the boil and then simmer gently until the potatoes are soft.
9. Strain off all the water put back into the pan and return to the heat. Mash well allowing the excess steam to escape
10. Mix in the salt, pepper, milk and butter and check the seasoning.

To assemble

1. In a earthenware dish place the portion of cooked fish and leeks.
2. Cover with the veloute sauce and allow to cool slightly.
3. Then pipe over the top with mash potato.
4. Sprinkle with Wensleydale cheese.
5. Cook for 30 minutes in a pre-heated oven at 180°c.

Richard Upton

The Butchers Arms, Hepworth

Tim is the award-winning chef proprietor of one of Yorkshire's best-loved dining pubs, The Butchers Arms at Hepworth (and recently The Kaye Arms at Grange Moor), and has built an enviable reputation for good, honest, local food. Standing true to his roots, this year he celebrated the best of Yorkshire food when he competed in BBC2's Great British Menu.

www.thebutchersarmshepworth.co.uk

THE BUTCHERS ARMS HEPWORTH

Warm Salad of Smoked Corn Fed local Chicken with Asparagus and Quails Eggs on a Field Mushroom

INGREDIENTS

4 field mushrooms
Rapeseed oil
A sprig of fresh thyme
Salt and freshly ground black pepper
60g butter
8 spears of local asparagus
A handful of mixed baby leaf salad
4 tbsp Womersley Blackcurrant and Rosemary Vinegar
300g prepared smoked chicken, cut into small pieces
8 softly boiled quails eggs, peeled and halved
4 rashers of pancetta – cooked until crispy

METHOD

1. Place the mushrooms on a baking tray, drizzle with a little oil, sprinkle with a few thyme leaves, salt and pepper and place a knob of butter in the centre of each mushroom. Bake at 180°c/gas 4 for approximately 10 minutes.
2. Prepare and trim the asparagus. Place in a roasting tin, sprinkle with salt and pepper and a drizzle of rapeseed oil. Roast at 180°c/gas4 for approximately 10 minutes, or until the stems are tender.
3. Dress the salad leaves in a bowl with a little of the Womersley vinegar and divide between 4 serving plates.
4. Sit the baked mushrooms on top of the salad, add the pieces of smoked chicken and roasted asparagus.
5. Scatter the halved soft boiled quails eggs in and around the dish to garnish.
6. Finish with a jauntily placed piece of crispy pancetta.

Serves 4

Tim Bilton

The Hare Inn, Scawton.
The Hare Inn's business partners Geoff and Jan Smith are committed to using local, seasonal produce wherever possible on the menus at their ancient and much-cherished 13th century dining inn. They say: "With quality seasonal ingredients provided by local suppliers, this dish is simple, clean and delicious!" **www.thehareinnn.co.uk**

THE HARE INN

Fillet of Whitby Seabass with Pickering watercress sauce and Sandhutton asparagus

INGREDIENTS

1/2 pint of double cream
4 fillets of Seabass
4 bunches of fresh Pickering watercress
16 stems of Sandhutton asparagus

Serves 4

METHOD

1. Remove stalks from the watercress and blanche in boiling salted water, remove and drain the puree in a food processor.
2. Place this sauce in a heavy based saucepan, add the cream and stir until smooth, season to taste.
3. Place the fish in a frying pan with knob of butter and cook gently.
4. Grill the asparagus with a sprinkling of sea salt and a splash of olive oil.
5. Place the Seabass in centre of plate, pour sauce around and place asparagus on top.

Enjoy!

The Magpie Café, Whitby
A British classic, fresh from Yorkshire's fine fishing ground – Whitby. Serve with your favourite accompaniment for the ultimate Yorkshire feast!
www.magpiecafe.co.uk

Traditional Fish and Chips

INGREDIENTS

4 fillets of fresh Whitby Haddock 200g each
2kg Maris Piper or King Edward potatoes
Beef dripping for cooking

For the Batter

500g plain flour
200g self raising flour
Half a tsp of baking powder
Approx 1 litre of chilled water (you may need a little more or less as flours can absorb differently)

Serves 4

METHOD

1. Firstly make the batter by sieving the flour into a bowl, add the baking powder then gradually add the water, whisking continuously to avoid any lumps. The batter should be the consistency of single cream (too thick and the batter will be crisp on the outside yet stodgy on the inside) – place in the fridge to chill.
2. Slowly heat the dripping to approx 150°c in a large pan (the dripping should come no more than half-way up the pan)
3. Peel and cut the potatoes into thick chips (the thicker the better as thicker chips absorb less fat), rinse and pat dry. Carefully add the chips to the fat and cook until soft but still slightly firm, remove and cool slightly.
4. Turn up the heat to 175°c, take the fillets of fish one at a time, dip them into the batter and gently lay them into the dripping. These should take about 7-8 minutes to cook and the batter should look light, golden and crispy. Remove and place onto kitchen paper to drain, next place the chips into the hot fat and cook until crisp.
5. Serve with your favourite accompaniments and enjoy!

The Old Farmhouse Restaurant
at Hinchliffes Farm Shop, Huddersfield
Chef Richard Greenway says: "This is a recipe I love to make for my family and friends at home. It's a really nice dish that allows for great interaction at the dinner table, allowing your family or guests the pleasure of digging in to a centrepiece dish of stunning quality." **www.oldfarmhouserestaurant.com**

Roasted Rib Eye beef with a pie of sautéed cabbage, morel mushrooms, onions, garlic and blue cheese

INGREDIENTS

4 thick cut Hinchliffes rib-eye steaks 2-3 inch in thickness - room temperature
Outer leaves of 1 Savoy cabbage
1 white onion
2 cloves of garlic
8 pre-cooked new potatoes
75g Yorkshire Blue cheese
225g button or chestnut mushrooms
1 beaten egg
200g of ready made puff pastry
Butter and olive oil

Serves 4

METHOD

1. Slice the pre-cooked new potatoes in half, wash and then slice the cabbage into strips, slice the mushrooms as thick as you like, half and slice the onion and cut the garlic roughly into large pieces.
2. Heat a non-stick frying pan over a medium heat with a little olive oil and add the sliced onion and cook until dark golden brown, move them to the side of the pan and add a knob or two of butter.
3. Put the potatoes in cut side down, then add the mushrooms, allowing the butter to foam and colour in the pan – do not move the pan throughout the cooking process. Once the potatoes have a nice nutty brown appearance you can throw in the garlic, turn the heat onto low and move it around a little. Cook the garlic for one minute and add the strips of cabbage cooking for a further minute while stirring. Season well and turn out into a pie dish. Finally add large chunks of the cheese to suit your taste. Roll out pastry, place on top, crimp edges and brush with beaten egg. Put in oven for 15-20 minutes at 200°c.
4. Generously season the beef. Heat two frying pans, adding enough oil to coat the base of the pan. When hot add two of the seasoned steaks into each pan, thus not over crowding. After four minutes turn the steaks over as quickly as possible, when evenly caramelised place them on a baking tray and put them in the oven at 200°c.

Rare – cook for further 6-8 minutes
Medium – 9-12 minutes
Well done – 12–15 minutes

5. Serve and enjoy.

The Westwood Restaurant, Beverley.
Showcasing simple stylish food, Matthew, Michele and their team use the highest quality locally sourced ingredients to evolve their seasonal menus and get the best out of the ingredients. This fish dish is seasonal, locally sourced and delicious! **www.thewestwood.co.uk**

THE WESTWOOD RESTAURANT

Wild Skipsea Seabass served with potato purée, clams, wild mushrooms, Bridlington brown shrimp and caper butter

INGREDIENTS

1 whole wild Skipsea Seabass, filleted, pin boned and scaled
20g shrimp, peeled
20g capers
100g clams
30g wild mushrooms
50ml white wine

Dressing

1 lemon
Chopped flat leaf parsley
3 tbsp extra virgin olive oil
Red vein sorrel leaves

Potato puree

3 Maris Piper potatoes
50g unsalted butter
50ml double cream

Serves 2

METHOD

1. Peel the potatoes and boil until cooked in salted water.
2. Drain and pass through a ricer to ensure there are no lumps.
3. Heat the double cream and butter together, when melted combine with mash potato and season. Should be a smooth puree, add more cream if needed, set aside keep warm.
4. Flour the skin of the wild Seabass and tap off any excess, fry in a pan on a medium heat, skin side down for 3 to 4 minutes, then turn on to the belly for a further 3 minutes until cooked.
5. Sauté the mushroom in a pan with a knob of butter, add the clams, then a splash of white wine. Cover the pan until the clams open, then add capers, shrimp, chopped parsley extra virgin olive oil and lemon juice.
6. Place a spoon of potato puree in the centre of the plate, place Seabass on top of the puree, then dress the fish with dressing, garnish with red vein sorrel leaves.

Matthew Barker

Whitby Seafish, Staithes
Why change a classic? This delicious pate, made with top quality fish, is a perfect starter or canapé.
www.whitbyseafish.co.uk

Staithes Oak Roast Salmon Pate

INGREDIENTS

255g/9oz Staithes oak roast salmon
110g/4oz cream cheese
2 tbsp double cream
½ lemon, juice only
Freshly ground pepper

Serves 4

METHOD

1. Pop all the ingredients into a blender and pulse until it has a consistency that you desire.
2. If serving as a starter, top with salad leaves alongside oatcakes or Melba toast.

Anthony's, Leeds
The mission at Anthony's Restaurants is simple: to appeal to all food lovers and not a chosen few. The group is committed to ensuring the best possible dining experiences at Anthony's Restaurant, Anthony's Patisserie and Piazza by Anthony. **www.anthonysrestaurant.co.uk**

Potted Smoked Ham Hock with Homemade Piccalilli

INGREDIENTS

Smoked Ham Hock
1 smoked ham hock
1 bay leaf
3 cloves
1 carrot
1 stick of celery

Piccalilli
½ cauliflower
1 onion (diced)
½ Cucumber (diced)
300g white wine vinegar
160g sugar
25g mustard
10g turmeric
3 tsp corn flour

Serves 4

METHOD

Ham Hock
Place the smoked ham hock in a pan of cold water with all the other ingredients. Boil for a couple of hours until you can freely remove the bone from the centre of the hock. Remove from the water and allow to cool just enough so you can handle it. Pick down the meat and press in to four kilna jars. Reduce a little of the ham water by half and pour over the hock. Set in the fridge.

Piccalilli
Salt the cauliflower and the onion for 24 hours and wash off the salt. Salt the cucumber for only 20 minutes and once again wash off the salt. Bring the vinegar and the sugar to the boil in a pan with the turmeric, mustard and the corn flour. Boil for 3-4 minutes and pour over the vegetables and leave to cool.

To serve
Remove the ham hocks from the fridge 15 minutes before serving. Place the jars on the plate and a good amount of the piccalilli next to it. Finish the dish with a little salad leaf and serve.

Tips
Don't throw the ham hock water away – add a couple of potatoes, some more carrots and a couple of rashers of bacon and any of the hock meat that is left over. Reduce by half. Add a splash of cream and a knob of butter and blitz until smooth. You have now a second dish of bacon and vegetable soup – ideal with a chunk of crusty bread.

Anthony Flinn

The Black Swan Tearoom and Patisserie, Helmsley
The award-winning Black Swan Tearoom & Patisserie presents its traditional Yorkshire scones. Served with traditional accompaniments this is afternoon tea at its best. **www.blackswan-helmsley.co.uk**

The HOTEL

Traditional Yorkshire Scones

INGREDIENTS

500g plain flour
100g caster sugar
125g butter
25g baking powder
A handful of sultanas
2 eggs (plus one for egg wash)
A dash of milk

Serves 10

METHOD

1. Place all dry ingredients in a bowl.
2. Rub in butter until it resembles breadcrumbs.
3. Add eggs and enough milk to bind into soft dough.
4. Roll out mixture and cut in rounds.
5. Place on a baking tray and wash the top of scones with beaten egg.
6. Bake in oven at 180°c for 20 minutes.

To serve
Stamfrey Farm clotted cream and York Preserves jam.

Cedar Court Grand Hotel & Spa, York

York's first five-star hotel presents their restaurant, **HQ at the Grand**. Combining traditional favourites with adventurous gastronomic delights – this is a recipe that Head Chef David Sharp hopes will establish The Grand as everyone's favourite York restaurant.

www.cedarcourtgrand.co.uk

Lemon sole with razor clams

INGREDIENTS

6 x 200g lemon sole fillets
30g langoustine mousse
2 razor clams
50ml bouillabaisse (see recipe below)
Twist of lemon juice
10g finely chopped chives
Salt and cayenne pepper

Bouillabaisse

40ml olive oil
2 leeks, sliced
1 fennel bulb, sliced
1 large onion, sliced
1 garlic head cut in half
½ tomato, chopped
1 tsp tomato purée
A few sprigs of parsley
A few sprigs of thyme
2 bay leaves
2 orange rinds, free of pith
1 ½ litre water
500ml fish stock
1 tbsp fennel seeds
1 tsp saffron
2 tbsp Pernod
Fish bones 300g

Serves 2

METHOD

To prepare fish

Fillet lemon sole leaving you with 2 fillets, trim excess fillet so they are neat and tidy. Place fillets on chopping board skin side up and using a pallet knife spread the langoustine mousse over the fillet. Roll fillets up into a wheel shape and leave on a grease proof tray.
Take the razor clam and blanch for 1 minute in boiling water, when cool take clam out and cut into 5 pieces on the diagonal, leave the shell to one side for later.

Bouillabaisse:

Place the pan on a medium heat and when hot add vegetables and garlic. Cook till soft. Add tomatoes, parsley, thyme, puree, fish bones, the stock and the water and bring to a simmer. When boiled remove impurities with ladle from the top and then leave to cook for 60 minutes. When it has boiled strain through a fine sieve and bring to the boil for 15 minutes adding Pernod, salt and pepper. Leave to cool. Grill till cooked, finishing with a twist of lemon.

To serve:

Take 50ml of bouillabaisse and reduce on the stove adding cut up clams and chives at the last minute. Place 3 lemon sole fillets on plate with razor clam, pour sauce over the clam and over the lemon sole, garnish with chopped chives.

David Sharp

What to eat

Poet William Cowper had it right when he said 'variety's the very spice of life, that give it all its flavour' – and there's no county in the country where you'll find as great a variety of nature's abundance as in Yorkshire. Prime, flavoursome fruits, vegetables and crops spring from countless acres of the richest soil.

Swathes of green pastures provide fertile grazing grounds for thousands of beasts, whose quality of life is directly reflected in the finest-tasting dairy, lamb, venison, pork and beef.

And where land meets sea you'll find the highest concentration of seafood businesses in the country in the heritage fishing ports of the Yorkshire and Humber coast.

All across the county, pride of tradition combines with entrepreneurial spirit in award-winning food and drink producers who are constantly looking for new ways to enhance nature's gifts. That's a flavour of what Yorkshire's burgeoning food and drink sector is about... now let's eat...

Glorious food

Shepherds Purse Cheeses, Thirsk

Best Cheese

Shepherds Purse Cheeses is flying high as it celebrates its 21st year of trading

Established by Judy Bell in the late 1980s as part of a diversification scheme on the Bell family farm, it was the first company to reintroduce artisan blue cheese making to Yorkshire since its disappearance in the 60s with the rationalisation of the dairy industry. It launched initially to fill a niche in the market to provide sheep's milk products, but now boasts a wide range of traditionally handmade premium quality cheeses available in major supermarkets, specialist cheese shops and delis nationwide and through a large wholesaler base.

The multi-award-winning range of cheeses, made to the family's own recipes, uses only locally-sourced cow's, ewe's and water buffalo milk. Cheeses include best-selling Yorkshire Blue, Mrs Bells Blue, Buffalo Blue, Byland Blue, Yorkshire Fettle, Olde York, Basilano, Monks Folly – winner of the cheese category at the deliciouslyorkshire awards 2009-2010 – Katy's White Lavender and Ryedale. The company continues to innovate year on year and the latest addition includes Bells Bluemin White, a mould-ripened blue-rind brie, a first for the region, available in Waitrose.

www.shepherdspurse.co.uk (Contact details on page 119)

Yorkshire Dales Meat Company, Bedale

Best Fresh Meat

The Yorkshire Dales Meat Company serves some of the leading quality hotels, restaurants and gastro-pubs throughout the North of England, as well as a number of large supermarkets and foodie events within the region.

Run by the Knox family, who have farmed in the Dales for three generations, the company is based in Bedale, where its range of rare breed sheep and cattle – including Aberdeen Angus – are reared on the farm's own pastures.

The company's success centres around its production ethos of naturally fed and humanely slaughtered animals, and meat that is traditionally hung for 28 days and professionally butchered. This produces the finest flavoured, specialist meat, which producer and farmer Stephen Knox says is 'full of flavour and cooks like a dream'.

In addition to beef, pork, lamb, poultry and game, the company's 'Flavour of the Dales' range includes marinated products, handmade burgers and sausages. Its Heavenly Honey Swaledale Sausage won the best prepared meat category in the deliciouslyorkshire awards 2008-2009 while its Aberdeen Angus 7 Week Matured Sirloin took the fresh meat honours in the deliciouslyorkshire awards 2009-2010.

www.yorkshiredalesmeat.com (Contact details on page 129)

> "The range of rare breed sheep and cattle – including Aberdeen Angus – are reared on the farm's own pastures"

Taste Tradition, Thirsk

Best Prepared Meat

Taste Tradition was founded five years ago by mother and son Joyce and Charles Ashbridge, at Cold Kirby Farm, on the North Yorkshire Moors, after Charles spotted a gap in the market for quality meat and decided to specialise in rare and traditional native British breeds.

Now one of the country's largest rare breed suppliers, Taste Tradition sells lamb, beef and pork from breeds such as Gloucester Old Spot, Saddleback and Longhorn, reared on the farm and by neighbouring farmers, supplying hotels, restaurants and independent retail outlets around Yorkshire and London. The suckling pig, dry cured hams and sausages are some of the best sellers.

Taste Tradition won the best prepared meat category at the deliciouslyyorkshire awards 2009-2010 for its Rare Breed Saddleback Hambleton Lightning Ham.

Charles says: "Our butchers shop and restaurant customers in London really make a big selling point of the fact that our meats are from Yorkshire."

www.tastetradition.co.uk (Contact details on page 128)

York Preserves, York

Best Preserve

Paul Mercer set up York Speciality Food Ltd in 2007 after acquiring Village Green Preserves and establishing the new brand – York Preserves.

York Preserves is one of the largest premium jam makers in England and produces a range of traditional luxury preserves and condiments, using locally-sourced ingredients where possible. It caters for small independent retailers, such as farm shops, delis and garden centres as well as National Trust sites and various museums and stately homes in the region.

York Preserves produces a few million jars a year, many bearing the historic York Crest and a fascinating fact about the historic city and are packed full of fruit offering great tastes. Best sellers include lemon curd and regular flavours such as strawberry and English breakfast marmalade. Its Double Raspberry Jam won the herbs, spices, oils, condiments and preserves category at the deliciouslyyorkshire awards 2009-2010.

Paul said: "Yorkshire has a good name for food and we're really proud to be a part of that and represent our region."

www.yorkpreserves.com

> Yorkshire has a good name for food and we're really proud to be a part of that and represent our region

Little Valley Brewery, Hebden Bridge

Best Drink

With years of brewing experience under his belt, Dutchman Wim van der Spek fulfilled his lifelong ambition in 2005 when he founded the Little Valley Brewery in Cragg Vale, near to Hebden Bridge, and started producing his own award-winning real ales.

Along with his partner Sue Cooper they produce some of Yorkshire's finest ales, using 100% organic ingredients sourced locally and from around the world.

Little Valley's broad range includes traditional English, continental and specialty style ales in cask and bottle. The brewery has won a string of accolades over the last few years. The bestseller, Withens IPA, was named best drink product in the deliciouslyorkshire awards 2009-2010 and is even the guest beer in the House of Commons' Strangers Bar. Wim's ales are already a huge hit in the local area and could soon be seen all over the world as he looks set to take the export market by storm.

The brewery has a shop on site open Monday to Friday, 9am-5pm. Real ale lovers can also buy Little Valley's bottled beers via its website.

www.littlevalleybrewery.co.uk (Contact details on page 198)

Little VALLEY BREWERY

ProperMaid
Ladies who bake!

ProperMaid, Huddersfield

deliciouslyyorkshire winner awards 2009-2010

Best Bakery Product

Allison Whitmarsh launched ProperMaid based on a hypothetical business plan she dreamt up at university in July 2008.

Allison started off making her cakes in her farmhouse-style kitchen and just six months later moved to bigger premises in Marsh, Huddersfield, in January 2009.

ProperMaid and its team of passionate bakers produce 'posh cakes from Yorkshire', creating traditional recipes using Yorkshire ingredients but with a twist. Its Dandelion and Burdock cake won best bakery product at the deliciouslyorkshire awards 2009-2010, and other indulgent flavours include Sticky Ginger and Fudge and Chocolate Chilli and Fudge.

Up until now, large cakes made up ProperMaid's core business, however, Allison recently launched individual retail packs tailored for customers of delis, farm shops and major multiples. From April 2010, ProperMaid cakes will be available in nine branches of Asda.

Allison said: "I find it rewarding when local people go into a cafe or deli and see our cakes and recognise it as a ProperMaid cake."

www.propermaid.co.uk (Contact details on page 197)

> "I find it rewarding when local people go into a cafe or deli and see our cakes and recognise it as a ProperMaid cake"

W S Bentley (Growers), Gomersal

deliciouslyyorkshire winner awards 2009-2010

Best Fresh Produce

Three generations of the Bentley family have been growing high quality, pesticide-free salad cress at Gomersal, West Yorkshire, for more than 50 years.

Crops of the company's delicate mix of cress and rape seedlings are produced every week at its two-hectare site and distributed to supermarkets, wholesalers and caterers.

Employing 25 people, Bentley's won the fresh produce category in the deliciouslyyorkshire awards 2009-2010 for its sprouting peas which the company launched last year and sells under its own washed and ready-to-eat brand: ...and sow on...

The brand also includes alfalfa and a selection of mixed beans, and this year will see the label expand with the launch of new products including pea shoots – the tender leaves and stems of the pea plant.

Managing director Jan Bentley says: "While salad cress has been our staple produce, it's important not to stand still and that's why we've adapted and expanded our offer to meet the needs of consumers. As ever, we're committed to delivering produce of the highest quality and freshness – nothing else will do!"

www.andsowon.co.uk ● www.wsbentley.co.uk (Contact details on page 202)

Yummy Yorkshire Ice Cream, Huddersfield

Supreme and Best Dairy Product

Delph House Farm is run by husband and wife Jeremy and Louise Holmes, and has been in Jeremy's family since the 1960s.

In April 2007, the farm launched the Yummy Yorkshire Ice Cream Company using the excess cream produced at the farm to make the ice cream. Since then, the business has gone from strength to strength, opening an ice cream parlour in July 2008, and now produces the region's most adventurous ice cream flavours using ingredients sourced from the farm or within the region. It is now sold by retailers such as Asda and the Cedar Court hotel chain.

Lou's Liquorice Ice Cream won best dairy product and supreme product of the year at the deliciouslyorkshire awards 2009-2010, which was inspired by the Pontefract Liquorice Festival and includes bits of the famous Pontefract Cake.

Louise said: "We were both born in Yorkshire so we are really passionate about producing something truly Yorkshire."

www.yorkshiremilk.co.uk (Contact details on page 200)

“We were both born in Yorkshire so we are really passionate about producing something truly Yorkshire”

Wold Top Brewery, Driffield

The Wold Top Brewery was set up in 2003 as a farm diversification by Tom Mellor on the Mellor family farm to add value to the excellent malt and barley produced on the farm and to utilise the pure chalk-filtered water from its own borehole.

Today, Wold Top Brewery supplies its award-winning cask ales to over 400 pubs, hotels and restaurants throughout Yorkshire and Lincolnshire, and produces seasonal ales and bespoke beers for local events.

Tom and wife Gill's award-winning traditionally made cask and bottled real ales are the toast of East Yorkshire, and the range includes Wold Top Bitter, Wold Gold blonde beer and Wolds Way.

This year, the brewery celebrated gold in the speciality bottled beer category at the Society of Independent Brewers Northern awards for its unique gluten free beer, Against the Grain. This latest award brings Wold Top Brewery's award tally to 12 in the time since the micro brewery was launched.

www.woldtopbrewery.co.uk (Contact details on page 153)

Side Oven Bakery, Driffield

Sustainable food that tastes good is the motto of husband and wife team Tim and Caroline Sellers.

The couple's Side Oven Bakery is based at Carr House Farm, a family run organic farm set on the edge of the Yorkshire Wolds. The bakery produces sustainable, tasty food using its own fuel for the wood-burning stove, its own spring water and stone ground mill for the flour.

One of the best sellers is honey toasted muesli, which is very popular among farm shops, delis and hotels. Other produce includes bread, cereal bars, flour, juices and cordials made from fruit grown on the farm.

Caroline said: "All our products are traceable and we always try to ensure that they have something in them from our farm."

Carr House Farm and the Side Oven Bakery encourage schools to visit and learn more about organic farming and food production – they even have their own nature trail where children can discover wildlife.

www.sideoven.com (Contact details on page 152)

> All our products are traceable and we always try to ensure that they have something in them from our farm

Yorkshire Outdoor Pork Company Ltd, Hull

Yorkshire Outdoor Pork was launched in 2008 when farmers and brothers Grant and Mark Burton joined forces with Yorkshire Farmers to produce top quality pork products from their outdoor pig herd.

The pigs are born and reared at Manor House Farm, Wilberfoss, which was originally purchased by Grant and Mark's great–grandfather who had been a butcher in York. The farm boasts 280 acres with the 500 sows allowed to roam on 50 acres, as well as another 230 acres used to grow crops and for stewardship schemes.

Yorkshire Outdoor Pork uses a local feed manufacturer and sources other ingredients from the farm or around the region.

Traditionally-made high quality sausages, dry cured bacon and fresh pork products are sold to a variety of retail outlets, multiples, caterers, hotels and restaurants.

Mark said: "We're unique in that we have control of the whole operation and are able to follow the process from conception to the plate."

www.yorkshireoutdoor.co.uk (Contact details on page 157)

Yorkshire Crisps, Sheffield

The Yorkshire Crisps Company, established in 2005, was founded by Ashley Turner whose family businesses have been established in Sheffield for over 100 years.

The company produces luxury hand-cooked crisps and prides itself in only using quality produce grown by local farmers. Potatoes are delivered to the factory by tractor from the farm just a few miles away. Perfect local potatoes are fried in pure sunflower oil and flavoured with only 100% natural ingredients – no MSGs, preservatives, colourings or artificial flavourings are used. All packaging is sourced in Yorkshire too.

Yorkshire Crisps have received a number of awards for their crisps, including a Caterer & Hotelkeeper Excellence Award, beating off stiff competition from established national brands.

There are 10 flavours in the range presented in 100g drums, which are unique to Yorkshire Crisps, as well as 40g and 150g bags and 500g re-sealable catering bags.

In addition to supplying farm shops and delis, Yorkshire Crisps are also available in larger retail outlets, nine European countries and as far away as Dubai.

www.yorkshirecrisps.co.uk (Contact details on page 176)

> **Perfect local potatoes are fried in pure sunflower oil and flavoured with only 100% natural ingredients**

A L Simpkin & Co Ltd, Sheffield

Brother and sister Adrian and Karen Simpkin are the third generation of the Simpkin family at the helm of the travel sweet firm which bears their name.

Since 1921, A L Simpkin & Co Ltd have been manufacturing high grade glucose travel sweets from their base in Sheffield. Today Adrian and Karen lead a team of 50 staff using methods and recipes first used by their forebears and enjoyed in over 40 countries across the globe.

The company is still the only English travel tin manufacturer, producing many varieties, from sugar free and gluten free to Fairtrade and chocolate centres.

Their main market is UK pharmacies, but they also supply to health food shops, hospitals, garden centres, airports, petrol stations and larger retailers such as Booths and Tesco.

And it's not just the founding family who have long-lasting links with the firm. As Adrian explains: "We have people who work here whose parents and grandparents worked here."

www.alsimpkin.com (Contact details on page 170)

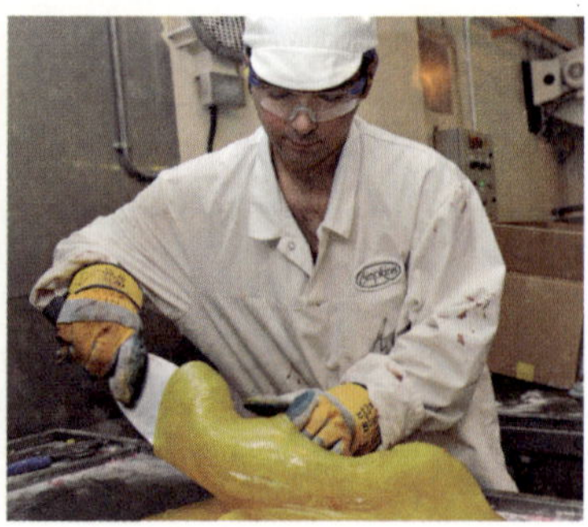

Ripley Store, Ripley

Best confectionery

Award-winning Ripley Store, North Yorkshire, is among the region's finest independent retailers committed to sourcing a range of local foods. It is world famous for its ice cream – made for decades to a secret recipe. The successful Ripley team has now extended its ice cream parlour to include a traditional fudge kitchen, making luxury fudge in the traditional way, using only the finest ingredients. And Ripley's homemade chocolate fudge won the confectionery category at the deliciouslyorkshire awards 2009-2010.

Contact details on page 135

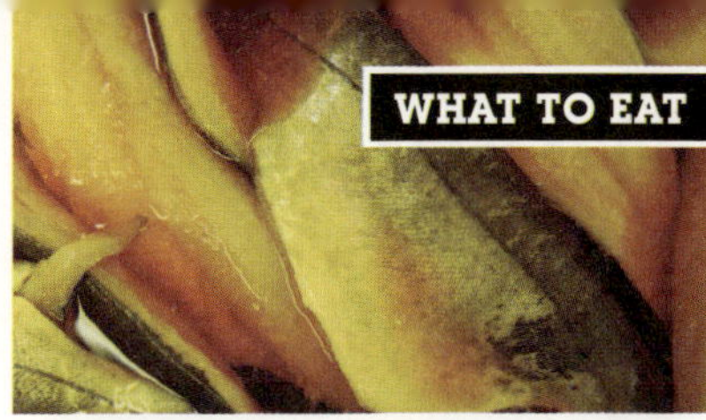

Alfred Enderby Ltd, Grimsby

Alfred Enderby Ltd was founded 50 years ago and is one of the few specialist fish smokers left in the country. Based in Grimsby, it is now run by Alfred's sons Richard and George and still operates from the 100-year-old traditional fish smoking factory on Fish Dock Road. It is a member of the Grimsby Traditional Fish Smokers Group.

Alfred Enderby specialises in smoked haddock fillets, and vacuumed-packed smoked salmon sides and supplies to top restaurants, caterers and hotels across the country.

Still using traditional, hands-on smoking methods, Alfred Enderby sources the finest fish from Iceland, and the Faroe Islands, where fish is plentiful and the perfect size, and smokes it overnight using tall chimneys giving it a richer aroma and fuller flavour.

It was recently awarded the Protected Geographical Indication (PGI), which is an EU protected status for products. The blue and yellow PGI symbol is now on each of Alfred Enderby's smoked haddock boxes.

www.alfredenderby.co.uk (Contact details on page 216)

PROTECTED GEOGRAPHICAL INDICATION

> Now only a small group of dedicated fish smokers – The Traditional Grimsby Fish Smokers Group – smoke cod and haddock in the authentic way, overnight in 100-year-old 10 metre high chimneys

Mackenzies Yorkshire Smokehouse, Blubberhouses

Best Fish and Seafood

Mackenzies Yorkshire Smokehouse was taken over by Robert and Stella Crowson in April 1997 and is a highly respectable business known nationally for its finest smoked products.

Specialising in smoked meats and fish and dry cured bacon, Robert and Stella are committed to buying the highest quality and freshest produce much of which is sourced from local suppliers.

Mackenzies smokes its fish and meat using sophisticated computerised kilns at the factory. They also run a large on-site restaurant, shop and butchery department specialising in local meat.

Stella said: "We love what we do and are proud of the Mackenzies brand and how it champions the Yorkshire cause."

Mackenzies was awarded best fish producer at the deliciouslyorkshire awards 2009-2010 and has also recently been awarded Grade A by the British Retail Consortium, a highly regarded food accolade.

www.yorkshiresmokehouse.co.uk (Contact details on page 135)

MACKENZIES Yorkshire SMOKEHOUSE

Where to eat

Did you know that Yorkshire has more Michelin-starred restaurants than any other UK county? And that's just the cherry on the cupcake. The fact is that our bountiful supply of fresh local ingredients is a magnet to the finest chefs the UK has to offer. If they're not actually born or bred here, they can't resist but come see... (often we don't let them leave!)

You'll find them in buzzing city bistros and fine dining restaurants, frenetically putting the art into a la carte for celebrities and city slickers. You'll find them in idyllic country inns and elegant parkland hotels, quietly honing their craft and paying 21st century homage to world-beating traditional dishes.

But culinary prowess is equally in evidence any day of the week at a multitude of individual cafes and tearooms – and if you want that just picked taste, then food doesn't come any fresher than in the growing number of farm shop eateries offering a 'gate to plate' service made to make your mouth water.

“This year’s guide proves that Yorkshire doesn’t just produce great cricketers, as it can boast of fielding more starred restaurants than any other county… what they all have in common is a commitment to making the best of Yorkshire’s wonderful produce”

Derek Bulmer, editor of the Michelin Guide

Six of the best

Howzat! 2010 is the year in which Yorkshire has finally made it to the top of the food and drink charts with the most Michelin-starred restaurants in the country. No fewer than six restaurants have been awarded prestigious stars, all producing amazing dishes served up by talented and passionate chefs – each with their own individual style. The six stars in Yorkshire's Michelin heaven are:

Pipe and Glass Inn, South Dalton, Beverley

The Pipe and Glass is a new addition (2010) to the Michelin star list and the first restaurant in East Yorkshire to be awarded a star.

The 17th century country inn at the entrance to Dalton Park has been refurbished by Kate and James Mackenzie. Chef James' approach to cooking is straightforward – due respect for timeless classics but with the thrill of a modern twist. See recipe p18

www.pipeandglass.co.uk

Box Tree, Ilkley

Renowned for its good taste, uncompromising quality and sense of luxury, the Box Tree was named Yorkshire Life magazine's Restaurant of the Year 2009-2010.

It's owned by husband and wife team Simon and Rena Gueller. Chef Simon produces a modern French classical menu using the freshest ingredients, with an emphasis on local suppliers, farmers and growers, and with an equally impressive and extensive wine list to match.

www.theboxtree.co.uk

The Yorke Arms, Ramsgill, Pateley Bridge

Frances Atkins, chef proprietor of The Yorke Arms, is one of only six female Michelin-starred chefs in the UK.

Her cooking is based on simple ideas and well-tried combinations, but with original touches that make the most of the restaurant's home-grown ingredients and a wealth of locally-sourced ingredients.

The Yorke Arms was this year named one of the Hardens Guide Top Ten UK Restaurants.

See recipe p19

www.yorke-arms.co.uk

The Old Vicarage, Ridgeway, Sheffield

The Old Vicarage – a splendidly restored 19th century country house and gardens – is Sheffield's only Michelin-starred restaurant and has been home to TV chef and cookery writer Tessa Bramley – one of only six female Michelin-starred chef's in the UK – since 1987.

Tessa is a country cook whose seasonal menus include many ingredients grown in the vicarage's magnificent kitchen garden and supplied by local farmers.

www.theoldvicarage.co.uk

The Burlington, Bolton Abbey

The Burlington Restaurant in the Devonshire Arms Country House Hotel is one of only 25 restaurants in the UK to receive a fourth AA Rosette.

The elegant setting is all about fine dining with head chef Steve Smith creating sumptuous five-course feasts whose hallmarks are seasonal game and fish from the Bolton Abbey Estate, together with vegetables and herbs from the hotel's gardens. See recipe p21

www.thedevonshirearms.co.uk

The Star Inn, Harome, near Helmsley

The Good Food Guide has called it 'the very model of an English pub'. The Star Inn at Harome, owned by Andrew and Jacquie Pern, prides itself on being a unique Yorkshire inn with relaxed yet efficient service.

Chef Andrew's style is 'sort of' traditional British with spiced-up old favourites and Anglicised classics using, wherever possible, seasonal produce from a strong network of both professional and amateur suppliers. See recipe p20

www.thestaratharome.co.uk

The Black Swan at Oldstead, York

Best use of regional produce

Named a Michelin 'Rising Star' for 2010, The Black Swan is owned by the Banks family, who have farmed at Oldstead for generations. The restaurant is ideal for those who wish to escape to the country. Diners are recommended by The Times to 'soak up the views' in this delightfully secluded spot.

As farmers, the Banks family are committed to supporting local suppliers. Meat from neighbouring farms and locally hunted game is supplied to the kitchen, along with herbs, salads and soft fruit grown from the family farm.

The Black Swan's commitment to regional produce was recognised by the deliciouslyyorkshire awards 2009-2010, where they won the best use of local produce category. For Tom Banks, the real reward comes from 'knowing that guests return because they enjoy the very best local food'.

www.blackswanoldstead.co.uk (Contact details on page 102)

Clocktower Restaurant, Harrogate

Set in the idyllic Rudding Park, just south of Harrogate, the Clocktower is one of the most popular restaurants in North Yorkshire. And it's not just the food that attracts people – the interior of the restaurant is every bit as dramatic as its surroundings, featuring an enormous limestone bar, a pink glass chandelier and a 400-year-old olive tree in the conservatory.

The Clocktower offers food cooked by a team of award-winning chefs, and is known for its exceptional customer service. The restaurant offers a monthly Yorkshire Food Heroes menu, a unique selection of dishes featuring a principal ingredient sourced within a 75-mile radius of Rudding Park.

Head chef Jerome Gaudre says: "Yorkshire offers a vast amount of fantastic ingredients, from the asparagus which is grown just three miles away to the honey that is produced on our own estate. I will often visit a farm before I agree to buy any products. This way we know exactly where each ingredient has come from."

www.ruddingpark.co.uk (Contact details on page 96)

"I will often visit a farm before I agree to buy any products. This way we know exactly where each ingredient has come from"

Cedarbarn Farm Shop & Café, Pickering

Best use of regional produce (cafe/tearoom)

Owned and run by Mandy and Karl Avison, the Cedarbarn Farm Shop & Café is in the grounds of the family's farm. It is clear to see why the café has won deliciouslyorkshire awards for best use of regional produce (in a café/tearoom) two years running as its menu reflects the farm's growing patterns. From asparagus in the spring, to soft fruits and new potatoes in the summer. On Sunday's the café offers a traditional Sunday lunch, featuring the farm's own Aberdeen Angus beef, home-reared lamb or pork from local farms.

The Avisons are not only committed to providing high-quality, locally-sourced food, but also pride themselves on their friendly, helpful service.

The café is set in a landscaped herb garden, allowing their customers to enjoy their meals outside in warmer weather. There is also a 'pick your own' area, play area and a seasonal maize maze, making the Cedarbarn a great day out for families.

www.cedarbarnfarmshop.co.uk (Contact details on page 139)

The Angel Inn, Hetton

Founded by Denis and Juliet Watkins nearly 30 years ago, the Angel Inn helped change the face of pub food when it moved from traditional pub fayre to establish the country's first dining pub.

Bruce Elsworth, chef director, continues Denis' legacy with seasonally adjusted menus that include the freshest seasonal produce from around the region including meat and game from the Yorkshire Dales, fresh fish from the East and West coasts and locally farmed fruit and vegetables. These ingredients are used to create modern twists on traditional dishes, such as ham and egg, crispy coated ham hock wedge with poached free range egg, pineapple and homemade pork scratchings. The Angel was proud to be one of the first pubs in Yorkshire to have traceability from gate to plate.

With origins in part over 500 years old, the inn is full of charm with oak beams, nooks, crannies and crackling log fires. The Angel has five exquisite bedrooms and a Wine Cave where it holds intimate wedding ceremonies and private 'Angel Auberge' dining events.

www.angelhetton.co.uk (Contact details on page 94)

"The Angel was proud to be one of the first pubs in Yorkshire to have traceability from gate to plate"

Green's of Whitby

Husband and wife team Rob and Emma Green are celebrating Green's of Whitby's 10th anniversary in style, having picked up multiple awards including best restaurant at the Northern Hospitality Awards 2010, restaurant of the year from the Yorkshire Moors and Coast Tourism Awards 2009 and Taste of Yorkshire Award at the White Rose Awards.

Green's offers a relaxed bistro downstairs and a restaurant upstairs. This year they also extended the business to include boutique apartments, allowing customers to enjoy wonderful dining and exquisite accommodation.

Renowned for its prime fish dishes, favourite catches include salt and pepper Whitby squid with lime and chilli mayonnaise. All the fish is sourced locally from the quay just around the corner, so customers can be certain that their meal is freshly landed in Whitby.

Head chef Rob, who was national seafood chef of the year 2009, believes: "The combination of the freshest local produce with a welcoming and relaxing atmosphere makes us stand out."

www.greensofwhitby.com (Contact details on page 98)

The Pipe and Glass Inn, South Dalton

East Yorkshire's first and only Michelin-starred restaurant, The Pipe and Glass Inn is on the site of the original gatehouse to Dalton Park where 15th century visitors were fed and entertained. Today, the inn continues to offer its visitors a warm Yorkshire welcome.

Recognised for its exquisite menus, the Pipe and Glass Inn has won numerous awards, including best chef at the Northern Hospitality Awards 2010 for its head chef and proprietor, James Mackenzie.

James is committed to sourcing as much local and seasonal produce as possible, and his menu allows diners to explore the region's culinary offerings. Dishes such as Taste of Yorkshire game provide modern twists on classic Yorkshire ingredients.

The drinks list is just as local, and the inn offers a wide selection of hand-pulled ales including Old Rosie hand-pulled cider and guest beers from the Wold Top, York and Cropton breweries.

www.pipeandglass.co.uk (Contact details on page 150)

"Dishes such as Taste of Yorkshire game provide modern twists on classic Yorkshire ingredients"

Artisan Restaurant, Hessle

Serving 'lovingly prepared food in an intimate setting', the Artisan last year received the highest rating for restaurants in East Yorkshire awarded by the Which? Good Food Guide. This year it has gone one better and been named North East of England Restaurant of the Year in the Which? Good Food Guide 2011.

And, with space for just 16 diners, this is a personal dining experience in the setting of a listed Georgian house. Diners can linger over their meal, as there is only one sitting.

Founded in 2004 by husband and wife team, Richard and Lindsey Johns, the restaurant remains a solely family venture. Chef Richard is passionate about local ingredients. "Yorkshire offers the chef a fantastic larder of produce. Having such great food on your doorstep and cooking by the seasons is a joy," he says.

Richard's passion is reflected in his intricate menus that are bursting with flavour. Typical dishes include slow-cooked duck egg with truffle wild mushrooms, bacon and brioche, or a mouth-watering dessert of warm vanilla rice pudding, compote of apples and calvados sultanas, with apple sorbet.

www.artisanrestaurant.com (Contact details on page 149)

The Wortley Arms, Sheffield

Providing hearty, classic pub dishes downstairs and a more sophisticated à la carte menu in its Montagu restaurant, the Wortley Arms has something for everyone.

Built in Wortley, Sheffield, in the 17th century, the pub has been trading for over 200 years, and despite extensive refurbishment it still has many of its original features, including solid oak beam and roaring open fires, providing bags of character. Chef patron and master chef of Great Britain Andy Gabbitas is keen to keep the pub's traditions alive and visitors can still see 'local shooters trading pints for pheasants' during the hunting season.

The menu is packed with seasonal, locally-sourced ingredients and almost everything is freshly made on the premises, including pasta, bread, ice-cream and even the burger buns. The menu changes regularly, but customers can expect to find classics such as the renowned Wortley venison pie which is one of the pub's specialities.

www.wortley-arms.co.uk (Contact details on page 170)

“The menu is packed with seasonal, locally-sourced ingredients and almost everything is freshly made on the premises”

The Butchers Arms, Hepworth

Set high in the Pennines, the Butchers Arms provides traditional Yorkshire food with a modern twist. The pub offers quick bar bites, including its unique 'Yorkshire Tapas & Things' or an à la carte menu in the chic dining area. In 2009 the Butchers opened its 'secret garden', allowing visitors to enjoy their meals in an intimate outside area.

The Butchers is a favourite of locals and critics alike, winning Yorkshire Life's best dining pub of the year 2009 and the Great Yorkshire Cookery Competition's professional chef of the year 2009 for head chef and owner, Tim Bilton.

The menu reflects Tim's passion, skill and commitment to sourcing local ingredients, with dishes such as Round Green Farm venison loin, served with baby venison cottage pie, roast winter vegetable and a Pontefract Cake jus. Tim competed in the 2010 Great British Menu representing the North East, and diners can try some of his competition dishes.

www.thebutchersarmshepworth.co.uk (Contact details on page 189)

Mumtaz, Leeds

Building on the success of its world-famous Bradford restaurant and popular food products range, Mumtaz opened its Leeds restaurant in 2009, to equal acclaim.

Mumtaz stands out from other curry houses on account of its unique Kashmiri menu, with dishes such as sweet and creamy Chicken Korma with pineapple, pistachio and coconut, lamb-on-the-bone and chilli paneer. There are also plenty of unusual sweet treats for dessert, for those who have room.

The dining experience is enhanced by Mumtaz's luxurious decoration, including an exquisite black and red chandelier and a grand piano, which is played live most nights. This is fine dining at its best, for a fraction of the usual price.

For those who prefer to eat their curries at home, Mumtaz also offers a takeaway service, chilled food counters and a delicatessen serving some of its renowned sauces, which are also stocked at Harrods.

www.mumtaz.com (Contact details on page 205)

"This is fine dining at its best, for a fraction of the usual price"

Piazza by Anthony, Leeds

It's probably little surprise to customers that Piazza by Anthony was this year named a Bib Gourmand in the Michelin Guide – an award given to restaurants offering excellent food at a reasonable price. As The Independent's reviewer points out: "This is an impressive place. To deliver food of this quality at a reasonable price in a setting this spectacular is not easy to do."

Set in the iconic Leeds Corn Exchange, this flourishing, family-run establishment is far from just a brasserie; it offers customers a bakery, patisserie, fromagerie, chocolaterie and a cafe. In fact, the brasserie sources its ingredients, where possible, from these in-house producers, guaranteeing its freshness.

Chef Anthony Flinn says: "People expect the finest, locally-sourced, quality ingredients when they visit the Piazza. Customers have the benefit of seeing the provenance of their food, such as the bread from our own bakery, fresh that day."

www.anthonysrestaurant.co.uk (Contact details on page 185)

Beverley Tickton Grange

The family-run Beverley Tickton Grange is one of Yorkshire's favourite independent hotels.

With the restaurant always at its heart, David Nowell and his brigade create inspirational seasonal dishes to AA two rosette standard.

This year marks the start of an exciting future for Beverley Tickton Grange. Having acquired 12 acres of adjacent pastureland, planning permission has been granted to create an East Yorkshire Hotel Estate.

The 10-year programme will create landscaped gardens and elements which include a farm restaurant and shop, artists studio, orangery, walled garden, Georgian bath house and business paddock. The development will be quite unique and will contribute to the exciting advancement of tourism to East Yorkshire.

Maggy Whymant, daughter of founders Peter and Sheila, said: "It would be wonderful if our own children could further develop the hotel as we are now doing. Our dream is that it will remain in Whymant hands through many generations to come."

www.beverleyticktongrange.co.uk (Contact details on page 151)

"With the restaurant always at its heart, David Nowell and his brigade create inspirational seasonal dishes to AA two rosette standard"

Nethergill Farm, Oughtershaw

Breakfast Member of the Year

Victorian farmhouse and B&B Nethergill Farm sits in Langstrothdale at the head of the River Wharfe and is perfectly placed for walkers on the Dales Way.

At the farm, run by Fiona and Chris Clark, guests can relax and unwind while taking in the breathtaking views, Yorkshire hospitality and great tasting locally-sourced food.

Fiona says that it's not only the home-from-home ambience of the farm that attracts the visitors: "We source most of our food from the farm such as our meat, or as local as possible such as our eggs, flour, sausages and Wensleydale cheese."

Every morning guests can enjoy a delicious breakfast of homemade bread, homecured bacon, lemon curd and marmalade which won the farm Breakfast Member of the Year in the deliciouslyyorkshire awards 2009-2010.

The farm also provides evening meals for guests, including the popular Beef in Black Sheep Ale, served with seasonal vegetables and rhubarb crumble for dessert.

www.nethergill.co.uk (Contact details on page 222)

Where to buy

There's no getting away from it, we like our food in God's Own County – with such a fantastic supply of local produce it would be a sin not to.

Sales at farm shops are booming as more and more consumers find quality locally-produced food and drink is fresher, tastier and more competitively priced than they thought.

Local provenance is right at home in these honest-to-goodness family-run food stores where the people behind the counter are often those who grew the crops and raised the animals in the first place.

Visiting them is often a day out in itself, combining an opportunity to enjoy the scenery, breathe fresh air and sample some of the produce while you're there in the farm shop cafe: the original 'gate to plate' experience.

Just down the road in the village, town or city, you'll also find specialist independent grocers, delicatessens, butchers, bakers, confectioners and cheesemongers at every twist and turn – all foodie Aladdin's caves where you're sure to find just the right 'little something' to take home for tea.

But if you can't make the trip all is not lost: many producers now sell online via their own websites or at the hallmark of great food www.deliciouslyorkshire.co.uk

Welcome
Hawes
Northallerton
Ripon
Harrogate
York
Leeds
Holmfirth
Sheffield
23
31
10
33
9
32
1
2
17
14
11
19
4
30
13
18
22
35
5
15
37
8
6
16
7
29
25
27
36
38

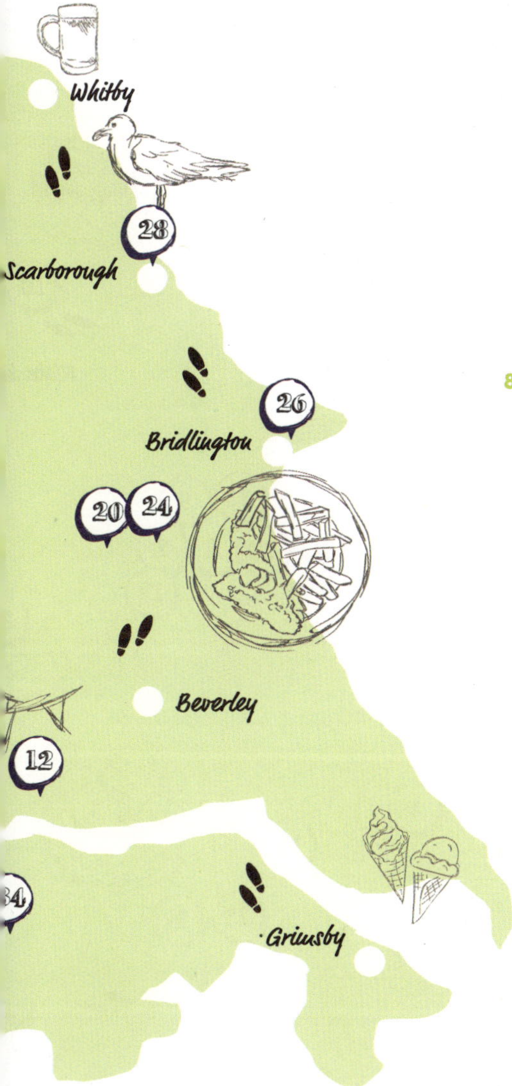

Farm shops

1. Ainsty Farms Direct p137
2. Beadlam Grange Farmshop & Tearoom p138
3. Billy's Hill Farm Shop p177
4. Birkhill Farm Shop p209
5. Blacker Hall Farm Shop p210
6. Bolster Moor Farmshop p210
7. Cannon Hall Farm Shop p177
8. Castle Hill Nurseries (Yorkshire Farm Shop) p210
9. Castle Howard Farm Shop p138
10. Cedarbarn Farm Shop & Cafe p139
11. Crimple Valley Fresh p139
12. Drewtons p160
13. Far Barsey Farm Shop p210
14. Fodder p140
15. High Bank Farm p140
16. Hinchliffes Farm Shop p211
17. Home Farm Shop p140
18. Ingfield Farm Shop p211
19. Keelham Hall Farm Shop p211
20. Kelleythorpe Farm Shop p160
21. Langlands Garden Centre p161
22. Langlands Garden Centre (Leeds) p212
23. Mainsgill Farm Shop p140
24. Manor Farm Shop p161
25. Marr Grange Farm Shop p177
26. Marton Manor Farm Shop & Tea Rooms p161
27. McCallum's Bank End Farm Shop p178
28. Redcliffe Farm Shop & Café p140
29. Rob Royd Farm Shop p178
30. Robinson's Farm Shop p212
31. Roots Farmshop & Cafe p141
32. The Balloon Tree Farm Shop & Café p138
33. The Farmers Cart p139
34. The Pink Pig Farm p219
35. Tomlinson's Farm Shop p212
36. Uncle Henry's Farm Shop p219
37. Villa Farm Shop p212
38. Whirlow Hall Farm Trust p178

Fodder, Harrogate

deliciouslyorkshire winner awards 2009-2010

Independent Retailer of the Year

Fodder opened its doors in June 2009 with the aim of both supporting small food producers in the region and bringing the best food and drink that Yorkshire has to offer to its customers. The business now employs 39 staff.

Fodder prides itself on quality and good value for money, offering the best in locally-produced food, at an affordable price. As well as fresh fruit and vegetables, dairy produce, and even beers and wine, at the store's heart is a butchers, which stocks meat reared in the region.

Fodder's Heather Parry said: "We are absolutely passionate about the food we sell and this enthusiasm rubs off on our customers and staff. Our ethos is that locally-produced food should be affordable and accessible for everyone."

The business was named best independent retailer in the deliciouslyorkshire awards 2009-2010 and takes an active role in encouraging people to buy local food from farm shops across the region.

www.fodderweb.co.uk (Contact details on page 139)

The Farmer's Cart, York

Farm Shop of the Year

Prior to opening The Farmer's Cart, the Sykes family were producers for large supermarkets. In 2001, they decided to sell directly to the customer by opening a farm shop and restaurant and have never looked back. Far from being a shop for special occasions, regular customers are rewarded with a popular loyalty card, offering attractive discounts.

Their motto when it comes to sourcing ingredients is 'farm first, then as locally as possible'. They offer over 50 varieties of home-grown fruits and vegetables.

The farm also rears Aberdeen Angus, rare breed old spot pork, lamb, free range chickens and turkeys, which are all sold in their butchery.

It is this home-grown produce that owner Ed Sykes believes sets their shop apart. "As customers drive up to the shop they are able to see our crops growing and the animals grazing in the fields so they can see exactly where their food is coming from."

The Farmer's Cart was named best farm shop retailer in the deliciouslyyorkshire awards 2009-2010.

www.thefarmerscart.co.uk (Contact details on page 141)

"Customers are able to see our crops growing and the animals grazing in the fields so they can see exactly where their food is coming from"

The Balloon Tree Farmshop and Café, Gate Helmsley

Innovation award

It was the Machin family's enthusiasm for fresh produce that led to the setting up of The Balloon Tree Farmshop and Café in 2004 to sell the freshest quality produce direct to the consumer.

Six years on, The Balloon Tree at Gate Helmsley is a favourite foodie destination operating under the mantra: 'Fewer food miles, more farm yards'. Everything grown on the 60-acre plot is picked and sold in either the shop or the café within a few hours, under the watchful eye of field manager Robert Sturrock.

A family-run business, established by Digby and Jill Machin, the shop, delicatessen and café are managed on a day-to-day basis by the couple's sons Will and Matthew who pride themselves on offering a wide range of 'super fresh' fruit and vegetables grown on site, together with traditional rare breed meat including Longhorn cattle, alongside their Gran's award-winning chutney, homemade ready meals, and free range eggs and dairy.

"We're passionate about quality local food and we are always striving to make our customer's experience enjoyable and unique," said Will. The Balloon Tree won the award for innovation at the deliciouslyorkshire awards 2009-2010.

www.theballoontree.co.uk (Contact details on page 141)

Roots Farm Shop & Cafe, East Rounton

Best Newcomer

Opened in August 2008 by cousins Barry and Katherine Hutchinson, Roots is brimming with quality local produce and delicious homemade food.

The business is housed in a converted 19th century Arts & Crafts red brick building at the heart of their family's working mixed beef and arable farm at East Rounton, near Northallerton, North Yorkshire, and was awarded outstanding newcomer in the deliciouslyyorkshire awards 2009-2010.

Roots is committed to providing a personal service throughout the business. The butchery team share information with customers about the local farms that supply the meat and offer advice on cooking it. In Roots cafe, visitors can take their time over tasty and freshly prepared food, served by staff who are happy to impart information regarding local sourcing.

Katherine says: "We provide the local community and the public with the 'full basket shop' while upholding high standards of freshness, flavour and traceability. Our family prides itself on sourcing from an array of quality local producers, including our own farm, as much as possible."

www.rootsfarmshop.co.uk (Contact details on page 140)

> "We provide the local community and the public with the 'full basket shop' while upholding high standards of freshness, flavour and traceability"

Blacker Hall Farm Shop, Wakefield

Three hundred years of family farming tradition has been the backbone of the success story of Blacker Hall Farm Shop.

The shop opened its doors in October 1999. Under the management of Edward Garthwaite, together with his parents, John and Anne, the business continues to grow.

What was once a collection of derelict stone barns is now a thriving family business, selling the best in local produce comprising a traditional Q Guild butchery, craft bakery, delicatessen and wine loft staffed by a dedicated team of 60 people. More than 90% of everything sold in the shop is produced on the farm. August 2010 will see the opening of a coffee shop/restaurant and children's attractions together with a purpose-built bakery and butchery production facility.

Edward says: "Last October we celebrated 10 years of bringing the best local produce to local people. We are a close team and enormously proud of what we do."

www.blackerhall.com (Contact details on page 210)

Kelleythorpe Farm Shop, Driffield

Housed in a beautiful red brick building, Kelleythorpe Farm Shop stocks the finest in local produce. From cheese, chutneys and jams to local milk and eggs, Kelleythorpe is most famous for its Aberdeen Angus beef – particularly its Angus burgers – and is the premier pedigree herd and cattle breeder in East Yorkshire.

Offering free delivery to homes in the Driffield area and selling its produce regularly at farmers' markets across East Riding are two ways Kelleythorpe maintains its loyal customer following and ensures that its top quality produce is easily accessible to all.

Manager Tiffy Hopper enthused: "The quality and taste of the food we sell is outstanding, and keeps our customers coming back again and again. You can't beat food that's local and fresh."

www.theinternetfarmshop.com/KelleythorpeFarmShop (Contact details on page 161)

> "The quality and taste of the food we sell is outstanding, and keeps our customers coming back again and again"

Uncle Henry's, Gainsborough

With over 100 years of farming behind it, Uncle Henry's is a showcase for the very best in Yorkshire and Lincolnshire produce. The store sits right on the border of the two counties and sells the best food the local area has to offer alongside pork, sausages, bacon, gammon, haslet, potatoes and fresh vegetables that are produced on the farm itself.

As well as the farm shop, Uncle Henry's boasts an award-winning cafe which serves more than 50 varieties of locally-produced sausages. Uncle Henry's and Grayingham Grange Farm are run by husband-and-wife team Steve and Meryl Ward who bought the business from Henry Wright after whom the store is named.

Steve said: "It's a credit to Yorkshire that the county supplies such a diverse range of high quality food which is sold locally, nationally and worldwide. Uncle Henry's is exceptionally proud to stock Yorkshire produce."

www.unclehenrys.co.uk (Contact details on page 177)

Cannon Hall Farm Shop, Barnsley

Famous for its home produced pork, beef and lamb, Cannon Hall Farm Shop relies on traditional farming and butchery methods handed down through generations to provide some of the highest quality meat available in the region.

The meat is sold alongside the freshest fruit and vegetables, preserves and cakes, all sourced form the best local producers.

Cannon Hall's Robert Nicholson says that when it comes to sourcing local produce, he and his staff take real care to make sure everything they stock is of the highest possible quality and taste.

Robert says: "Our beef is hung for maximum flavour, our lambs thrive on the rich natural pastures around the farm and our pigs are specially reared for flavour and tenderness. We pride ourselves on this level of attention to detail, which is why we have experienced such tremendous growth in demand in the 10 years since we opened our doors."

www.cannonhallfarm.co.uk (Contact details on page 177)

> "Our beef is hung for maximum flavour, our lambs thrive on the rich natural pastures around the farm and our pigs are specially reared for flavour and tenderness"

700425

Source it

You know you want it – but where are you going to find it? Right here actually.

Yorkshire and Humber is home to some of the world's best known food companies and the highest concentration of small, passionate enterprises delivering innovative products.

What follows is deliciouslyorkshire's comprehensive directory of members split by region (North, South, East and West Yorkshire and North/ North East Lincolnshire), by category (producer, retailer, hospitality etc) and by speciality (bakers, brewers, hotels, restaurants etc).

You want to find a rare breed meat supplier? Dip in. You want to order handmade chocolates direct from their creator? Look it up. You want to eat somewhere special? It's all here.

There's so much wonderful food and drink out there, the hardest bit will be making a decision – but then no-one said it was going to be easy!

Key to icons

- Internet Sales
- Mail Order
- Own Retail Outlets
- On Site Cafe / Restaurant
- Children's Play Area

North Yorkshire

There's a taste of everything for visitors to North Yorkshire, home to the magnificent Yorkshire Dales National Park and the Nidderdale Area of Outstanding Natural Beauty. Take in the historic city of York with its Gothic Minster and cosmopolitan Harrogate and the popular Valley Gardens. Or take a trip across the North York Moors to seafaring Whitby. But don't forget to have a bite of the very best in local food at award-winning farmshops, cafes, gastropubs, restaurants and hotels.

SHERBURN IN ELMET

1. Holme Farmed Venison p110

YORKSHIRE MOORS

2. North York Moors Shearling Group p111

RICHMOND

3. Just Williams p116

CARNFORTH

4. Country Harvest p133

HAWES

5. Wensleydale Dairy Products Ltd p104

THIRSK

6. The Black Lion p121
7. Fauconberg Arms p125
8. The Hare Inn p127
9. Herbs Unlimited p106
10. Shepherds Purse Cheeses Ltd p103

RIPON

11. Appletons of Ripon p109
12. Bare Earth Ltd p114
13. Black Sheep Brewery p98
14. Brymor Ice Cream Ltd p102
15. Fountains Abbey & Studley Royal p119
16. Hambleton Ales p98
17. The Harrogate Cake Company Ltd p94
18. Independent Foods p95
19. Lightwater Shopping Village p128
20. R & J Catering Butchers Ltd p112
21. Rosebud Preserves p116
22. Swinton Park p131

SKIPTON

23. The Bull p123
24. The Coniston Hotel p124
25. Whitakers Chocolates Ltd p97
26. Yorkshire Dales Real Food p115

MALTON

27. Flamingoland p126
28. The Market Place Bistro Wine Bar p130
29. Yorkshire Rapeseed Oil p107

BOROUGHBRIDGE

30. The Ship Inn p132
31. Paynes Dairies p102
32. The Laden Table p134

NORTHALLERTON

33. Lewis & Cooper Ltd p134
34. Yorkshire Dales Cheese Company p137
35. Roots Farmshop & Cafe p141
37. Vale of Mowbray Ltd p113

PICKERING

47. The Black Bull Inn (Punch Taverns) p121
48. Cedarbarn Farm Shop & Cafe p139
49. The Chocolate Factory Ltd p93

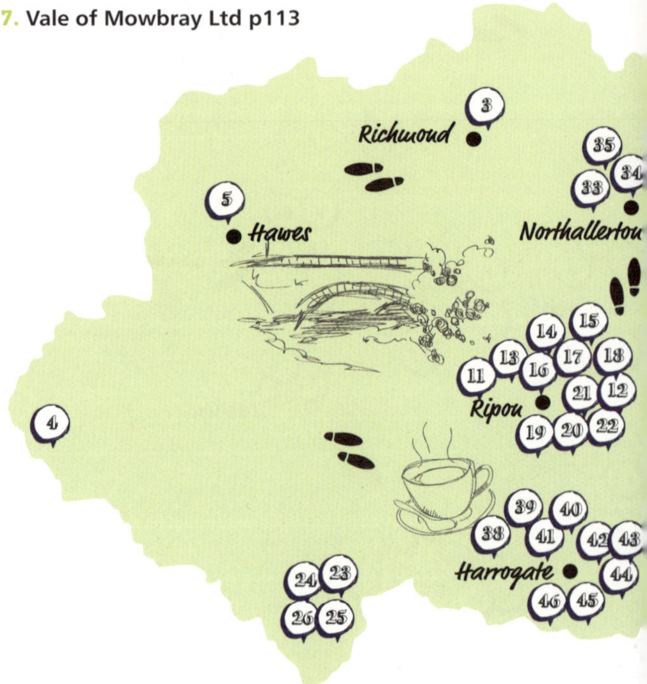

HARROGATE

38. Bettys & Taylors of Harrogate p118
39. Bleikers At The Malt Shovel p122
40. Clocktower at Rudding Park p124
41. Daleside Brewery p98
42. Fodder p140
43. The General Tarleton Inn p126
44. Harrogate Spring Water Ltd p99
45. LH Fine Foods p135
46. Weetons p136

Food highlights

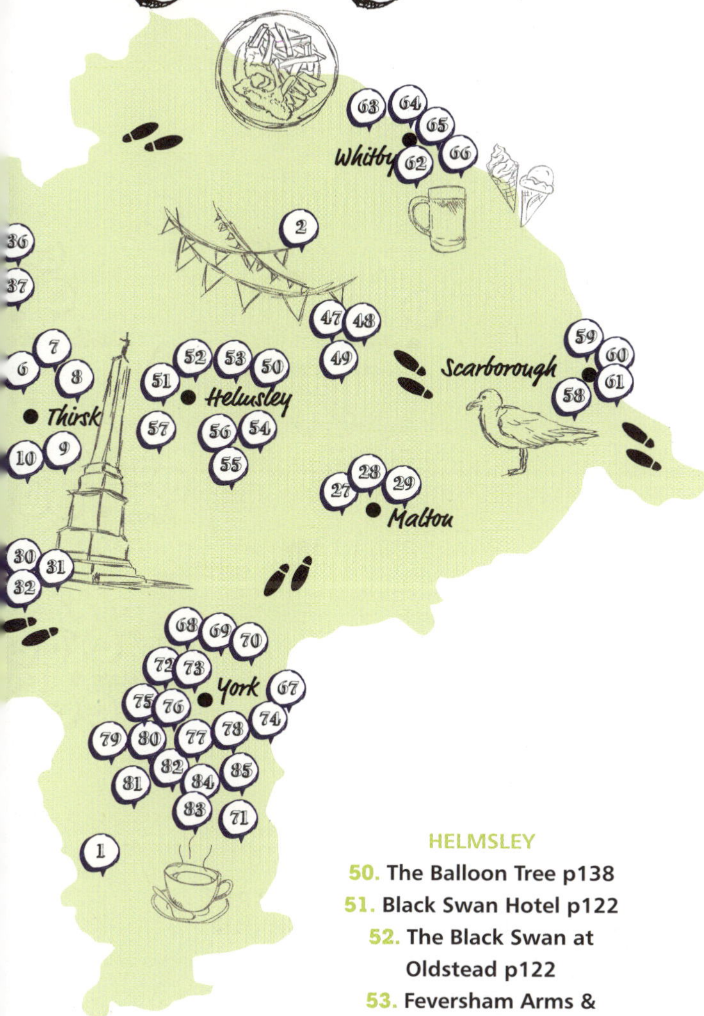

HELMSLEY

50. The Balloon Tree p138

51. Black Swan Hotel p122

52. The Black Swan at Oldstead p122

53. Feversham Arms & Verbena Spa p125

54. Hunters of Helmsley p134

55. The Inn at Hawnby p128

56. Makins at Helmsley p129

57. Ryeburn of Helmsley p103

SCARBOROUGH

58. Beiderbecke's Hotel & Restaurant p121

59. The Glass House Cafe Bistro p119

60. Lanterna p128

61. Trotters Farm Shop p112

WHITBY

62. Botham's of Whitby p92

63. Green's Restaurant, Bistro & Boutique Apartments p127

64. The Magpie Cafe p129

65. Plough Inn p131

66. Whitby Seafish Ltd p106

YORK

67. The Abbey Inn p120

68. About Foods Ltd p108

69. The Alice Hawthorn (Punch Taverns) p120

70. Beadlam Grange Farmshop & Tearoom p138

71. Burn Hall Hotel p123

72. Castle Howard Farm Shop p138

73. Dooley's p133

74. The Farmers Cart p139

75. The Fruity Kitchen p117

76. GF Foods Ltd p94

77. Herb Fed p110

78. The Malt Shovel (Punch Taverns) p129

79. The National Trust Beningbrough Hall p130

80. The Red Lion p131

81. Raisthorpe Manor Fine Foods p99

82. SLOE motion p100

83. Tollerton Stores p136

84. Voakes Pies p114

85. The Yorkshire Food Company p137

Bakers & Confectioners

The Bakery

Family run craft bakery producing a vast selection of standard and speciality bread, rolls, cakes and slices. Fresh sandwiches and quiches. Visit our bakery shop.

DETAILS:
Sally Hudson
01653 693343
17 Church Street, Norton, Malton, YO17 9HP, North Yorkshire

E: sally@nortonbakery.co.uk
W: www.dolcevitacakedesign.co.uk

Basically Baking

A company striving to deliver top quality homemade desserts and baking for all. Wholesale customers buy in products for cafe's, restaurants and farm shops. Direct sales through shows and fairs.

DETAILS:
Louise Krier
01765 601850
May Lodge, 4 Springfield Close, Ripon, HG4 2RR, North Yorkshire

E: basicallybaking@googlemail.com
W: www.basicallybaking.co.uk

Bakers & Confectioners

Botham's of Whitby

Botham's of WHITBY

Family run craft bakers and confectioners in Whitby since 1865. Selling a wide range of wrapped goods for wholesale nationally and internationally. Also worldwide mail-order and award winning tearooms.

DETAILS:
Michael Jarman
01947 602823
35/39 Skinner Street, Whitby, YO21 3AH, North Yorkshire

E: sales@botham.co.uk
W: www.botham.co.uk

Bakers & Confectioners

Choc-Affair

Here at Choc-Affair we believe that chocolate should be an experience, not just a treat. We are committed to producing a wonderfully delicious, ethically made range of Fairtrade chocolate indulgences.

DETAILS:
Linda Barrie
01904 541541
Station Yard, York Road, Naburn, York, YO19 4RW, North Yorkshire

E: linda@choc-affair.com
W: www.choc-affair.com

We like our food in God's Own County – with such a fantastic supply of local produce it would be a sin not to

Bakers & Confectioners

The Chocolate Factory Ltd

The Chocolate Factory produces fresh handmade chocolates, handmade chocolate figures and a full range of diabetic chocolate. Everything made by hand with real Belgian chocolate. Watch the chocolatiers in action at The Chocolate Factory in Hutton Le Hole.

DETAILS:
Gareth East
01751 417084

Unit 2, Hutton le Hole,
YO62 6UA, North Yorkshire

E: sales@the-chocolate-factory.co.uk
W: www.the-chocolate-factory.co.uk

Bakers & Confectioners

Confectionery Craft Ltd

Confectionery Craft, trading under the Parrs brand name, manufacturers a range of traditional sugar confectionery products including fruit jellies, lollipops, cinder toffee and rock.

DETAILS:
John Grimshaw
01636 706163

The Sweet Factory,
23-25, Sherwood Street,
Scarborough, YO11 1SR

E: john@grimshawcc.fsnet.co.uk
W: www.parrsrock.co.uk

Country Fare

Winner of 21 Great Taste Awards, cakes are made by hand, using free range eggs, local milk and butter. All cakes made from family recipes in an artisan bakery on a working hill farm.

DETAILS:
Dianne Halliday
01768 371173

Dalefoot Farm,
Mallerstang, Kirkby
Stephen, CA17 4JT

E: countryfareuk@aol.com
W: www.country-fare.co.uk

Bakers & Confectioners

Cupcakes by Charley

A gourmet cupcake boutique established in the stylish Montpellier Quarter, Harrogate. Good quality simple ingredients sourced from local suppliers for cakes that taste as good as they look.

DETAILS:
Hayley Kelly
01423 524330

5a Royal Parade,
The Montpellier Quarter,
Harrogate, HG1 2SZ

E: enjoy@cupcakesbycharley.co.uk
W: www.cupcakesbycharley.co.uk

Davill's Patisserie

An accredited and award winning Independent Master Baker based in Ripon. We produce a variety of fresh breads, delicious cakes, couverture chocolate and seasonal goods.

DETAILS:
Ken Davill
01765 603544

24 Westgate, Ripon,
HG4 2BQ, North Yorkshire

E: kenandshirleydavill@hotmail.com

Bakers & Confectioners

Fudge Kitchen

Fudge handmade to a traditional 1830's recipe for 25 years. Produced in 20+ flavours using natural ingredients. Available by mail-order and as wedding and corporate favours. New fudge sauces also available.

DETAILS:
Jack Wilkinson
01904 645596
58 Low Petergate, York, YO1 7HZ, North Yorkshire

E: york@fudgekitchen.co.uk
W: www.fudgekitchen.co.uk

The Gluten Free Kitchen

After winning a third award for their Victoria sponge, The Gluten Free Kitchen is clearly doing something right! Producers of quality gluten free foods including cakes, breads and confectionery products.

DETAILS:
Sue Fleming
01969 622222
Leyburn Business Park, Leyburn, DL8 5QA, North Yorkshire

E: info@theglutenfreekitchen.co.uk
W: www.glutenfreefood.info

Bakers & Confectioners

GF Foods Ltd

gff trade

Wholesale and distributor of an extensive range of gluten and wheat free products including our own range Feel Free. Feel Free is a range of savoury pastry products produced in North Yorkshire and the North East using only the finest, freshest, local ingredients.

DETAILS:
Sally Allister
01757 289200
Unit 5b, Blackwood Business Park, North Duffield, Selby, YO8 5DD, North Yorkshire

E: info@gffdirect.co.uk
W: www.gffdirect.co.uk

Bakers & Confectioners

The Harrogate Cake Company Ltd

The HARROGATE cake company limited

Award winning producer of luxury, handmade fruitcakes, The Harrogate Cake Company uses locally sourced, quality ingredients. Winning recipes remain unchanged for over 40 years, and once made, each cake is carefully hand-wrapped to ensure that each looks as great as it tastes.

DETAILS:
Heather Cawthorne
01765 641267
3 Barugh Close, Barker Business Park, Melmerby, HG4 5NJ, North Yorkshire

E: sales@harrogatecakeco.com
W: www.harrogatecakeco.com

Bakers & Confectioners

Independent Foods

I's Pies puts the emphasis is on using fresh, Yorkshire ingredients. Enjoy our generous fillings with melt in the mouth pure butter pastry. Try our delicious range of gourmet pies, quiches and tarts for yourself and look out for our seasonal specials too! Handmade, natural, delicious...

DETAILS:
Anthony Sterne
01765 641200
Unit 7 Barugh Close, Barker Business Park, Melmerby, Ripon, HG4 5NB, North Yorkshire

E: info@independentfoods.co.uk
W: www.independentfoods.co.uk

Bakers & Confectioners

It's Nut Free

Manufacturer and packer of cakes, cereal bars, snack bags and chocolate in purpose-built, nut-free factory. Supply to education and health sectors, major retailers, delis, cafes, farm shops, export and mail order.

DETAILS:
Angela Russell
01609 775660
Moxon Court, Northallerton, DL6 2NG, North Yorkshire

E: sales@itsnutfree.com
W: www.itsnutfree.com

J Stringer & Sons

A family run farm on the Yorkshire Wolds. Flours, bread mixes and breakfast foods produced from organic cereals grown and milled on the farm. deliciouslyorkshire award winner.

DETAILS:
Lisa Cardy
01759 369859
High Callis Wold, Bishop Wilton, York, YO42 1TD, North Yorkshire

E: highcalliswold@aol.com
W: www.bigbarn.co.uk

Bakers & Confectioners

Just Puds Ltd

A deliciously naughty experience for all pudding lovers, skillfully crafted from our favourite recipes. We're proud to make our puds from only the finest ingredients, sourced locally wherever we can. Serve with cream, ice cream or simply on its own, and indulge yourself in pure pud pleasure.

DETAILS:
Rosemary Robinson
0845 4097009
Lamb Hill Farm, Masham, Ripon, HG4 4DJ, North Yorkshire

E: rosemary@justpuds.co.uk
W: www.justpuds.co.uk

Bakers & Confectioners

Little Barn Limited

We source the finest ingredients from local producers to hand make high quality refrigerated, ready-to-bake cake and biscuit mixes that are 100% natural. Handmade by us, home baked by you.

DETAILS:
Nicola Grant
01423 871466
Highfield House, Brackenthwaite Lane, Harrogate, HG3 1PQ, North Yorkshire

E: nicsgrant@talktalk.net

Bakers & Confectioners

Little Pretty Things

Gorgeous little chocolates hand made just for you! We use the best Yorkshire ingredients and natural flavours from local produce to make our fresh Yorkshire chocolates perfect.

DETAILS:
Sophie Jewett
01904 898393
17 York Eco Business Centre, Amy Johnson Way, Clifton Moor, York, YO30 4AG

E: littleprettything@googlemail.com
W: www.littleprettything.co.uk

Bakers & Confectioners

Sally Middlewood Farm Bakery

Farm and tea room serving homemade bakery items and light lunches, plus local vegetables and free-range eggs. Visit us Monday to Saturday 9.30am to 5.30pm and Sunday 10.30am to 4.00pm.

DETAILS:
Sally Middlewood
01944 710256
Glebe Farm, Potter Brompton, Scarborough, YO12 4PE, North Yorkshire

E: sandcottage@btinternet.com
W: www.glebefarmbakery.co.uk

The Little Chocolate Shop Ltd

A unique attraction in the Yorkshire Dales. Our Visitor Centre is perfect for everyone to watch delicious chocolates being hand crafted. There's a shop too.

DETAILS:
Clare Gardiner
01969 625288
Leyburn Business Park, Harmby Road, Leyburn, DL8 5QA, North Yorkshire

E: info@thelittlechocolateshop.co.uk
W: www.thelittlechocolateshop.co.uk

Mama Doreen's Cupcake Company

Producers of scrumptious Yorkshire cupcakes, made using the freshest ingredients, which are sourced locally where possible. Mama Doreen's supplies to only the best deli's, eateries and caters for special occasions.

DETAILS:
Jessica Bradley
07969 306583
Harrogate, North Yorkshire

E: info@mamadoreenscupcakes.co.uk
W: www.mamadoreenscupcakes.co.uk

Stickylicious

Producers of scrumptious handmade cakes, tray bakes and award-winning luxury fruit cakes, lovingly baked in our farmhouse AGA to tantalise your taste buds. Using locally sourced ingredients wherever possible.

DETAILS:
Carolyn Chapman
01677 450202
Hessleton Farm, Hunton, Bedale, DL8 1LU, North Yorkshire

E: stickylicious@hotmail.co.uk

Bakers & Confectioners

Toftly Treats

A family run business specialising in handmade chocolate buttons with a twist! Coming in a variety of designs, varying according to season. You'll be in chocolate heaven with Toftly Treats.

DETAILS:
Anthony Hobbs
01751 476126
The Old Vicarage, Newton Upon Rawcliffe, Pickering, YO18 8QD, North Yorkshire

E: treats@toftlyview.co.uk
W: www.toftlytreats.co.uk

Bakers & Confectioners

Whitakers Chocolates Ltd

Whitakers Chocolates Ltd

Supplying quality confectionery products for over 100 years, this family run company has evolved into a leading supplier of confectionery for both foodservice and retail markets in the United Kingdom. Products include indulgent truffles, wafers, cremes and selection boxes.

DETAILS:
Deborah Beresford
01756 791317
22 High Street, Skipton, BD23 1DT, North Yorkshire

E: sales@whitakerschocolates.com
W: www.whitakerschocolates.com

Bakers & Confectioners

Woodheads Scarborough Ltd

Family owned bakery business based in Yorkshire, baking pies for over 60 years, using the finest quality ingredients, the best recipes and experienced craft bakers who make it all happen.

DETAILS:
Philip Davis
01723 363561
Beaconsfield Street, Scarborough, YO12 4EL, North Yorkshire

E: phildavis7@btconnect.com
W: www.thepiepeople.com

Beverages (Alcoholic & Non)

Averre Group Ltd

Harrogate based producer of high quality non-alcoholic beverages, distributing their products throughout the region and beyond.

DETAILS:
Ray & Jayne Averre
01423 341966
Rosemary, Copgrove, Harrogate, HG3 3SZ, North Yorkshire

E: rayaverre@msn.com

There's no county in the country where you'll find as great a variety of nature's abundance as in Yorkshire

Beverages (Alcoholic & Non)

Black Sheep Brewery

Visitor centre offers 'shepherded' tours around the brewery so guests can experience the brewing processes and sample the award-winning ales at the Baa...r. The bistro provides locally sourced culinary delights and the Sheepy Shop is full of ewe-nique gifts.

DETAILS:
Helen Allison
01765 689227

Wellgarth, Masham, Ripon, HG4 4EN, North Yorkshire

E: helen.wilkinson@blacksheep.co.uk
W: www.blacksheepbrewery.co.uk

Beverages (Alcoholic & Non)

Daleside Brewery

An independent brewer of award-winning traditional cask and premium bottled beers, the Daleside Brewery was established in the mid 1980's in the Victorian spa town of Harrogate.

DETAILS:
Eric Lucas
01423 880022

Camwal Road, Starbeck, Harrogate, HG1 4PT, North Yorkshire

E: ericlucas@dalesidebrewery.com
W: www.dalesidebrewery.com

Beverages (Alcoholic & Non)

Hambleton Ales

Brewers of real ale and bottlers of the finest quality premium ales from the heart of Yorkshire available from the brewery, in pubs, off licenses, supermarkets and restaurants all over the UK. Also the leading British brewed gluten free ale and lager in the world.

DETAILS:
Nick Stafford
01765 640108

The Brewery, Melmerby Green Road, Melmerby, Ripon, HG4 5NB, North Yorkshire

E: nick@hambletonales.co.uk
W: www.hambletonales.co.uk

Beverages (Alcoholic & Non)

Harrogate Spring Water Ltd

HARROGATE
SPRING WATER

Award-winning naturally sourced spring water from the UK's original spa town. Competitively priced, this is an everyday premium product offering distinctive design and water of the highest quality.

DETAILS:
Nicky Reeve
01423 730000
Harlow Moor Road, Harrogate, HG2 0QB, North Yorkshire
E: info@hswl.co.uk
W: www.harrogatespringwater.co.uk

Beverages (Alcoholic & Non)

New Inn & Cropton Brewery

At the edge of the North York Moors - home cooked food combined with relaxing, peaceful accommodation with a brewery too! What more can you ask for?

DETAILS:
Andy Davidson
01751 417330
Cropton, Nr Pickering, YO18 8HH, North Yorkshire
E: info@croptonbrewery.com
W: www.croptonbrewery.com

Yorkshire and Humber is home to some of the world's best known food companies and the highest concentration of small, passionate enterprises

Beverages (Alcoholic & Non)

Raisthorpe Manor Fine Foods

RAISTHORPE
FINE FOODS

Established company and Yorkshire's Finest Taste Awards Winner 2009 situated on the Yorkshire wolds, our ingredients are locally sourced and hand crafted on the premises. We offer high quality products from liqueurs and preserves to confectionery and gifts. As seen on ITV's Emmerdale!

DETAILS:
Julia Medforth
01377 288295
Raisthorpe Manor, Thixendale, York, YO17 9TF, North Yorkshire
E: enquiries@raisthorpemanor.com
W: www.raisthorpemanor.com

Beverages (Alcoholic & Non)

Richmond Brewing Company Limited

Micro brewery situated in the Station in Richmond. Supplying bottle and cask beers to both station visitors and business customers around Richmond and the Yorkshire area.

DETAILS:
Andrew Hamilton
01748 828266
The Station Brewery, Richmond, DL10 4LD, North Yorkshire

E: andy@richmondbrewing.co.uk
W: www.richmondbrewing.co.uk

Beverages (Alcoholic & Non)

SLOE motion

SLOE motion's SLOE gin (Gold Star, Great Taste Awards 08) Brandy, Whisky (two Gold Stars, Great Taste Awards 09) and Vodka are produced in the traditional way using high concentrations of fruit to ensure a fabulous flavour. We then use the liquor infused sloes in our unique chocolate truffles and chutney.

DETAILS:
Jonathan Curtoys
0844 8001911
Green Farm, Barton Le Willows, York, YO60 7PD, North Yorkshire

E: info@sloemotion.com
W: www.sloemotion.com

Beverages (Alcoholic & Non)

Thorncroft Ltd

National Trust sites, farm shops, delis, garden centre's, and consumer shows throughout Yorkshire – that's where to look for Thorncroft's unique range of botanical cordials and sparkling drinks.

DETAILS:
Michael Haigh, 01642 791792
Unit 4 Food Enterprise Centre, Conygarth Way, Leeming Bar Business Park, Leeming Bar, DL7 9EE

E: info@thorncroftdrinks.co.uk
W: www.thorncroftdrinks.co.uk

Yorkshire Country Wines

Produce quality country wines from fruits and flowers; including elderberry, elderflower, gooseberry, blackberry and damson - each variety has its own distinctive character and flavour. Idyllically located tearoom overlooking the River Nidd.

DETAILS:
Richard Brown
01423 711947
The Riverside Cellars, The Mill, Glasshouses, Harrogate, HG3 5QH

E: info@yorkshirecountrywines.co.uk
W: www.yorkshirewines.co.uk

Have you heard?

"Yorkshire produce gets better and better as every year goes by. Just like rhubarb, Yorkshire products will soon be known as the best in the world"

Brian Turner

Dairy & Eggs

Acorn Dairy

Process and distribute organic milk, cream and butter produced with milk from own herd. Recognised for excellent service and organic milk in the region, supplying doorsteps, retail and wholesalers.

DETAILS:
Caroline Tweddle
01325 466999
Archdeacon Newton, Darlington, DL2 2YB, North Yorkshire

E: organic@acorndairy.co.uk
W: www.acorndairy.co.uk

Dairy & Eggs

Beacon Farm Ice Cream

We make traditional diary ice cream and luxury sorbets in a variety of flavours. Supplying to the retail and catering trade alongside our ice cream parlour and tearooms here on the farm.

DETAILS:
Michael Shardlow
01947 605212
Beacon Farm, Beacon Way, Sneaton, Whitby, YO22 5HS, North Yorkshire

E: beaconfarm@hotmail.com
W: www.beaconfarmicecream.co.uk

Dairy & Eggs

Brown Eggs Ltd

Brown Eggs produces and packs fresh farm and free range eggs. We provide a reliable delivery service throughout North and East Yorkshire.

DETAILS:
Daniel Brown
01723 582937
Redcliffe Farm, Lebberston, Scarborough, YO11 3NT, North Yorkshire

E: daniel@browneggs.co.uk
W: www.browneggs.co.uk

Archers Jersey Ice Cream

Our range of flavours is increasing all the time - we keep flavours seasonal, introducing champagne rhubarb that was grown in the farm garden from seed, along with many fruits.

DETAILS:
Sue Archer
01325 300336
The Station, Station Yard, Richmond, DL10 4LD, North Yorkshire

E: sue@archersjerseyicecream.com
W: www.archersjerseyicecream.com

Birchfield Family Dairies and Farmshop

Luxury Jersey dairy ice cream, farmhouse butters,clotted cream and luxury yoghurts all made on the farm. Our farm shop stocks local produce and we have a cafe serving delicious wholesome food.

DETAILS:
Martin Whitley
01423 781792
Oakmount House, Birchfield Farm, Summerbridge, Harrogate, HG3 4JS

E: birchfieldicecream@live.co.uk
W: www.birchfieldicecream.co.uk

deliciouslyorkshire – championing and celebrating delicious locally-sourced, lovingly-made food that is the authentic, pukka product with full traceability

Dairy & Eggs

Brymor Ice Cream Ltd

BRYMOR

Producing 32 different flavours of award-winning ice cream, using our own milk from the pedigree Guernsey herd. On-site ice cream parlour with 250,000 visitors per annum.

DETAILS:
Nicola Moore
01677 460337
High Jervaulx Farm, Masham, Ripon, HG4 4PG, North Yorkshire

E: nicola@brymordairy.co.uk
W: www.brymordairy.co.uk

Dairy & Eggs

Chippindale Foods Ltd

Supplying free range eggs to major retailers and food service specialists, we focus on bespoke packaging and traceability.

DETAILS:
Nick Chippindale
01423 884042
Kingsley Farm, Kingsley Road, Harrogate, HG1 4RF, North Yorkshire

E: info@chippindalefoods.co.uk
W: www.chippindalefoods.co.uk

Laceys Cheese Ltd

We take great pride in our craft to bring you a high quality, locally produced product. Definitely worth a visit for any cheese enthusiast.

DETAILS:
Simon Lacey
01748 828264
Unit 1, Station Buildings, Richmond, DL10 4LD, North Yorkshire

E: simon@laceyscheese.co.uk
W: www.laceyscheese.co.uk

Dairy & Eggs

Paynes Dairies

PAYNES DAIRIES LTD
FOR QUALITY AND SERVICE

Paynes Dairies Ltd is one of the largest independent dairies in the UK, trading across all sectors including manufacturing, retail, foodservice and independents. We pride ourselves on quality and service, producing a full range of fresh milk and creams in all pack sizes.

DETAILS:
Kevin Leech
01423 326058
Bar Lane, Boroughbridge, York, YO51 9LU, North Yorkshire

E: sales@paynesdairies.co.uk
W: www.paynesdairies.com

Dairy & Eggs

The Ribblesdale Cheese Company

Artisan cheese maker and wholesaler, using local goat and ewes milk. All of our cheese is hand-waxed and we smoke our own cheese over oak chippings. Grade A BRC quality accreditation.

DETAILS:
Iona Hill
01969 667788
Upper Wensleydale Business Park, Brunt Acres Road, Hawes, DL8 3UZ

E: ionahill@gmail.com
W: www.yorkshiredalescheese.co.uk

Have you heard?

"Yorkshire has plenty of coastline and great fish to be found swimming off it, so try to support our fishing folk"

Nigel Barden

Dairy & Eggs

Ryeburn of Helmsley

Ryeburn Of Helmsley

Producing delicious award-winning dairy ice cream and sorbet for 21 years, we have one of the largest selections of flavours in the country. We are very much a family run firm who enjoy the recognition of the quality of our products.

DETAILS:
David Otterburn
01439 770331
Church Farm, Cleveland Way, Helmsley, YO62 5AT, North Yorkshire

E: info@ryeburn.com
W: www.ryeburn.com

Dairy & Eggs

Shepherds Purse Cheeses Ltd

Shepherds Purse CHEESES

Best Cheese Product - deliciouslyyorkshire awards 2009-10.
Producing multi award-winning cheeses in our SALSA accredited dairy, using cows, ewes and water buffalo milk. Our brands include Yorkshire Blue, Mrs Bell's Blue, Buffalo Blue, and the delicious Olde York. Watch out for the new Bells Bloomin White!

deliciouslyyorkshire winner awards 2009-2010

DETAILS:
Judy & Katie Bell
01845 587220
Leachfield Grange, Newsham, Thirsk, YO7 4DJ, North Yorkshire

E: katie@shepherdspurse.co.uk
W: www.shepherdspurse.co.uk

Dairy & Eggs

St Helen's Farm

Fantastic family run goat farming business and supplier of fresh goat's milk, butter, yogurts, cream and cheese to supermarkets across the country, from their dairy near York.

DETAILS:
Mike Hind
01430 861400
Seaton Ross, York, YO42 4NP, North Yorkshire

E: info@sthelensfarm.co.uk
W: www.sthelensfarm.co.uk

Dairy & Eggs

The Swaledale Cheese Company

A family run business set in the heart of the Yorkshire Dales making award-winning, artisan Swaledale cheeses with PDO status. Range of 14 cheeses including goat, sheep and cow varieties.

DETAILS:
Mandy Reed
01748 824932
Mercury Road, Gallowfields, Richmond, DL10 4TQ, North Yorkshire

E: sales@swaledalecheese.co.uk
W: www.swaledalecheese.co.uk

Dairy & Eggs

Wensleydale Dairy Products Ltd

As the only makers of Real Yorkshire Wensleydale Cheese in the world, we are proud to achieve global acclaim for our award-winning cheeses. We are dedicated to ensuring all of our cheeses are made using traditional recipes that have been handed down through the generations.

DETAILS:
David Hartley
01969 667664
Gayle Lane, Hawes, Wensleydale, DL8 3RN, North Yorkshire

E: creamery@wensleydale.co.uk
W: www.wensleydale.co.uk

Stamfrey Farm Organics

Award-winning organic clotted cream and yoghurt, handmade using traditional methods on our own dairy farm. Suppliers to some of the finest eateries in Yorkshire. Available in selected farm shops and delis.

DETAILS:
Sue Gaudie
01609 882297
Stamfrey Farm, West Rounton, Northallerton, DL6 2LJ, North Yorkshire

E: info@stamfrey.co.uk
W: www.stamfrey.co.uk

Town Head Farm Products

Keeping dairy farming alive in the lower dales – we have our own herd of over 100 cows, supplemented by eight other local dairy farmers we supply milk to the region's NHS facilities.

DETAILS:
David Oversby
01756 752296
Town Head Farm, Grassington, Skipton, BD23 5BL, North Yorkshire

E: thfp@btconnect.com

Dairy & Eggs

Yoghurt Delights

The healthy alternative to ice cream, each frozen yoghurt is made using live yoghurt cultures. deliciouslyorkshire and deliciously low fat – come and see us at the region's shows and events!

DETAILS:
Elaine Newham
01723 870048
Highlands Farm, Lindhead Road, Burniston, Scarborough, YO13 0DL, North Yorkshire
E: elaine.newham@btconnect.com

Dairy & Eggs

Yorvale Ltd

Using only the milk from our cows, natural flavourings and locally sourced cream, we have created 28 ice creams and ten sorbet flavours that taste divine.

DETAILS:
Lesley Buxton
01904 706702
Fossfield Farm, Fossfield Lane, Acaster Malbis, York, YO23 2XA, North Yorkshire
E: customerservice@yorvale.co.uk
W: www.yorvale.co.uk

Fish (Fresh & Smoked)

Bleikers Smokehouse Ltd

Traditionally cure and smoke a broad range of the finest quality fresh fish. Our provenance and quality is recognised by numerous awards from the Guild of Fine Food Retailers.

DETAILS:
Charlie & Annabel Andrew
01423 711411
Unit 88, Glasshouses Mill, Glasshouses, Harrogate, HG3 5QH, North Yorkshire
E: annabel@bleikers.co.uk
W: www.bleikerssmokehouse.co.uk

Yorkshire Dales Ice Cream Ltd

Manufacture on the farm. Retail and sell from own fleet of vans and, from summer 2010, our fabulous new ice cream parlour here at the farm. Take home tubs are also available.

DETAILS:
Mandy Rogers
01756 710685
Calm Slate Farm, Halton East, Bolton Abbey, Skipton, BD23 6EU, North Yorkshire
E: mandy@yorkshiredalesicecream.co.uk
W: www.yorkshiredalesicecream.co.uk

Fish (Fresh & Smoked)

Artisan Cooks

Specialists in seafood deli items, oyster bar and canapes. Dedicated to using the best local produce - mobile seafood deli, corporate and private hire. See us with deliciouslyorkshire and taste our seafood dishes.

DETAILS:
David Hunter
01423 569910
4 Harlow View, Harrogate, HG2 9LX, North Yorkshire
E: mail@artisancooks.co.uk
W: www.artisancooks.co.uk

Scarborough Shell and Fish Company

A seafood equivalent to a farm shop. Providing sustainable caught fish (long line) and shellfish caught by our own and other local boats (whenever possible). Also, ethically killed shellfish.

DETAILS:
Clive Crosby
01723 372782
Market Hall, St Helens Square, Scarborough, YO11 1EU, North Yorkshire
E: clivecrosby72@hotmail.com

Fish (Fresh & Smoked)

Whitby Seafish Ltd

WHITBY SEAFISH LTD
Suppliers of fresh, hand prepared fish from Whitby & Scarborough

Processors of fresh and naturally smoked fish, all prepared by hand at our facility in the historic fishing village of Staithes. We pride ourselves on supplying excellent produce to the catering Industry throughout the UK.

DETAILS:
Matthew Asquith
01947 841236

Unit 1a Whitegate Close, Staithes, Saltburn, TS13 5BB

E: whitby-seafish@btconnect.com
W: www.whitbyseafish.co.uk

Fresh Ingredients

Bluebell Farm – Askham Bryan

We grow quality summer fruits and vegetables. (Open June to August). Visit us to pick your own or take home our ready picked fruits and vegetables. Local delivery.

DETAILS:
Andrew Sykes
01904 798426

Askham Bryan, York, YO23 3QY, North Yorkshire

E: apandje@hotmail.com

Have you heard?

“Yorkshire is teeming with the very best produce served up by hard-working, ingenious folk, passionate about what they do”

Alan Titchmarsh

Fresh Ingredients

Herbs Unlimited

Specialists in growing, importing, washing and processing fresh herbs and salads for both consumers and manufacturing industries. Products include freshly cut herbs, salads, spinach as well as unusual herb mixes.

DETAILS:
Alison Dodd
01845 587694

Hawker Lane, Sandhutton, Thirsk, YO7 4RW, North Yorkshire

E: sglltd@btconnect.com
W: www.herbsunlimited.co.uk

Fresh Ingredients

Stuart's Foods Ltd

High quality, fresh food wholesaler based in Scarborough, specialising in fresh fruit and vegetables. Sourcing only the freshest and best quality ingredients for local and national customers.

DETAILS:
Damian Howarth
01723 582252
Howarth House, Dunslow Court, Eastfield, Scarborough, YO11 3XT

E: info@stuartsfoods.co.uk
W: www.stuartsfoods.co.uk

The Organic Pantry

We pride ourselves on being amongst the foremost growers of organic salad and vegetables in the North. Our produce is available through our shop, box scheme, farmers markets and wholesale.

DETAILS:
Fanny Watson
01937 531693
St. Helens Farm, Newton Kyme, Tadcaster, LS24 9LY, North Yorkshire

E: office@theorganicpantry.co.uk
W: www.theorganicpantry.co.uk

Fresh Ingredients

Yorkshire Rapeseed Oil

Based near Thixendale on the Yorkshire Wolds, we offer high quality oils and dressings to the region's small retailers. For more information about our products, please visit our website.

DETAILS:
Adam Palmer
01759 368337
Thixendale, Malton, YO17 9LS, North Yorkshire

E: info@yorkshirehealthoil.co.uk
W: www.yorkshirehealthoil.co.uk

Ingredient Suppliers

Food Design Ltd

Bakers, confectioners and manufacturer of fudge and toffee inclusions for baking. Chilled and frozen desserts, chocolate confectionery, ice cream and breakfast cereals.

DETAILS:
Craig Hindmarsh
01423 870875
Valley House, Hornbeam Park Avenue, Harrogate, HG2 8QT, North Yorkshire

E: info@food-design.co.uk
W: www.food-design.co.uk

Hobson Farming Limited

We supply freshly dug, quality unwashed carrots to farm shops and greengrocers. Far better than washed carrots with superior taste, we are accredited to Natures Choice and Marks and Spencer.

DETAILS:
Vicky Hobson
01904 628670
Naburn Hill Farm, Crockley Hill, York, YO19 4SR, North Yorkshire

E: vlhobson@googlemail.com
W: www.hobsonfarming.co.uk

Ingredient Suppliers

J. E. Hartley Ltd

Using locally sourced vegetables wherever possible, we process, freeze and pack harvested vegetables, before supplying food manufacturers all over the UK and Europe.

DETAILS:
Jane Hartley
01904 448556
Roth Hill Lane, Thorganby, York, YO19 6DJ, North Yorkshire

E: tom@jehartleyfrozenveg.co.uk
W: www.jehartley.com

Metcalfe Food 2 Survive

Vegetable grower, packer and processor. Supply the carrots for the School Fruit and Vegetable scheme for Yorkshire and Humber (240 000 pieces /week). Washed or unwashed potatoes and carrots.

DETAILS:
Steven Metcalfe
01423 322605
Low House Farm, Aldborough, Boroughbridge, York, YO51 9HD

E: sales@metcalfeorganic.co.uk
W: www.food2survive.eu

Fresh Ingredients

Rafi's Spicebox

Specialising in the unique 'Curry Pack', invented by founder Rafi Fernandez, choose from 27 varieties, all spices blended to your taste. Simple Indian food, no need for chopping or oil.

DETAILS:
Kevin Fernandez
01904 638119
17 Goodramgate, York, YO1 7LW, North Yorkshire

E: york@spicebox.co.uk
W: www.spicebox.co.uk

Yorkshire Organic Millers

We are proud of the fact that we mill only locally grown organic grain. We supply the finest artisan bakers, hotels and restaurants. Try us and see for yourself!

DETAILS:
Joe Coughlan
01751 417799
Hill Top Farm, Spaunton, YO62 6TR, North Yorkshire

E: organicmillers@hotmail.com
W: www.yorkshireorganicmillers.co.uk

Meat, Poultry & Game

About Foods Ltd

Specialising in meat components for manufacturers and meal centre proteins for foodservice we are a BRC A grade meat processor. We supply cooked and raw meat, portioned, sliced, diced or shredded. Contract cooking service also available.

DETAILS:
Nigel Upson
0845 8800138
Oaklands, Church Lane, Moor Monkton, York, YO26 8LA, North Yorkshire

E: nigel@about-foods.co.uk
W: www.about-foods.co.uk

Meat, Poultry & Game

Appletons of Ripon

APPLETONS

Established in 1867, Appletons of Ripon's famous pork pies are made fresh every day with great ingredients to Appletons secret recipe. As a traditional pork butcher, other delicious cooked and fresh meats are available including handmade sausages, black pudding, haslet, polony, bacon and ham.

DETAILS:

Anthony Sterne
01765 603198

6 Market Place East, Ripon, HG4 1BP, North Yorkshire

E: info@independentfoods.co.uk

Meat, Poultry & Game

Arthur Haigh Ltd

Arthur Haigh's are based at Dalton near Thirsk in the centre of Herriot country. A second generation family business, excelling in premium award-winning cooked meats and champion pork sausage varieties.

DETAILS:

Duncan Haigh
01845 578227

Feedemwell, Unit G Dalton Airfield Industrial Estate, Dalton, Thirsk, YO7 3HE

E: duncan_haigh@btconnect.com
W: www.yorkshireblackpudding.co.uk

Meat, Poultry & Game

Colin M Robinson Award Winning Family Butchers

We are the premier retailer of Limestone Country beef, home reared Rock View pork and lamb, as well as our award-winning homemade sausages and home dry cured bacon.

DETAILS:

Colin Robinson
01756 752476

41 Main Street, Grassington, Skipton, BD23 5AA, North Yorkshire

E: info@colinmrobinson.co.uk
W: www.colinmrobinson.co.uk

The Blue Pig Company

Family run business with free range, rare breed pigs in the Yorkshire Dales. We produce gourmet sausages, dry cured bacons, gammon, black pudding and pork available from our online shop.

DETAILS:

Andrew Bradley
01729 840218

Mearbeck, Long Preston, Skipton, BD23 4QP, North Yorkshire

E: andrew@bluepigcompany.com
W: www.bluepigcompany.com

Debbie & Andrew's

Producers of quality sausages, we also produce dry cured bacon and hams and supply supermarkets and delis on a nationwide basis.

DETAILS:

Debbie Keeble
0800 7836481

Berryhills, Kirklington, Bedale, DL8 2NL, North Yorkshire

E: debbie@debbieandandrews.co.uk
W: www.debbieandandrews.co.uk

Meat, Poultry & Game

Farmhouse Direct

Farmers and producers of rare breed meats and sausages. Handmade rare breed pork pies with delicious toppings - Brandsby Pies which can be purchased at top class deli's throughout Yorkshire.

DETAILS:
David & Jacqui Kitson
01347 889354

Seaves Farm, Brandsby, York, YO61 4RT, North Yorkshire

E: info@farmhousedirect.com
W: www.farmhousedirect.com

There's so much wonderful food in Yorkshire – the hardest bit will be making a decision but then no-one said it was going to be easy!

Meat, Poultry & Game

Herb Fed

HERB FED
For A Bird With Taste

Producer and supplier of free range chickens and ducks throughout the year, as well as traditionally reared bronze turkeys for Christmas. All of our birds are fed on locally produced feed and fresh herbs to provide a bird with a difference and a flavour to be enjoyed by all.

DETAILS:
Edward Wilkinson
07765 044245

Woodmans House, Pilmoor, York, YO61 2QG, North Yorkshire

E: info@herbfed.co.uk
W: www.herbfed.co.uk

Meat, Poultry & Game

Holme Farmed Venison

Holme Farmed Venison

Providing high quality venison farmed to the highest standards, our deer are naturally reared on grass pastures in Yorkshire, guaranteeing a beautifully lean and tender meat. We currently supply Michelin starred restaurants, gastro pubs, hotels and major retailers.

DETAILS:
Nigel Sampson
01977 686440

9 First Avenue, Aviation Road, Sherburn in Elmet, Leeds, LS25 6PD, North Yorkshire

E: nigel@hfv.co.uk
W: www.hfv.co.uk

Meat, Poultry & Game

Masham Sausages

A family business, run by Paul and Michelle Dennis and now in its eleventh year of trading. Quality products made using good quality meat and the best quality seasonings.

DETAILS:

Paul Dennis
01765 640099

5 Hallikeld Close, Barker Business Park, Melmerby, Ripon, HG4 5GZ

E: j.p.dennis@talk21.com
W: www.mashamsausages.com

Yorkshire's bountiful supply of fresh local ingredients is as a magnet to the finest chefs the UK has to offer

Meat, Poultry & Game

North York Moors Shearling Group

We supply shearlings which have lived nearly all their lives on our heather moors. Properly matured on hook, our meat is considered the best in the area. We distribute to caterers via Taste Tradition and frozen meat to our Consumer Supported Agriculture Schemes (see the Shearling website within www.scarborough-local-food.org.uk).

DETAILS:

Philip & Nelly Trevelyan
01751 417351

Hill Top Farm, Spaunton Bank, Appleton Le Moors, YO62 6TR, North Yorkshire

E: organicmillers@btconnect.com
W: www.yorkshireorganicmillers.com

Meat, Poultry & Game

Paganum

Online farmers market – producer and supplier of quality, Yorkshire dales meat and produce. Family run farm supplying restaurants, pubs, hotels and direct. Free national delivery.

DETAILS:

Chris Wildman
01729 830727

Church End Farm, Kirkby Malham, Skipton, BD23 4BU, North Yorkshire

E: chris@paganum.co.uk
W: www.paganum.co.uk

Paynes Turkeys

An established, family-run farming business, rearing turkeys since 1953, producing day-old turkey poults, growing turkeys and traditional farm fresh and barn-reared white and bronze turkeys for a perfect Christmas.

DETAILS:

Christopher Payne
01430 872455

East Bursea Farm, Holme on Spalding Moor, York, YO43 4DB, North Yorkshire

E: sales@paynesturkeys.co.uk
W: www.paynesturkeys.co.uk

Meat, Poultry & Game

R & J Catering Butchers Ltd

A well established, family run business comprising of our active Yorkshire farm and purpose built cutting plant. We specialise in supplying the very best Yorkshire beef, lamb, pork, poultry and game to catering establishments throughout the county. We work with farmers and producers to ensure consistency from field to fork.

DETAILS:
Ryan Atkinson
01765 658611

Watersedge, Long Swales Lane, Kirkby Malzeard, Ripon, HG4 3RJ, North Yorkshire

E: ryan_rjc@hotmail.co.uk

Meat, Poultry & Game

Robinsons Pork Butchers Knaresborough Ltd

A well established family business in Knaresborough, Robinson's make handmade, award winning speciality pork pies and sausages. We are a traditional business with a modern twist.

DETAILS:
Mick Robinson
01423 863077

46 Market Place, Knaresborough, HG5 8AG, North Yorkshire

E: m.wrobinson@btopenworld.com

Taste Tradition Ltd

Best Prepared Meat Product - deliciouslyorkshire awards 2009-10. A family run business producing the highest quality rare and native breed meat. Served in the finest restaurants, stores and butchers nationwide.

DETAILS:
Charles Ashbridge
01845 525330
Units I & J Lumley Close, Thirsk Industrial Park, Thirsk, YO7 3TD

E: joyce@tastetradition.co.uk
W: www.tastetradition.co.uk

Meat, Poultry & Game

Trotters Farm Shop

Specialise in our own free range pork. Our pigs have the freedom to root and roam, giving a traditional tasting pork. Fresh cuts of pork, award-winning sausages, dry cured bacon and hams. Also a selection of locally reared beef, lamb and poultry.

DETAILS:
Paul Bradbury
01944 710721

Gladvic Farm, Potter Brompton, Scarborough, YO12 4PF, North Yorkshire

E: info@trotterspork.com
W: www.trotterspork.com

Meat, Poultry & Game

The York Sausage, Meat & Pie Shop

We offer free range eggs, meat and bacon and a growing range of freshly prepared award-winning sausages, cooked meats and pies using fresh Yorkshire produce.

DETAILS:
Julie Wilson
07752 606050
45 The Shambles, York, YO1 7LX, North Yorkshire

E: juliedoubleyou@hotmail.com
W: www.yorksausageshop.co.uk

Meat, Poultry & Game

Yorkshire Game Ltd

Suppliers of fresh, oven ready game and specialist foods to the catering trade, operating in North Yorkshire. Offering wild Scottish venison, grouse, pheasant, partridge, wild duck, woodpigeon, hare and rabbit.

DETAILS:
Richard Townsend
01748 810212
Station Road Industrial Park, Brompton on Swale, Richmond, DL10 7SN

E: ben@blackface.co.uk
W: www.yorkshiregame.co.uk

Pies

Vale of Mowbray Ltd

Producing pork pies in Leeming Bar since 1928, our crispy baked pastry filled with succulent cured meat provides the "Flavour to Savour" throughout the UK. We are proud of the products we produce and once experienced you will see why!

DETAILS:
Paul Keeton
01677 422661
20 Leases Road, Leeming Bar, DL7 9AW, North Yorkshire

E: paulkeeton@valeofmowbray.co.uk
W: www.valeofmowbray.co.uk

Yorkshire Dales Meat Company Ltd

Best Fresh Meat Product - deliciouslyyorkshire awards 2009-10. One of the largest premier catering butchers in Yorkshire supplying quality and well matured meat. See us at farmers markets and festivals.

DETAILS:
Stephen Knox
01748 810042
Mill Close Farm, Patrick Brompton, Bedale, DL8 1JY, North Yorkshire

E: info@yorkshiredalesmeat.com
W: www.yorkshiredalesmeat.com

Have you heard?

"I'm always proud to shout about our great Yorkshire produce and our brilliant array of suppliers"

James Mackenzie

Pies

Voakes Pies

Award-winning pork pie producer. Pies made at our purpose built factory at Whixley Grange Farm. Using our own herd of pigs and the best ingredients we take great care in producing a delicious pork pie for all food lovers!

DETAILS:
Andrew Voakes
01423 339988

Whixley Grange, Whixley, York, YO26 8AY, North Yorkshire

E: enquiries@voakespies.co.uk
W: www.voakespies.co.uk

Prepared Food

Bare Earth Ltd

Produce a range of healthy air dried meat snack products. Our range includes beef biltong, beef droewors (dried sausage) and organic beef jerky under Elizabeth Hurley Organics brand.

DETAILS:
Gary Quinn
01765 641824

8 Hallikeld Close, Barker Business Park, Melmerby, Ripon, HG4 5GZ, North Yorkshire

E: info@bare-earth.co.uk
W: www.bare-earth.co.uk

Prepared Food

R & R Tofu

Supplying organic tofu to wholesale and restaurants in the independent organic sector. At R & R Tofu, smoked tofu is our speciality!

DETAILS:
Ron Malarkey
01653 690235

Unit 5 Plot 8, Rye Close, York Road Business Park, Malton, YO17 6YD

E: RandRTofu@dsl.pipex.com
W: www.clearspottofu.co.uk

Westler Foods Ltd

Westlers are best known for manufacturing foodservice hotdogs. However, we also produce some well known retail brands including Tyne, Chesswood, Wayfayrer and numerous supermarket private label brands.

DETAILS:
Robert Burns
01653 693971

Amotherby, Malton, YO17 6TQ, North Yorkshire

E: robert.burns@westler.com
W: www.westlerfoods.com

Prepared Food

Whitby Seafoods Ltd

Specialists in frozen seafood coated in batter and breadcrumbs located in the iconic fishing port of Whitby, North Yorkshire. With a grade A for BRC accreditation ensuring quality products.

DETAILS:

Sarah Cox
01947 829015
Fairfield Way, Whitby Business Park, Whitby, YO22 4PU, North Yorkshire

E: sarah.cox@whitby-seafoods.com
W: www.whitby-seafoods.com

The Yorkshire Provender

We dare to go where no soup manufacturer has gone before! Using fresh and seasonal produce to achieve innovative new flavour combinations that really work.

DETAILS:

Terry Williams
01765 641212
Unit 5E Keld Close, Barker Business Park, Melmerby Ripon, HG4 5NB

E: info@theyorkshireprovender.co.uk
W: www.theyorkshireprovender.co.uk

Prepared Food

Yorkshire Dales Real Food

YORKSHIRE DALES REAL FOOD

Tasty granola fresh from the Dales! Our delicious granola is made from freshly milled wholegrains, bound together with an emulsion of olive oil and honey all hand-baked in small batches every day. Visit our website for all the delicious details.

DETAILS:

Stuart & Elizabeth Hird
01756 760835
Yockenthwaite Farm, Buckden, Skipton, BD23 5JH, North Yorkshire

E: info@yorkshiredalesrealfood.co.uk
W: www.yorkshiredalesrealfood.co.uk

Preserves/Honey/Condiments/Spices

Asharun Spices

Quality masala and spices uniquely blended to family recipes, perfect for homemade gourmet Indian cuisine.

DETAILS:

Syndi Duke
01423 541931
2 Back Chatsworth Grove, Harrogate, HG1 2AF, North Yorkshire

E: syndi.duke@chillinspice.co.uk
W: www.asharunspices.com

Visit our farm shops – an opportunity to enjoy the scenery, breathe fresh air and sample some of the produce: the original 'gate to plate' experience

Preserves/Honey/Condiments/Spices

Just Williams

Our ranges of award-winning products are all handmade in traditional open pans. Most of the fruit we use is handpicked from local gardens, orchards and wild hedgerows. From bullace jelly to hedgerow butter, quince cheese to wild bramble jam, we specialise in the unusual. Treat yourself.

DETAILS:
William Ramsbottom
07775 670134

9 High Street, Gilling West, Richmond, DL10 5JB, North Yorkshire

E: william@just-williams.com
W: www.just-williams.com

Preserves/Honey/Condiments/Spices

Raman's Kitchen

Producers of a wide range of hand-cooked relishes with a twist, using Yorkshire grown fruit and vegetables infused with spices to make these versatile accompaniments that give a kick!

DETAILS:
Priya Vardhan
07877 172503

4 The Willows, Strensall, York, YO32 5YG, North Yorkshire

E: ramanskitchen@googlemail.com

Raydale Preserves

Located in the heart of the Yorkshire Dales, preserve suppliers established by Derek and Lesley Kettlewell produce over 40 varieties of jam, honey, chutney and jelly, using traditional production methods.

DETAILS:
Derek Kettlewell
01969 650233

School House Farm, Stalling Busk, Leyburn, DL8 3DH, North Yorkshire

E: kraydale@aol.com
W: www.raydalepreserves.co.uk

Preserves/Honey/Condiments/Spices

Rosebud Preserves

Producer of sweet and savoury preserves since 1989. Our preserves are made by hand, in small batches, using traditional methods, and are characterised by bold, fresh flavours and natural sets.

DETAILS:
Elspeth Biltoft
01765 689174

Rosebud Farm, Healey, Masham, Ripon, HG4 4LH, North Yorkshire

E: elspeth@rosebudpreserves.co.uk
W: www.rosebudpreserves.co.uk

Preserves/Honey/Condiments/Spices

The Fruity Kitchen

The Fruity Kitchen

Handmade all the way! A family run business producing handmade preserves and chutneys made in small batches. Using locally sourced, quality ingredients including handpicked fruits, vegetables and free range eggs.

DETAILS:
John Southern
01347 810300
Unit 9/16, Green Park Business Centre, Sutton on the Forest, York, YO61 1ET, North Yorkshire
E: thefruitykitchen@tiscali.co.uk
W: www.thefruitykitchen.co.uk

Preserves/Honey/Condiments/Spices

The One Stop Hot Shop

Fine fiery fayre from home grown chillies! From Chocolate to 'Smart Arse Sauce' there is something for everyone! We are committed to promoting the humble yet fabulous chilli throughout Yorkshire.

DETAILS:
Andrea Wood
01845 537056
2 Primrose Hill, Kirby Knowle, Thirsk, YO7 2JF, North Yorkshire
E: awood824@btinternet.com
W: www.theonestophotshop.co.uk

York Speciality Foods

Best Preserves Product - deliciouslyorkshire awards 2009-10. Makers of preserves for 25 years, we offer a range of traditional luxury preserves and condiments, locally produced by hand in small batches.

deliciouslyorkshire winner awards 2009-2010

DETAILS:
Paul Mercer
01904 444949
Millfield Industrial Estate, Wheldrake, York, YO19 6NA, North Yorkshire
E: paul@yorkpreserves.com
W: www.yorkpreserves.com

Cafés & Tearooms

The Arches Cookery School

Based on a farm in East Cleveland, the main ingredients for all our recipes are sourced from local suppliers. Providing the perfect environment to learn and find fun in cooking.

DETAILS:
Sarah Muir
0845 5439005
Grinkle Park Farm, Loftus, Saltburn, TS13 4UD
E: sarah@archescookeryschool.co.uk
W: www.archescookeryschool.co.uk

Yorkshire has made it to the top of the food charts with the most Michelin-starred restaurants – six – in the country

Cafés & Tearooms

Bettys & Taylors of Harrogate

Bettys EST. 1919

Bettys is a traditional family business, and a trip to Yorkshire isn't complete without a visit to one of our six café tea rooms - find us in Harrogate, Ilkley, Northallerton and York. Or why not learn to make some of our signature dishes at our cookery school in Harrogate?

DETAILS:
01423 814000

1 Parliament Street, Harrogate, HG1 2QU, North Yorkshire

W: www.bettys.co.uk
www.bettyscookeryschool.co.uk

Cafés & Tearooms

Bishopthorpe Cookery Club

Retired caterer Diana Naish runs a cookery club at The Chantry for the local junior school as well as adult cookery classes. She also offers dinners for her B&B guests.

DETAILS:
Diana Naish
01904 709767

The Chantry, Chantry Lane, Bishopthorpe, York, YO23 2QF, North Yorkshire

E: diananaish@athomecatering.freeserve.co.uk

Café Harlequin

Regarded as one of the best coffee shops worldwide. It also offers a fantastic lunch menu and a fine afternoon tea. Their award winning coffee is available retail and wholesale.

DETAILS:
Marie Howell
01904 630631

2 Kings Square, York, YO1 8BH, North Yorkshire

E: marie@cafeharlequin.talktalkbusinesshosting.co.uk

Cafés & Tearooms

The Cooking Rooms

Whether you want to learn the basics, or take a master class, The Cooking Rooms in York allows you to hone your skills. Also available for private events and parties.

DETAILS:
Luke Norbury
01904 500700

Workshops 7 & 8, York Eco Business Centre, Amy Johnson Way, York, YO30 4AG

E: info@thecookingrooms.com
W: www.thecookingrooms.com

D'oyly's Tearoom

Traditional farmhouse tearoom drawing from Yorkshire's unique food and farming heritage to provide delicious homemade fare for your enjoyment whilst supporting small scale local producers.

DETAILS:
Victoria Houseman
01904 744354

North House, Bolton Percy, York, YO23 7AN, North Yorkshire

E: henryhouseman@yahoo.co.uk
W: www.doylys.co.uk

Cafés & Tearooms

Fountains Abbey & Studley Royal

National Trust

Celebrating every element of Yorkshire food, we aim to inspire our supporters to eat local and seasonal food in our large restaurant and relaxing tearoom. Our venison is free range from the estate, and we support many local suppliers by using their produce.

DETAILS:
Andi Aikman
01765 608888

Estate Office, Fountains Abbey, Ripon, HG4 3DY, North Yorkshire

E: info@fountainsabbey.org.uk
W: www.fountainsabbey.org.uk

Cafés & Tearooms

The Glass House Cafe Bistro

The GLASS HOUSE Cafe Bistro

Situated in beautiful park land, an elegant modern cafe transforming into a bistro on Thursday, Friday and Saturday from 6:30pm. Serving Italian coffees, fine teas and light snacks during the day, inside or outside. We cater for food allergies and intolerances and aim to make your visit a memorable experience.

DETAILS:
Lesley Humphreys
01723 368791

Northstead Manor Gardens, Burniston Road, Scarborough, YO12 6PF, North Yorkshire

E: info@glasshousebistro.co.uk
W: www.glasshousebistro.co.uk

Cafés & Tearooms

Harmony House Cookery School

Day and residential cookery courses for adults and children of all abilities. Offering cookery demonstrations, home tuition, culinary team building, food hygiene training and food solutions for easy home entertaining.

DETAILS:
Hilary Finney
01904 720933

The Green, Stillingfleet, York, YO19 6SH

E: hilary@harmonyhousecookeryschool.co.uk
W: www.harmonyhousecookeryschool.co.uk

Just-Delicious

Producing award winning products in their Harrogate based coffee shop, offering a display of stunning cakes, scones and savouries. Why not pop in to eat or take home some treats?

DETAILS:
Donna Clark
01423 711595

9-10 Kings Court, Pateley Bridge, Harrogate, HG3 5JW, North Yorkshire

E: de_clark2004@yahoo.co.uk
W: www.just-delicious.co.uk

Cafés & Tearooms

The Lime Tree Cafe & Delicatessen

Popular cafe and deli located in a family owned garden centre midway between Harrogate & Knaresborough. Freshly prepared meals, genuine home baking along with a selection of 250 fine wines.

DETAILS:
Nick Iles
01423 869800
Moorland Nurseries, Forest Moor Road, Knaresborough, HG5 8JY

E: nick@limetreecafe.co.uk
W: www.limetreecafe.co.uk

Hotels & Restaurants

Angel Inn

Picturesque pioneering gastro pub in the heart of the Yorkshire Dales. Locally sourced seasonally changing menus with full vegetarian menu options. Daily fish blackboard. New Angel Auberge dining experience.

DETAILS:
Bruce Elsworth
01756 730263
Main Street, Hetton, Skipton, BD23 6LT, North Yorkshire

E: info@angelhetton.co.uk
W: www.angelhetton.co.uk

Hotels & Restaurants

The Abbey Inn

18th century inn with stunning views of Byland Abbey, serving Yorkshire food with a modern spin. Seasonal menu using fresh local produce. Three ensuite bedrooms.

DETAILS:
Melanie Drew and David Robbins
01347 868204
Byland Abbey, Coxwold, YO61 4BD, North Yorkshire

E: theabbey-inn@btconnect.com
W: www.theappletree.org

Hotels & Restaurants

The Alice Hawthorn (Punch Taverns)

Emma and Mark welcome you to the newly refurbished Alice. The pub stands for all that is great about village inns; freshly prepared, homemade dishes featuring the highest quality locally sourced ingredients from our various menus in beautiful surroundings.

DETAILS:
Emma & Mark Jordon
01423 330303
The Green, Nun Monkton, York, YO26 8EW, North Yorkshire

E: emma@the-alice.co.uk
W: www.the-alice.co.uk

Hotels & Restaurants

Beiderbecke's Hotel & Restaurant

Beiderbecke's
HOTEL & BRASSERIE

A boutique hotel overlooking a quiet leafy crescent just a street away from Scarborough town centre. It has excellent service and a contemporary brasserie, Marmalade's.

DETAILS:
Jean-Yves Cottard
01723 365766

1-3 The Crescent, Scarborough, YO11 2PW, North Yorkshire

E: info@beiderbeckes.com
W: www.beiderbeckes.com

Hotels & Restaurants

The Black Bull Inn (Punch Taverns)

Tina and local chef Andrew (formally of Middlethorpe Hall) welcome you to the newly refurbished Black Bull. Enjoy traditional home cooked food, using wherever possible, locally sourced ingredients in a relaxed and child friendly atmosphere.

DETAILS:
Andrew Walker
01751 471590

Malton Road, Pickering, YO18 8EA, North Yorkshire

E: theblackbullpickering@googlemail.com

Hotels & Restaurants

The Black Lion

Sitting in the market square of Thirsk offering visitors a unique atmosphere and dining experience, the Black Lion is open for morning coffee, luncheon and dinner. Providing homemade cakes, scones and an extensive lunch and dinner menu using locally sourced ingredients with Yorkshire flair.

DETAILS:
Richard Bainbridge
01845 574302

8 Market Place, Thirsk, YO7 1LB, North Yorkshire

E: info@blacklionthirsk.co.uk
W: www.blacklionthirsk.co.uk

Hotels & Restaurants

The Black Swan at Oldstead

Best use of Regional Produce on a Menu (restaurant/pub/inn) - deliciouslyorkshire awards 2009-10.
Expect seriously good food with stylish luxury accommodation in a stunning rural location. This Michelin Rising Star pub and restaurant is becoming established as one of the best places to eat in the area.

DETAILS:
Anne Banks
01347 868387

Oldstead, Coxwold, Nr Helmsley, York, YO61 4BL, North Yorkshire

E: enquiries@blackswanoldstead.co.uk
W: www.blackswanoldstead.co.uk

Hotels & Restaurants

Black Swan Hotel

Yorkshire is famed for its high quality food and the cuisine at the Black Swan Hotel doesn't disappoint, with its two AA rosette restaurant serving up locally sourced dishes, and its own award winning tearoom. Voted Top Tea Place 2010 serving a wide selection of teas from around the world.

DETAILS:
Chris Falcus
01439 770466

Market Place, Helmsley, YO62 5DJ, North Yorkshire

E: chrisf@blackswan-helmsley.co.uk
W: www.blackswan-helmsley.co.uk

Hotels & Restaurants

Bleikers At The Malt Shovel

The Bleiker family has a wealth of experience in food, hospitality and the world of opera. Committed to using the finest local ingredients, fine wine and cask ales.

DETAILS:
Jane Bleiker
01423 862929

The Malt Shovel, Main Street, Brearton, Harrogate, HG3 3BX, North Yorkshire

E: bleikers@themaltshovelbrearton.co.uk
W: www.themaltshovelbrearton.co.uk

Hotels & Restaurants

The Bull

THE BULL

Situated four miles from Skipton, The Bull at Broughton showcases the finest Yorkshire produce on its menus, created by chef Nigel Haworth, celebrity chef and finalist of BBC2's Great British Menu. Recipes include Barnsley chop, Yorkshire curd tart, a true accolade to the regions finest ingredients.

DETAILS:
01756 792065

Broughton, Skipton, BD23 3AE, North Yorkshire

E: enquiries@thebullatbroughton.com
W: www.thebullatbroughton.co.uk

Hotels & Restaurants

Burn Hall Hotel

THE garden ROOM

The Burn Hall Hotel is proud to launch a new fine dining experience - The Garden Room is an intimate restaurant with the focus on quality local produce. The first crops have been harvested from our garden, making the distance from ground to fork a matter of yards.

DETAILS:
Claire Waterhouse
01347 825400

Tollerton Road, Huby, York, YO61 1JB, North Yorkshire

E: enquiries@burn-hall.co.uk
W: www.burnhall.com

Hotels & Restaurants

The Cayley Arms (Punch Taverns)

A warm welcome and exceptional home cooked fayre using the best seasonal ingredients from the local area await you. Our extensive range of wines and ales complement your dining experience.

DETAILS:
Jo Massingham & Laura Hutton
01723 859372

High Street, Brompton-By-Sawdon, Scarborough, YO13 9DA, North Yorkshire

E: joannabou@hotmail.com

Cedar Court Grand Hotel & Spa

York's first five star hotel presents their restaurant, HQ at the Grand. Combining traditional favourites with adventurous gastronomic delights will establish The Grand as everyone's favourite York restaurant.

DETAILS:
Andrew Coney
0845 4096430

Station Rise, York YO1 6HT

E: reservations@cedarcourtgrand.co.uk
W: www.cedarcourtgrand.co.uk

Hotels & Restaurants

Clocktower at Rudding Park

Rudding Park

deliciouslyorkshire award winner in 2008-9 for their use of local produce, The Clocktower's chefs take inspiration from local ingredients when creating their Yorkshire menu. Serving local and seasonal dishes in stunning surroundings, this is a must visit for all with a passion for food!

DETAILS:

Rebecca Hill
01423 871350

Rudding Park, Follifoot, Harrogate, HG3 1JH, North Yorkshire

E: eat@ruddingpark.com
W: www.ruddingpark.co.uk

Hotels & Restaurants

The Coniston Hotel

The Coniston Hotel

Breathtaking views, stunning hospitality, delightful warm welcome and delicious locally sourced food make The Coniston Hotel a wonderful destination to eat, rest and play! Located on the A65 Skipton to Kendal, the Hotel has facilities for weddings, conferences and corporate activities such as shooting, falconry, archery, 4x4 driving and fishing.

DETAILS:

Louise Bolton
01756 748080

Coniston Cold, Skipton, BD23 4EA, North Yorkshire

E: info@theconistonhotel.com
W: www.theconistonhotel.com

Hotels & Restaurants

The Corner Café Ltd

Whether it's a morning coffee, snack or light lunch in the café-bar or a full blown evening meal in our fully licensed restaurant, we have something to offer everyone.

DETAILS:

Paul Carline
01723 512261

16 Bellvue Crescent, Filey, YO14 9AD, North Yorkshire

E: thecornercafeltd@googlemail.com
W: www.thecornerfiley.co.uk

Crossbutts Stable Restaurant in Whitby

A family run restaurant with rooms offering quality meals to suit every taste, our suppliers are proud of what they do and we're proud of them too.

DETAILS:

Louise King
01947 820986

Guisborough Road, Whitby, YO21 1TL
North Yorkshire

E: info@crossbutts.co.uk
W: www.crossbutts.co.uk

Hotels & Restaurants

The Crown Inn Roecliffe

A refurbished 16th century coaching Inn with four beautiful letting bedrooms and a medieval barn function room. The food emphasis is on locally sourced, fresh, classic pub dishes with daily blackboard fish specials. With their own smokehouse for local salmon they ensure superb quality dishes.

DETAILS:
Karl Mainey
01423 322300

Roecliffe, Boroughbridge, YO51 9LY, North Yorkshire

E: karl.mainey@btconnect.com
W: www.crowninnroecliffe.com

Hotels & Restaurants

Fauconberg Arms

Pub of the Year 2009 – come and see what all the fuss is about! Our menu boasts traditional cuisine given a contemporary Fauconberg twist. Unwind in the relaxing ambience of our dining room, or enjoy the lively atmosphere of the bar. Check our website for regular events throughout the year.

DETAILS:
Verity Rheinberg
01347 868214

Coxwold, Thirsk, YO61 4AD, North Yorkshire

E: info@fauconbergarms.com
W: www.fauconbergarms.com

Hotels & Restaurants

Feversham Arms & Verbena Spa

AA Hotel of the Year for England 2010, situated in the picturesque market town of Helmsley, this luxurious spa hotel has an award winning restaurant that serves delicious, fresh seasonal food. With a variety of menus to choose from, the Feversham Arm's showcase the very best quality Yorkshire fayre.

DETAILS:
Simon Rhatigan
01439 770766

High Street, Helmsley, York, YO62 5AG, North Yorkshire

E: marketing@fevershamarmshotel.com
W: www.fevershamarmshotel.com

Hotels & Restaurants

Flamingoland

The all-new Coach House brings alive a traditional family pub atmosphere in the heart of Flamingo Land. Our menu is full of family favourites as well as our chef's signature dishes and seasonal specials. Offering a selection of real ales and fine wines, it is the ideal place to dine.

DETAILS:
Shaun Franks
01653 668788

Kirbymisperton, Malton, YO17 6UX, North Yorkshire

E: coachhouse@flamingoland.co.uk
W: www.flamingoland.co.uk

Hotels & Restaurants

The General Tarleton Inn

The General Tarleton

Serving food with Yorkshire roots – AA five star accommodation and two rosettes for food. Michelin Bib Gourmand. Sourcing the best local seasonal produce from farmers and producers who care as passionately as we do about food.

DETAILS:
John Topham
01423 340284

Boroughbridge Road, Ferrensby, Knaresborough, HG5 0PZ, North Yorkshire

E: gti@generaltarleton.co.uk
W: www.generaltarleton.co.uk

Hotels & Restaurants

Grassington House Hotel

Featuring the culinary expertise of three-time national award winning chef John Rudden, Grassington House Hotel restaurant and bar is the area's premier location for fine dining and local entertainment.

DETAILS:
John & Sue Rudden
01756 752406

The Square, Grassington, BD23 5AQ, North Yorkshire

E: bookings@grassingtonhousehotel.co.uk
W: www.grassingtonhousehotel.co.uk

Yorkshire and Humber is home to some of the world's best known food companies and the highest concentration of small, passionate enterprises

Hotels & Restaurants

Green's Restaurant, Bistro & Boutique Apartments

Green's of Whitby
RESTAURANT & BISTRO

An award winning combination of dining experiences - a 'buzzy bistro' and gourmet restaurant. We only use the finest local produce, whether it is fresh turbot from Whitby or lamb from Ryedale. We are committed to serving you the best quality Yorkshire produce available in the majority of our dishes.

DETAILS:
Rob Green
01947 600284

13 Bridge Street, Whitby, YO22 4BG, North Yorkshire

E: info@greensofwhitby.com
W: www.greensofwhitby.com

Hotels & Restaurants

The Hare Inn

THE HARE INN

Observer Food Awards 2009 - runner - up: Best Sunday Lunch. The way it should be - fresh local ingredients, friendly staff and a stunning location, this 600 year old inn nestles on the edge of the stunning Rievaulx Valley. Enjoy award-winning ploughman's and a pint or a candlelit supper.

DETAILS:
Jan Smith
01845 597769

Scawton, Nr Thirsk, Y07 2HG, North Yorkshire

E: info@thehareinn.co.uk
W: www.thehareinn.co.uk

Hotels & Restaurants

The Highwayman (Punch Taverns)

Indulge in a fine menu, composed entirely from locally sourced supplies. Alternatively take a Yorkshire pint from the cask ale range and relax in the beautiful beer garden.

DETAILS:
Gavin & Lucy Greenbank
01347 878328

The Square, Sheriff Hutton, York, YO60 6QZ

E: highwaymanyork@aol.com
W: www.thehighwaymanyork.co.uk

Have you heard?

We like our food in God's Own County – with such a fantastic supply of local produce it would be a sin not to

Hotels & Restaurants

The Inn at Hawnby

The INN at Hawnby

This delightful country inn is at the top of the hill in the peaceful village of Hawnby. There are stunning panoramic views of the North Yorkshire Moors. Elegant restaurant and cosy bar with one rosette and Taste of Yorkshire award.

DETAILS:

Dave and Kathryn Young
01439 798202

Hawnby, Helmsley,
YO62 5QS, North Yorkshire

E: info@innathawnby.co.uk
W: www.innathawnby.co.uk

Hotels & Restaurants

Lanterna

Piemontese/Italien restaurant using mainly Yorkshire ingredients specialising in local fresh fish sourced directly from Scarborough harbour at the early morning fish market. Fresh white and black truffles from Giorgio's native Piemonte, North West Italy.

DETAILS:

Giorgio Alessio
01723 363616

33 Queen Street,
Scarborough, YO11 1HQ,
North Yorkshire

E: info@giorgioalessio.co.uk
W: www.lanterna-ristorante.co.uk

Hotels & Restaurants

Lightwater Shopping Village

the granary
Restaurant and Coffee Shop

With a great range of locally sourced meals and snacks, including a mouth-watering Sunday carvery and a sinful range of homemade cakes, why not take a fresh look at The Granary Restaurant at Lightwater Shopping Village?

DETAILS:

Ashley Young
0871 7200011

North Stainley, Ripon,
HG4 3HT, North Yorkshire

E: ashley@lightwatervalley.co.uk
W: www.lightwatervalley.co.uk

Hotels & Restaurants

The Magpie Cafe

Housed in a distinctive black and white building overlooking the harbour in the Port of Whitby, the dining rooms command excellent views of the Harbour, Abbey and St Mary's Church. Given the proximity of the fish market, it is not surprising that The Magpie specialises in fresh Whitby fish.

DETAILS:
Ian Robson
01947 602058

14 Pier Road, Whitby, YO21 3PU, North Yorkshire

E: info@magpiecafe.co.uk.
W: www.magpiecafe.co.uk

Hotels & Restaurants

Makins at Helmsley

Makin's restaurant and takeaway gives a fresh, modern take on the classic fish and chip formula. We use fresh locally sourced ingredients to produce delicious home-cooked food prepared with pride. Fresh, honest food is at the heart of Makin's.

DETAILS:
Jane Makin
01439 772465

6 Bridge Street, Helmsley, YO62 5BG, North Yorkshire

E: chris.makin@makins.co.uk
W: www.makinsathelmsley.co.uk

Hotels & Restaurants

The Malt Shovel (Punch Taverns)

A warm greeting awaits at this local situated in a picturesque village. The menu boasts fine local meats and produce and is completed by a range of cask ales .

DETAILS:
Steve Smith
01653 628264

Main Street, Hovingham, York, YO62 4LF, North Yorkshire

E: info@themaltshovelhovingham.co.uk
W: www.themaltshovelhovingham.co.uk

Hotels & Restaurants

The Market Place Bistro Wine Bar

the MARKET PLACE restaurant

We offer delicious food prepared using the finest local ingredients and pride ourselves on our friendly, attentive service. We are open 10.30am till 4.00pm Tuesday to Saturday and Friday and Saturday evenings. We are fully licensed and customers are always welcome to join us just for a drink and relax.

DETAILS:

Tanya Wells
01653 697100

46 The Market Place, Malton, YO17 7LW, North Yorkshire

E: tanya.wells@fsmail.net
W: www.the-market-place.co.uk

Hotels & Restaurants

National Railway Museum Milburns Restaurant

Sample fabulous Yorkshire produce in the museum's restaurant and cafe or experience first class dining in our award-winning conference centre, unique galleries and luxurious events carriage.

DETAILS:

Rachel Fox
01904 686219

Leeman Road, York, YO26 4XJ, North Yorkshire

E: rachel.fox@nrm.org.uk
W: www.nrm-events.org.uk

There's no county in the country where you'll find as great a variety of nature's abundance as in Yorkshire

Hotels & Restaurants

The National Trust Beningbrough Hall

National Trust

Beningborough Walled Garden restaurant is set in the grounds of a National Trust 18th century Georgian mansion. All produce is either freshly picked from our own walled garden or locally sourced. Family friendly facilities include a counter restaurant, ice-cream kiosk, snack kiosk, picnic areas and wilderness play area.

DETAILS:

Jayne Wallace
01904 472027

Beningbrough, York, YO30 1DD, North Yorkshire

E: jayne.wallace@nationaltrust.org.uk
W: www.nationaltrust.org.uk

Hotels & Restaurants

Plough Inn (Punch Taverns)

A great place to relax and enjoy cask ales and home cooked food in traditional pub surroundings. Greeting you with open fires and a warm welcome, relax in the beer garden and enjoy stunning views over North Yorkshire and perhaps extend your stay in one of the pub's letting rooms.

DETAILS:

Richard Nattriss
01947 810412

Sleights, Whitby, YO22 5EN, North Yorkshire

Hotels & Restaurants

Swinton Park

Luxury castle hotel, set in 200 acres of parkland in the Yorkshire Dales, with gardens, lakes and four acre-walled kitchen garden. Lavishly furnished with award-winning cuisine. Bird of Prey Centre, spa and cookery school. Garden lunches and garden design days. Alfresco food festival with culinary trail and guided tours. Open all year, non residents welcome

deliciouslyyorkshire winner awards 2009-2010

DETAILS:

01765 680900

Swinton Park, Masham, Ripon, HG4 4JH, North Yorkshire

E: enquiries@swintonpark.com
W: www.swintonpark.com

£

Hotels & Restaurants

The Red Lion

The Red Lion is all about serving delicious traditional English pub meals. The pub serves a full menu of starters, mains and desserts featuring all the classic pub favourites and a daily changing specials board full of seasonal dishes.

DETAILS:

Annie Prescott
01904 793957

Main Street, Knapton, York, YO26 6QG, North Yorkshire

E: annie@redlionpubyork.com
W: www.redlionpubyork.com

Hotels & Restaurants

The Ship Inn

Described by visitors from home and around the world as "This Is England", The Ship Inn serves top quality British food with care and pride. Celebrity chef Gordon Ramsay endorses our Sunday Lunch as the best in the Country as part of his 'Real Gravy Campaign'.

DETAILS:
Elaine Howden
01423 322749

Low Road, Aldborough, Boroughbridge, York, YO51 9ER, North Yorkshire

E: info@shipinnaldborough.co.uk
W: www.shipinnaldborough.co.uk

Hotels & Restaurants

The Shoulder of Mutton

David has been cooking for over 25 years and combines this experience together with his love for the best quality local ingredients in the food at the Shoulder of Mutton.

DETAILS:
Kate Deacon
01423 871205

Main Street, Kirkby Overblow, HG3 1HD North Yorkshire

E: katedeacon@btconnect.com
W: www.shoulderatkirkbyoverblow.com

The Star Inn

The restaurant glows with the bonhomie of a proper old fashioned auberge - run with style! Unpretentious, good hearted genius on every plate - "Adore every second of being there".

DETAILS:
Andrew Pern
01439 770397

Harome, Helmsley, YO62 5JE, North Yorkshire

E: jpern@thestarinnatharome.co.uk
W: www.thestarinnatharome.co.uk

Hotels & Restaurants

Ye Old Sun Inn

Charming olde world pub, oozing with charm run by Ashley and Kelly McCarthy who are enthusiastic about giving their best. Monthly menus bursting with flavours- all locally sourced!

DETAILS:
Ashley & Kelly McCarthy
01904 744261

Main Street, Colton, Tadcaster, LS24 8EP, North Yorkshire

E: info@yeoldsuninn.co.uk
W: www.yeoldsuninn.co.uk

Yorkshire and Humber is home to some of the world's best known food companies and the highest concentration of small, passionate enterprises

Deli & Independent Grocers

Country Harvest

Country Harvest is the quality shopping outlet and deli-cafe ideally situated where the Dales meet the Lakes. Open seven days a week, our packed to the rafters foodhall is every gourmet's dream; while our licensed coffee shop serves a day-long feast of light bites and home-style lunches. For sweet tooths, there's also a new instore fudge kitchen.

DETAILS:
Mike Clark
01524 242223

Ingleton, Carnforth, LA6 3PE

E: info@countryharvest.co.uk
W: www.country-harvest.co.uk

Deli & Independent Grocers

Dooley's

Here in Easingwold, our bright and modern food hall hosts a huge variety of products. Our produce includes local fruit, vegetables, meat, deli, wine as well as our new cake-craft department which caters for all your sugar-craft needs, whether you are an expert or novice.

DETAILS:
Phil Lancaster
01347 821403

Chapel Street, Easingwold, YO61 3AF, North Yorkshire

E: philtollerton@yahoo.com
W: www.dooleys-retail.co.uk

Deli & Independent Grocers

Holmesterne Farm Food Co Ltd

Committed to delivering the finest food products for our food service partner customers, we provide fresh products including BPEX's Pork Product of the Year 2010 Khmer Pork Curry.

DETAILS:
Steven Holden
01748 818283

Gatherley Road, Brompton on Swale, Richmond, DL10 7JQ, North Yorkshire

E: steven.holden@holmesterne.com
W: www.holmesterne.com

Have you heard?

" Yorkshire produce gets better and better as every year goes by. Just like rhubarb, Yorkshire products will soon be known as the best in the world "

Brian Turner

Deli & Independent Grocers

Hunters of Helmsley

HUNTERS of HELMSLEY

Fine food and wine emporium specialising in local, regional and international gourmet food. A family business based on good teamwork, excellent customer service and excellent local produce.

DETAILS:
Chris & Christine Garnett
01439 771307

13 Market Place, Helmsley, YO62 5BL, North Yorkshire

E: contact@huntersofhelmsley.com
W: www.hunterofhelmsley.com

Deli & Independent Grocers

The Laden Table

the LADEN TABLE

A cafe and creative community located in Boroughbridge. From book groups to children's weekly story-time to the best homemade food locally,
The Laden Table is child friendly and has disabled access and dog parking outside.

DETAILS:
Nicola Dixon
07801 544711

7-8 Foundry Yard, New Row, 14 St James Meadow, Boroughbridge, YO51 9AX, North Yorkshire

E: info@theladentable.com
W: www.theladentable.com

Deli & Independent Grocers

Lewis & Cooper Ltd

LEWIS & COOPER
• PURVEYORS OF FINE FOOD AND WINE SINCE 1899 •

Long before buying locally became fashionable, Lewis & Cooper strove to bring to its shelves the best food and drink the region has to offer, complemented by the world's finest goods.

DETAILS:
Bettina Bell
01609 772880

92 High Street, Northallerton, North Yorkshire, DL7 8PT

E: sales@lewisandcooper.co.uk
W: www.lewisandcooper.co.uk

Deli & Independent Grocers

LH Fine Foods

LH Fine Foods

After gaining enormous experience working with Michael Roux, Paul Heathcote and Sally Clarke, Lucinda opened LH Fine Foods in 2005, as a place where people can shop and enjoy Illy coffee in a relaxed atmosphere. Specialising in canapés, soups, pastries, English cheeses, preserves, luxury chocolates, and much more!

DETAILS:
Lucinda Hyman
01423 506400

135 Otley Road, Harrogate, HG2 0AG, North Yorkshire

E: info@lucindahyman.co.uk

Deli & Independent Grocers

Mackenzies Yorkshire Smokehouse

Best Fish and Seafood Product - deliciouslyyorkshire awards 2009-10. Famous for award-winning smoked and cured foods. Sample the exquisite foods produced in the restaurant or purchase in the shop.

DETAILS:
Robert Crowson
01943 880369

Units 1-6, Woodnook Farm, Hardisty Hill, Blubberhouses, LS21 2PQ

E: sales@yorkshiresmokehouse.co.uk
W: www.yorkshiresmokehouse.co.uk

Deli & Independent Grocers

Richardsons of Woodthorpe Ltd

Butcher, pie maker and delicatessen, producing to the highest standards. Retailer of the year, York Press business awards winner 2009.

DETAILS:
Martin Richardson
01904 707876

55-57 Moor Croft Road, Woodthorpe, York, YO24 2RQ, North Yorkshire

E: jane.richardson12@ntlworld.com
W: www.richardsonsofwoodthorpe.co.uk

Proudfoots

Based in Scarborough, Proudfoots have a long history as an independent, family- run, grocery retailer. Throughout three stores we provide a unique shopping experience and offer support for local suppliers.

DETAILS:
Valerie Aston
01723 585960

Blinking Sike, Caxton Way, Eastfield Business Park, Scarborough, YO11 3YT

E: valerie@proudfootgroup.com
W: www.proudfootgroup.com

Ripley Store

Best Confectionery Product - deliciouslyyorkshire awards 2009-10. See fudge being made at this village store and taste their world famous ice cream, made for decades to a well kept secret recipe!

DETAILS:
01423 770044

Beechwood, Ripley, Harrogate, HG3 3AX, North Yorkshire

E: info@ripleyicecream.com

Deli & Independent Grocers

Taste...

A family run sandwich shop also providing high quality outside catering. Most of our sandwich fillings and all our cakes, quiches and soups are homemade on the premises.

DETAILS:

Annette Harker
01904 651932
74 Clarence Street, York, YO31 7EW, North Yorkshire
E: taste09@ymail.com

deliciouslyorkshire – championing and celebrating delicious locally-sourced, lovingly-made food that is the authentic, pukka product with full traceability

Deli & Independent Grocers

Tollerton Stores

A well stocked shop selling local produce in a thriving village just outside York.

DETAILS:

Phil Lancaster
01347 838436
The Green, Tollerton, YO61 1PX, North Yorkshire
E: philtollerton@yahoo.com

Deli & Independent Grocers

Weetons

WEETON'S
FRESH FROM THE FARM

Over 3000 sq ft dedicated to the finest and freshest Yorkshire produce. You can watch the butchers and bakers at work in this state-of-the-art farm shop, listed by The Daily Express newspaper as one of the Top 100 shops in the world. The bustling cafe is a popular meeting place.

DETAILS:

Andrew Loftus
01423 507100
23-24 West Park, Harrogate, HG1 1BJ, North Yorkshire
E: andrew@weetons.com
W: www.weetons.com

Deli & Independent Grocers

Yorkshire Dales Cheese Company

yorkshiredales cheeseco.

Showcasing award-winning cheeses, this specialist supplier of hand crafted Yorkshire cheeses can be found at markets, agricultural shows and food festivals throughout the region. Creating mouth-watering cheese themed gifts and fabulous cheese wedding cakes now available to buy online.

DETAILS:
David Harris
01677 423248
Lowlands, Low Street, Leeming Bar, Northallerton, DL7 9BN, North Yorkshire

E: info@yorkshiredalescheese.co.uk
W: www.yorkshiredalescheese.co.uk

Deli & Independent Grocers

The Yorkshire Food Company

The Yorkshire Food Company

Located in the heart of the city, we pride ourselves on our extensive array of locally sourced and speciality foods. Spend time browsing or relax and enjoy a bite to eat in our busy eatery. For the best produce in the heart of Yorkshire's capital, visit the Yorkshire Food Company.

DETAILS:
Kerry Brooks
01904 630497
130-134 Micklegate, York, YO1 6JX, North Yorkshire

E: kerry@theyorkshirefoodcompany.co.uk
W: www.theyorkshirefoodcompany.com

Farm Shops

Ainsty Farms Direct

Farm shop with in-house butchery selling traditionally hung, quality local beef, pork, lamb, poultry and game. The shop also houses a bakery, an extensive deli and a coffee shop.

DETAILS:
Stuart & Lily Beaton
01423 331897
The Farm Shop, York Road, Green Hammerton, York, YO26 8EQ, North Yorkshire

E: info@ainstyfarmshop.co.uk
W: www.ainstyfarmshop.co.uk

Have you heard?

"Yorkshire has plenty of coastline and great fish to be found swimming off it, so try to support our fishing folk"

Nigel Barden

Farm Shops

The Balloon Tree Farm Shop & Café

Innovation Award - deliciouslyorkshire awards 2009-10.
Renowned farm shop and café supplying super fresh fruit and vegetables - specialising in seasonal asparagus and strawberries when available. Our award-winning bakery and in-house kitchen supply meals to our cafe, providing exquisite meals to the visiting public.

DETAILS:
Matthew Machin
01759 373023

Stamford Bridge Road, Gate Helmsley, York, YO41 1NB, North Yorkshire

E: info@theballoontree.co.uk
W: www.theballoontree.co.uk

Farm Shops

Beadlam Grange Farmshop & Tearoom

Award-winning farm shop and tearoom. Customers can enjoy a unique farm shopping experience in lovely traditional surroundings. We have an excellent butchers counter with home produced meat and deli counter selling vegetables, chutneys and cheeses. Try our delicious home-cooked food in our Granary Tearoom.

DETAILS:
Jenny Rooke
01439 770303

Beadlam Grange, Pockley, York, YO62 7TD, North Yorkshire

E: info@beadlamgrange.co.uk
W: www.beadlamgrange.co.uk

Farm Shops

Castle Howard Farm Shop

Open all year with free admission, Castle Howard's Farm Shop offers a range of local meat at the butcher's counter - most sourced within 15 miles of the estate - including our own Aberdeen Angus. Well stocked delicatessen, plus homemade cakes and fresh bread. Selection of gift foods, grocery items and seasonal fruit and vegetables.

DETAILS:
Kelly Smith
01653 648444

Castle Howard Estate Ltd, York, YO60 7DA, North Yorkshire

E: rjack@castlehoward.co.uk
W: www.castlehoward.co.uk

Farm Shops

Cedarbarn Farm Shop & Cafe

cedarbarn
FARM SHOP & CAFE

Best use of Regional Produce on a Menu (cafe/tearoom) - deliciouslyorkshire awards 2009-10.
Specialising in own pure bred Aberdeen Angus beef and lamb, local outdoor reared pork, homemade sausages and beef burgers, home-grown and local vegetables, homemade cakes, pies and ready meals. Award-winning café in a beautiful setting.

deliciouslyorkshire winner awards 2009-2010

DETAILS:
Karl Avison
01751 475614
Thornton Road, Pickering, YO18 7JX, North Yorkshire
E: cedarbarn@btconnect.com
W: www.cedarbarnfarmshop.co.uk

Farm Shops

Crimple Valley Fresh

Family run company based in Harrogate, specialising in home delivery of local produce, alongside our Ripley based shop. We also offer a chilled and ambient distribution service.

DETAILS:
Steve Willis
01423 873636
Fulwith Mill Farm, Fulwith Mill Lane, Harrogate, HG2 8HJ, North Yorkshire
E: sales@crimplevalleyfresh.com
W: www.crimplevalleyfresh.com

Have you heard?

"Yorkshire is teeming with the very best produce served up by hard-working, ingenious folk, passionate about what they do"
Alan Titchmarsh

Farm Shops

The Farmer's Cart

THE FARMER'S CART

Farm Shop Retailer of the Year – deliciouslyorkshire awards 2009-10.
Pet the animals in the fields, browse the plethora of Yorkshire produce in the farm shop or just relax and enjoy a light lunch or afternoon tea in the cafe.

deliciouslyorkshire winner awards 2009-2010

DETAILS:
Edward Sykes
01904 499183
Towthorpe Grange, Towthorpe Moor Lane, York, YO32 9ST, North Yorkshire
E: ed@thefarmerscart.co.uk
W: www.thefarmerscart.co.uk

Farm Shops

Fodder

Independent Retailer of the Year – deliciouslyorkshire awards 2009-10.
Fodder is the new home for Yorkshire food. Fodder celebrates and sells the very best of food and drink from our region in a spectaular purpose-built shop and cafe. Tasty local meat, vegetables, cheese, breads, eggs, oils and so much more.

DETAILS:
Heather Parry
01423 546111

Great Yorkshire Showground, Harrogate, HG2 8NZ, North Yorkshire

E: HeatherP@eventcentre.co.uk
W: www.fodderweb.co.uk

Farm Shops

High Bank Farm

Darlington based farm shop specialising in dairy products, ice cream, alcoholic beverages, meat, game, poultry, as well as prepared foods such as soups and sauces.

DETAILS:
Lesley Thompson
01325 365883

Cleasby Road, Stappleton, DL2 2QE

E: lesley@highbankfarm.co.uk

Home Farm Shop

Next to Beningbrough Hall. Home reared Aberdeen Angus beef, local and seasonal fruit and vegetables, home baking, speciality breads and a mouth-watering deli counter.

DETAILS:
Lucy Jackson
01904 470562

Beningbrough Home Farm, Beningbrough, York, YO30 1DB, North Yorkshire

E: homefarmshop@btinternet.com
W: www.homefarm-beningbrough.com

Farm Shops

Mainsgill Farm Shop

Tea room and farm shop selling local produce including fruit and vegetables, chutneys, cakes, meats, cheeses and cooked meats.

DETAILS:
Maria Henshaw
01325 718860

East Layton, Richmond, DL11 7PN, North Yorkshire

E: mainsgillfarm@btconnect.com
W: www.mainsgillfarm.co.uk

Redcliffe Farm Shop & Café

Enjoy lunch at our deli-style farm shop, offering a comprehensive selection of fresh meat, local seasonal vegetables, eggs, dairy, Yorkshire cheeses, ice cream and locally made preserves.

DETAILS:
Martin Brown
01723 583194

Redcliffe Lane, Lebberston, Scarborough, YO11 3NT, North Yorkshire

E: office@redcliffefarmshop.co.uk
W: www.redcliffefarmshop.co.uk

Farm Shops

Roots Farmshop & Cafe

Outstanding Newcomer - deliciouslyorkshire awards 2009-10.
Real farm retail experience and personal service - our team of butchers are happy to advise you. In the farm shop find out about our wide range of local produce and relax in Roots Cafe with our delicious home-cooked food.

DETAILS:
Katherine Hutchinson
01609 882480

Home Farm, East Rounton, Northallerton, DL6 2LE, North Yorkshire

E: info@rootsfarmshop.co.uk
W: www.rootsfarmshop.co.uk

Have you heard?

"It's no secret that I think Yorkshire is the garden of England. It has a massive range of quality produce: fantastic meat, poultry and veg, and then all the way to the coast at Brid, Scarborough and Whitby for the best tasting seafood. There's so much going on and every part of Yorkshire has something to offer"

James Martin

Class One Fresh Produce Ltd

Starting life as a family-run market stall in Skipton fifteen years ago, Class One supplies hotels and restaurants throughout the region with produce from Bradford markets and local producers.

DETAILS:
Ben Cluny
01756 700244
Unit 19, Snaygill Industrial Estate, Keighley Road, Skipton, BD23 2QR, North Yorkshire

E: class1produce@btconnect.com

Crofter's Foods Ltd

Providing marketing and distribution services for small and medium food manufacturers, retailers and caterers located in the region.

DETAILS:
Grahame Armitage
01642 711155
Seamer Hill Farm, Seamer, Stokesley, Middlesbrough, TS9 5NQ, North Yorkshire

E: info@croftersfoods.co.uk
W: www.croftersfoods.co.uk

Miller Food Service

Leading independent food wholesale offering a range of chilled, fresh, ambient, frozen and non food products. Wide range of products, including many from local manufacturers, supplied to caterers throughout the region.

DETAILS:
Gareth Wilson
01904 655368
27 Hospital Fields Road, Fulford, York, YO10 4DZ, North Yorkshire

E: gareth@davidmillerfrozenfoods.co.uk
W: www.millerfoodservice.co.uk

Country Products Limited

Suppliers of quality food products, including healthy snacking range, for the farm shop, delicatessen, grocery, health food and leisure industry. Soil Association registered, SALSA accredited.

DETAILS:
Mark Leather
01423 358858
Unit 6 Centre Park, Tockwith, York, YO26 7QF, North Yorkshire

E: mark.leather@countryproducts.co.uk
W: www.countryproducts.co.uk

Hebden & Poole Fine Foods

Wetherby based food manufacturers specialising in the distribution and wholesale of top quality, fresh fruit and vegetables.

DETAILS:
Gary Poole
01937 843085
Unit 423 D, Thorp Arch Trading Estate, Wetherby, LS23 7BJ, North Yorkshire

E: gary@hpfoods.net

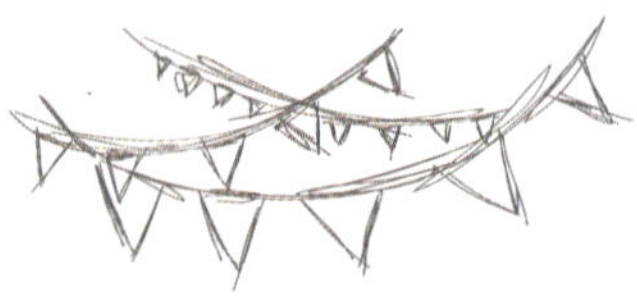

Yorkshire has made it to the top of the food charts with the most Michelin-starred restaurants – six – in the country

East Yorkshire

Countryside, coastline and city combine to make East Yorkshire a truly diverse destination. Ramble in the stunning Yorkshire Wolds before venturing to the coast and taking the sea air at the traditional resorts of Bridlington and Hornsea. Travel south and you'll find Hull with its bustling waterfront providing a vibrant mix of shopping, nightlife and maritime culture. Favourite food flavours include excellent pies and preserves lovingly made by the region's artisan producers.

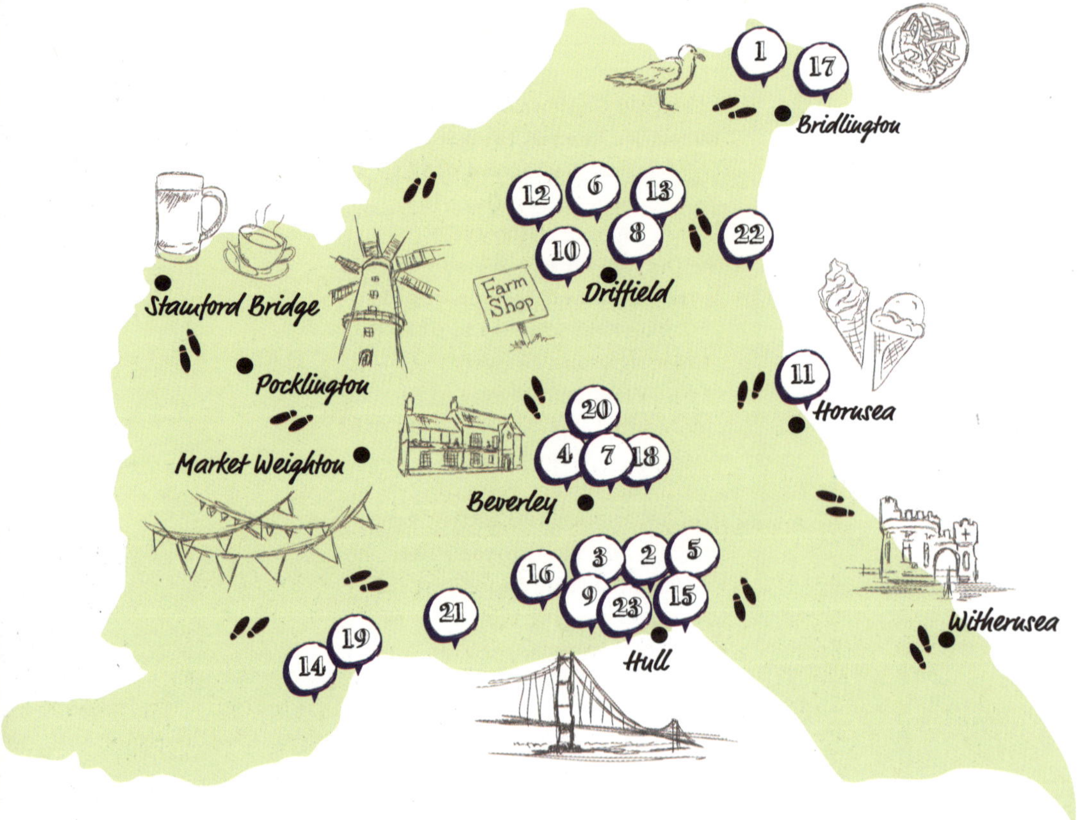
1
17
Bridlington
12
6
13
8
10
22
Driffield
Farm Shop
Stamford Bridge
Pocklington
11
Hornsea
20
4
7
18
Market Weighton
Beverley
3
2
5
16
9
23
15
21
19
14
Hull
Withernsea

Food highlights

Bakers & Confectioners

Brownie Heaven

Brownie Heaven available to buy at Dine on the Rowe Brasserie Beverley to try as a delicious sophisticated dessert or takeaway as Brownie Mountain's, Brownie Boxes. Also available gluten free. Can be ordered online.

DETAILS:
Jason Rowe
01482 623933
12-14 Butcher Row, Beverley, HU17 0AB, East Yorkshire

E: divine@brownieheaven.co.uk
W: www.brownieheaven.co.uk

Bakers & Confectioners

Kitchen

A family business producing beautiful breads, pretty pastries and Supa-Dupa meringues. All sold at our deli in Snaith and many shows throughout the region.

DETAILS:
Debbie Falkingham
01405 862662
10 Market Place, Snaith, Goole, DN14 9HE, East Yorkshire

Bakers & Confectioners

Shepcote Distributors Ltd

Quality manufacturer of cake decorations, and distributor of sugars, syrups, nuts, cereals, dried fruit and confectionery, supplying the bakery, ice cream and other speciality trade partners.

DETAILS:
Richard Shepherdson
01377 252537
Pexton Road, Kelleythorpe Industrial Estate, Driffield, YO25 9DJ, East Yorkshire

E: enquiries@shepcote.com
W: www.shepcote.co.uk

Fullers Bakery

We are a family run craft bakery, providing freshly baked bread morning goods and confectionery to our own shops and a comprehensive range of specialty breads to the wholesale market.

DETAILS:
Heather Fuller
01405 768302
159 Pasture Road, Goole, DN14 6DR, East Yorkshire

E: heather@fullersqualitybakers.co.uk

Riva Foods

Producer of bread and bakery products - pizzas, garlic bread and curry paste.

DETAILS:
Mandy Bailey
01482 837285
32 Copenhagen Road, Sutton Fields Industrial Estate, Hull, HU7 0XQ, East Yorkshire

E: mandy.bailey@rivafoods.co.uk

Side Oven Bakery

A range of homemade organic breads, croissants, honey toasted mueslis, juices and cordials. All wheat, spelt and oats are grown and processed on the farm using a stone ground mill.

DETAILS:
Caroline Sellers
01262 488376
Carr House Farm, Foston-on-the-Wolds, Driffield, YO25 8BS, East Yorkshire

E: bakery@sideoven.com
W: www.sideoven.com

Bakers & Confectioners

The Ultimate Candy Company Limited

Award winning hand-broken 16% butter fudge is one of the fantastic products available from the Ultimate Candy Company. For other Fairtrade, organic, sugar-free and indulgent treats contact us.

DETAILS:
Dave Richardson
01482 891754
4 Sheriff Highway, Hedon, Hull, HU12 8HD, East Yorkshire

E: ultimatecandy@aol.com
W: www.ultimatecandy.co.uk

White Rabbit Chocolate Company

Award-winning, handmade chocolate including our bestselling Yorkshire Honeycomb Slab. Our chocolate tastes delicious and looks beautiful - a feast for the eyes as well as the palate!

DETAILS:
Sally Hawkes
01482 679325
16 Dyer Lane, Beverley, HU17 8AE, East Yorkshire

E: whiterabbitchocolate@hotmail.co.uk
W: www.white-rabbit-chocolate.co.uk

Beverages (Alcoholic & Non)

Blue Keld Springs Ltd

A family run business based in the heart of the Yorkshire Wolds. Drawn from our natural artesian spring, the mineral water is high in calcium and low in sodium. We supply a range of natural and flavoured water, conference glass and our world renowned blue artesian glass bottles.

DETAILS:
Annabelle Marr
01377 271207
Throstle Nest, Cranswick, Driffield, YO25 9RE, East Yorkshire

E: info@bluekeld.co.uk
W: www.bluekeld.co.uk

Beverages (Alcoholic & Non)

Great Newsome Brewery Ltd

Situated on the East Yorkshire coast close to the city of Hull and run by the Hodgson family at Great Newsome Farm, the brewery produces a range of award-winning cask and five different bottled real ales which are all named after local locations, words and dialects.

DETAILS:
Matthew Hodgson
01964 612201
Great Newsome Farm, South Frodingham, Winestead, Hull, HU12 0NR, East Yorkshire

E: enquiries@greatnewsomebrewery.co.uk
W: www.greatnewsomebrewery.co.uk

Beverages (Alcoholic & Non)

Wold Top Brewery

Award-winning small brewery situated high on the Yorkshire Wolds producing cask and bottled real ales using home-grown malting barley and pure chalk filtered water from the farm's borehole.

DETAILS:
Gill Mellor
01723 892222
Hunmanby Grange, Wold Newton, Driffield, YO25 3HS, East Yorkshire

E: enquiries@woldtopbrewery.co.uk
W: www.woldtopbrewery.co.uk

Beverages (Alcoholic & Non)

Yorkshire Wolds Apples

Traditional apple juice farm-pressed in East Yorkshire. Sugar-free, healthy and contains no additives - a perfect addition to your healthy '5 a day'.

DETAILS:
Ray Kirby
07531 597267
28 Springdale Road, Market Weighton, YO43 3JT, East Yorkshire

E: rayk@mktw.karoo.co.uk
W: www.yorkshirewoldsapplejuice.co.uk

Dairy & Eggs

Eggsell Ltd

Yorkshire based, free range egg co-operative, working with the producer aiming to bridge the gap between farmers and the retailers.

DETAILS:
Barry Jackson
01964 541828
Manor House Farm, Routh, Beverley, HU17 9SR, East Yorkshire

E: barry@eggsell.com
W: www.eggsell.com

Dairy & Eggs

Chestnut Dairies Ltd

Family owned and run dairy farm in East Yorkshire, passionate about supporting our local producers. We deliver quality local milk and cream throughout the area.

DETAILS:
Eric & Sue Varley
01964 535061
Stud Farm, Seaton, Hull, HU11 5RJ, East Yorkshire

E: chestnutdairies@hotmail.com

Elliott Eggs Ltd

Lion Code and Freedom Food Eggs produced on the farm, hens are fed home-grown wheat, with eggs being packed and delivered out from the farm to retailers, butchers and caterers.

DETAILS:
Tom Elliott
01964 533718
Manor House, Bewholme, Driffield, YO25 8DX, East Yorkshire

E: tom@elliotteggs.co.uk
W: www.elliotteggs.co.uk

Dairy & Eggs

Mr Moo's Real Dairy Ice Cream

MR MOO'S

Made on our farm ice cream as it used to be, using fresh whole milk and double cream to which quality, natural flavours are added, producing a deliciously rich and creamy ice cream. Products sizes 120ml, 500ml, 1ltr, 4.75ltr.

DETAILS:
Stephen Foreman
01262 469829

Southfield House Farm, Hornsea Road, Hornsea, Driffield, YO25 8SY, East Yorkshire

E: info@mrmoos.co.uk
W: www.mrmoos.co.uk

Fish (Fresh & Smoked)

W Simpson Ltd (Seafish)

The UK's largest family fresh and frozen fish processors based in Hull since 1982. We specialise in traditional smoking of species such as cod and haddock using natural colours, sustainable oak chips and traditional kilns.

DETAILS:
David Orr
01482 585109

35 West Dock Street, Hessle, Hull, HU3 4HH, East Yorkshire

E: david@simpson-seafish.co.uk
W: www.simpson-seafish.co.uk

Fresh Ingredients

Humdinger Ltd

A leading supplier of grocery and snack products in partnership with Sunsweet, Ocean Spray and Community Foods. Our growing range of brands includes Humzinger Fruit Sticks and Apple Crisps.

DETAILS:
Emma Woodmansey
01482 625790

Gothenburg Way, Sutton Fields Industrial Estate, Hull, HU7 0YG, East Yorkshire

E: phil.whitfield@humdinger-foods.co.uk
W: www.humdinger-foods.co.uk

Fresh Ingredients

Snaith Salad Growers Ltd

Independent grower co-operative and one of the leading glasshouse producers of wholehead leafy salads. We are ideally situated to service the whole of the UK with our products.

DETAILS:
Simon Deighton
01405 860354

West Bank, Carlton, Goole, DN14 9PZ, East Yorkshire

E: enquiries@salads-yorkshire.com
W: www.salads-yorkshire.com

W Clappison Ltd

Clappison's of Risby are East Yorkshire's main producer of brussel sprouts. Using the best quality seeds, fertile Yorkshire soils, and plenty of TLC our brussels are the highest quality.

DETAILS:
John Clappison
01482 848132

Beverley, HU17 8SS, East Yorkshire

E: john@risby.karoo.co.uk

Fresh Ingredients

Yorkshire Peas

Grown by Swaythorpe Growers, a partnership of over 40 family farms across the Yorkshire Wolds and the Vale of York. This experience and devotion helps make our peas taste sweeter. We know when to pick crops to bring you the freshest, tender peas. We're not a faceless company, we're farmers!

DETAILS:
Ian Keyes
01377 229491

Southburn, Driffield, YO25 9ED, East Yorkshire

E: info@yorkshirepeas.co.uk
W: www.yorkshirepeas.co.uk

Ingredient Suppliesr

Bannisters' Farm

BANNISTERS' farm

Farmhouse Potato Bakers is a family-run business which has been baking potatoes for 25 years, serving the foodservice and retail sectors. Now sold under Bannisters' Farm brand in retail outlets.

DETAILS:
Marie Medhurst
01262 605650

Lancaster Road, Carnaby Industrial Estate, Bridlington, YO15 3QY, East Yorkshire

E: marie@farmhousepotatobakers.co.uk
W: www.bannistersfarm.co.uk

Meat, Poultry & Game

Anna's Happy Trotters Yorkshire Free Range Pork

anna's happy trotters yorkshire free range pork www.annashappytrotters.com

Our pigs enjoy a free range lifestyle from beginning to end. Being part of only 2% of pigs reared in this way in the UK they are undoubtedly lucky well looked after pigs. And just like their quality of life, the quality of meat from our pigs is second to none.

DETAILS:
Anna Longthorp
01430 433030

Burland, Holme Road, Howden, DN14 7LY, East Yorkshire

E: anna@longthorp.com
W: www.annashappytrotters.com

Meat, Poultry & Game

Burton's of Wilberfoss

Burton's of Wilberfoss produce the highest quality pork sausages and dry cured bacon from our own herd of free range pigs, ensuring full traceability.

DETAILS:
Grant Burton
01759 380244
Manor House Farm, Wilberfoss, York, YO41 5NY, East Yorkshire

E: grant@wilberfoss.com

Meat, Poultry & Game

Rose Cottage Pies

Producing speciality homemade savoury pies using the finest local ingredients. Our products are sold at farmers markets, food festivals and shows throughout Yorkshire.

DETAILS:
Rupert Clemmit
01377 257700
Rose Cottage, Main Street, Garton-on-the-Wolds, Driffield, Y025 3ET

E: rosecottagefoods@aol.com
W: www.rosecottagepies.co.uk

Meat, Poultry & Game

T Soanes & Son (Poultry) Ltd

Making delicious poultry products has been a tradition in the Soanes family for over 65 years. Bringing customers the freshest, tastiest and most nutritious products available.

DETAILS:
Richard Holey
01377 217243
Church Hill Farm, Middleton on the Wolds, Driffield, YO25 9UG

E: richard.holey@soanespoultry.co.uk
W: www.soanespoultry.co.uk

Givendale Prime Beef

Our farmers believe in rearing succulent, tender, free-range grass-fed beef to exemplary animal welfare standards and are confident that every cut follows a traceable route to your plate.

DETAILS:
Ursula Taylor
01377 227790
Southburn Offices, Driffield, YO25 9ED, East Yorkshire

E: ursula.taylor@jsr.co.uk
W: www.givendaleprime.co.uk

Sledmere Estate

Carefully designed by Sir Christopher Sykes 2nd Baronet and nurtured by successive generations, this very special place brings new devotees every year. Venison produced from own herd on the Sledmere Estate.

DETAILS:
Stephen Greenfield
01377 236221
Sledmere Estate Office, Sledmere, Driffield, YO25 3XG, East Yorkshire

E: stephengreenfield@sledmere-estate.com
W: www.sledmerehouse.com

Yorkshire Outdoor Pork Company Limited

Using top quality, traceable, outdoor reared pork, we make our products available to local consumers via a selection of retail outlets. Products include traditionally made speciality sausage and bacon.

DETAILS:
Mark Burton
01482 337990
Malmo Park, Malmo Road, Sutton Fields, Hull, HU7 0YH, East Yorkshire

E: sales@yorkshireoutdoor.com
W: www.yorkshireoutdoor.com

Prepared Food

Aarhus Karlshamn

AAK
AarhusKarlshamn

AAK are the UK's leading manufacturer of speciality oils, mustards, condiments and salad dressings. Our brands include Chalice, Lion, Midsummer Organic and L<C Cooking Sprays.

DETAILS:
Helen Flower
01482 701271

King George Dock, Hull,
HU9 5PX, East Yorkshire

E: uk.info@aak.com
W: www.aakuk.com

Prepared Food

Bantaba Foods

Bantaba Foods is a range of popular Afro-Caribbean ready prepared meals. Each has been lovingly made using traditional African and Caribbean ingredients with recipes passed down through generations of ancestors.

DETAILS:
Mo Bah
07908 820081

173 Spring Bank, Hull,
HU3 1LP, East Yorkshire

E: info@bantabafoods.co.uk
W: www.bantabafoods.co.uk

There's so much wonderful food in Yorkshire – the hardest bit will be making a decision but then no-one said it was going to be easy!

Prepared Food

William Jackson Food Group

A BUSINESS TO BE PROUD OF Est. 1851
WILLIAM JACKSON FOOD GROUP

A fifth generation family business (established 1851) comprising four manufacturing divisions: Aunt Bessie's (traditional frozen food), Hazeldene (prepared salads), Jackson's Bakery (sandwich/speciality breads) and Parripak (prepared vegetables).

DETAILS:
Di Kirby
01482 224939

The Riverside Building,
Livingstone Road, Hessle,
HU13 0DZ, East Yorkshire

E: djk@wjfg.co.uk
W: www.wjfg.co.uk

Prepared Food

Yorkshire Hemp Limited

Provide organic and conventional bulk hemp to the baking and food manufacturing industry as well as branded hemp food products to the health, speciality and fine food market.

DETAILS:

Paul Jenkinson
01377 272790

Twydale Business Park, Unit 8b, Skerne Road, Driffield, YO25 6JX

E: info@yorkshirehemp.com
W: www.yorkshirehemp.com

Yorkshire's bountiful supply of fresh local ingredients is as a magnet to the finest chefs the UK has to offer

Preserves/Honey/Condiments/Spices

Gold From The Wold Ltd

Our cold-pressed rapeseed oil is simply pressed once and allowed to naturally settle on our farm where it has been grown on the Yorkshire Wolds by Paul. This makes our oil ideal for all culinary uses. Enjoy!

DETAILS:

Paul Jackson
01262 672293

Carnaby House Farm, Carnaby, Bridlington, YO16 4UJ, East Yorkshire

E: info@goldfromthewold.co.uk
W: www.goldfromthewold.co.uk

Preserves/Honey/Condiments/Spices

Kitchen Guru

Winner of 12 industry awards, Kitchen Guru is the founder of the 'cook your own' made easy concept. The products offer consumers to cook from scratch fresh, truly authentic, healthy delicious meals at home. The range includes Indian, Thai and other world cuisines for you to enjoy.

DETAILS:

Chandra Parmar
01482 864799

Petunia Lakeside Park, Plaxton Bridge Road, Woodmansey, Nr Beverley, HU17 0RT, East Yorkshire

E: info@kitchenguru.co.uk
W: www.kitchenguru.co.uk

Cafés & Tearooms

The Atrium Cafe

Situated in the historic market town of Beverley, The Atrium Cafe provides a quality, fresh and diverse daily menu using ingredients sourced locally as possible. Also provide outside catering.

DETAILS:
Kaye Walker
01482 872143
3-4 Cross Street, Beverley, HU17 9AX, East Yorkshire

E: kayewalker@live.co.uk

The Gallery

A cafe and Aladdin's cave gift shop by day and Italian restaurant by night – The Gallery is truly unique. Authentic Italian food, including stone-baked pizzas, is served to happy customers.

DETAILS:
Gaynor Edson
01430 470042
67 Market Place, South Cave, HU15 2AS, East Yorkshire

E: info@thegallerysouthcave.co.uk
W: www.thegallerysouthcave.co.uk

Cafés & Tearooms

Eastfield Garden Centre Ltd

Browse our food hall for a variety of Yorkshire products, quintessentially artisan cheeses, eggs, confectionery, plus our homemade cakes, pies and quiches. Enjoy the atmosphere of Autumn Bliss Coffee Bar serving speciality teas and coffees, breakfasts and snacks, or take comfort in our homemade meals in the Potting Shed Café.

DETAILS:
Joan Stephenson
01262 676285
Easton Road, Bridlington, YO16 4XF, East Yorkshire

E: info@eastfield-gardencentre.co.uk
W: www.eastfield-gardencentre.co.uk

Cafés & Tearooms

Millers Tea Room & Farm Shop

Set in beautiful, rural countryside, award winning Millers offers a relaxed and friendly atmosphere. Meals are prepared on the premises using fresh local produce. We bake a wide selection of homemade cakes and pastries. The farm shop sells locally sourced produce plus unusual and exciting gifts.

DETAILS:
Elaine Townend
01482 631702
Raywell Lodge Park, Riplingham Road, Raywell, HU16 5YL, East Yorkshire

E: elaine@etownend.karoo.co.uk
W: www.millerstearoomandfarmshop.co.uk

Hotels & Restaurants

Artisan Restaurant

ARTISAN restaurant www.artisanrestaurant.com

Yorkshire Life Restaurant of the Year 2009/10 and most recently Which? Good Food Guide - voted the North East Restaurant of the Year 2010/11. Set within a Georgian townhouse, we can seat up to 16 guests to serve lovingly prepared food in an intimate setting.

DETAILS:

Lindsey Johns
01482 644906

22 The Weir, Hessle,
HU13 0RU, East Yorkshire

E: eat@artisanrestaurant.com
W: www.artisanrestaurant.com

Hotels & Restaurants

Cerutti '2' Beverley

Cerutti 2

Just a five minute walk from Beverley's historic town centre, Cerutti 2 boasts a diverse a la carte menu and is renowned for its cookery masterclasses, giving customers a sneak preview of what goes on behind the scenes.

DETAILS:

Tina Cerutti
01482 874774

Station Square, Beverley,
HU17 0DS, East Yorkshire

E: tinaceru2@tinaceru2.co.uk
W: www.ceruttis.co.uk/beverley.php

Hotels & Restaurants

Cerutti's Hull

Cerutti's

Situated on Hull's picturesque pier in the old town, looking out across the Humber, Cerutti's serves an extensive range of fish delicacies and remains as popular today as it was when it first opened in 1974.

DETAILS:

Tony Cerutti
01482 328501

10 Nelson Street, Hull,
HU1 1XE, East Yorkshire

E: ceruttis@ceruttisltd.karoo.co.uk
W: www.ceruttis.co.uk

Hotels & Restaurants

The Old Mill Hotel & Restaurant

The Old Mill Hotel & Restaurant, where we are passionate about local food - keeping it local, keeping it fresh and keeping it tasty.

DETAILS:
Kathie Oliver-Heaton
01377 267284

Mill Lane, Langtoft, Driffield, YO25 3BQ, East Yorkshire

E: enquiries@old-mill-hotel.co.uk
W: www.old-mill-hotel.co.uk

Hotels & Restaurants

The Pipe and Glass Inn

East Yorkshire's first and only Michelin Star 18th century country inn situated in the heart of East Yorkshire. Stylish restaurant area, serving modern British food with an East Riding accent!

DETAILS:
James Mackenzie
01430 810246

West End, South Dalton, Beverley, HU17 7PN, East Yorkshire

E: email@pipeandglass.co.uk
W: www.pipeandglass.co.uk

Rags Restaurant with Rooms

On the harbour edge with views of South Bay, serving local produce such as Bridlington crab and seabass there is something to suit every taste at Rags Restaurant with Rooms.

DETAILS:
Julie Dyl
01262 400355

South Pier, Bridlington, YO15 3AW, East Yorkshire

E: ragshotel@tesco.net
W: www.ragshotel.co.uk

Hotels & Restaurants

Smorrebrod

Enjoy the relaxed and friendly atmosphere of Beverley-based Smorrebrod. All meals prepared on the premises using local fresh produce. Wide selection of home baked cakes and quiches. Gluten free options menu.

DETAILS:
Kaye Walker
01482 860153

1 Well Lane, Beverley, HU17 9BL, East Yorkshire

E: kayewalker@live.co.uk

Tickton Grange

We have a real Yorkshire passion which is reflected in our choice of suppliers. This wealth of produce allows our chefs to develop vibrant dishes for the most discerning diners.

DETAILS:
David Nowell
01964 543666

Main Street, Tickton, Beverley, HU17 9SH, East Yorkshire

E: info@ticktongrange.co.uk
W: www.beverleyticktongrange.co.uk

Hotels & Restaurants

The Westwood Restaurant

Situated in the historic market town of Beverley, the Westwood Restaurant is one of the jewels in the region's restaurant scene. Showcasing simple stylish food, Matthew, Michele and their team use the highest quality locally sourced ingredients to evolve their seasonal menus and get the best out of the ingredients.

DETAILS:
Michele & Matthew Barker
01482 881999

New Walk, Beverley,
HU17 7AE, East Yorkshire

E: dine@thewestwood.co.uk
W: www.thewestwood.co.uk

Deli & Independent Grocers

The 'C' Horse Deli

Conveniently located next door to Cerutti 2, The 'C' Horse Deli provides a delicious range of ready meals allowing customers to take the taste of Cerutti's to the comfort of their own home. Seasonal menus ensure the freshest ingredients are used.

DETAILS:
Tina Cerutti
01482 874774

Station Square, Beverley,
HU17 0AS, East Yorkshire

E: tinaceru2@tinaceru2.co.uk
W: www.ceruttis.co.uk/deli.php

Deli & Independent Grocers

Flourish and Prosper

Located close to Howden Minster, Flourish and Prosper is a wine shop, delicatessen and wine school. Speciality cheeses, affordable wines, bespoke hampers and so much more.

DETAILS:
Sean Welsh
01430 430006

64 Bridgegate, Howden,
DN14 7JH, East Yorkshire

E: sean@flourish-and-prosper.com
W: www.flourish-and-prosper.com

Deli & Independent Grocers

James Patrick Delicatessen

Hessle based delicatessen providing a wide range of sandwiches and seasonal hamper creation, along with in-house catering services.

DETAILS:
Malcolm Crease
01482 641053
11 The Weir, Hessle, HU13 0SB, East Yorkshire

E: hello@james-patrick.co.uk
W: www.james-patrick.co.uk

Taste....

Independent delicatessen, selling Yorkshire food and drink of exceptional quality as well as other products from around Britain and Europe, supporting small artisan producers as much as we can.

DETAILS:
Joy Swift
01482 890944
14 Market Place, Hedon, Hull, HU12 8JA, East Yorkshire

E: joyous@afslimited.karoo.co.uk
W: www.tasteofhedon.co.uk

Farm Shops

Drewtons

Opening in October 2010 - a new and exciting farm shop, bakery and deli! Enjoy regional produce from cheeses to fish and meat, including Aberdeen Angus beef from the Drewton Estate.

DETAILS:
Katie Taylor
07977 375432
The Drewton Estate, South Cave, Nr Brough, HU15 2AG, East Yorkshire

E: katie@drewtons.co.uk
W: www.drewtons.co.uk

Farm Shops

Kelleythorpe Farm Shop

Specialising in tender, well hung, expertly butchered Aberdeen Angus beef, you will also find local seasonal fruit and vegetables, home baked goods and English cheeses at Kelleythorpe Farm Shop.

DETAILS:
Tiffy Hopper
01377 256627
Kelleythorpe, Driffield, YO25 9DW, East Yorkshire

E: hoppertiffy@hotmail.com
W: www.kelleythorpefarmshop.co.uk

“I'm always proud to shout about our great Yorkshire produce and our brilliant array of suppliers”

James Mackenzie

Farm Shops

Manor Farm Shop

Only high quality Yorkshire produce available here! Along with our home-cooked meats, patés, salads and delicious baking, we offer takeaway sandwiches and drinks. Plus we have fresh fruit and vegetables, meats and poultry and delicious Yorkshire ice cream in cornets or tubs to take away.

DETAILS:
Helen Stones
01377 271038
Manor Farm, Hutton Cranswick, Driffield, YO25 9PQ, East Yorkshire

E: adrian.manorfarm@virgin.net

Farm Shops

Langlands Garden Centre

An established farm shop selling a range of produce – we have a passion for home cooked Yorkshire fayre made from locally produced ingredients and cooked the old fashioned way.

DETAILS:
Robert Ducker
01430 873426
York Road, Shiptonthorpe, YO43 3PN, North Yorkshire

E: robert.ducker@langlands-nurseries.co.uk
W: www.langlandsgardencentre.co.uk

Marton Manor Farm Shop & Tea Rooms

Situated on a working farm, come and try our homemade produce in our newly opened tea rooms, sample the delights in our farm shop, and even pick your own strawberries.

DETAILS:
Jane Waind
01262 672522
Marton Manor, Flamborough Road, Sewerby, Bridlington, YO15 1DU, East Yorkshire

E: martonmanor@btconnect.com
W: www.martonmanor.com

Have you heard?

“I like to teach all the students at my cookery school at Swinton Park about fresh seasonal local food and sustainability because it's so important at every level – it's best for communities, best for the future, and it tastes the best!”

Rosemary Shrager

Hider Food Imports Ltd

Family owned company specialising in wholesale distribution of quality nuts and dried fruits for cake and confectionery producers. Covering the country with our own fleet of lorries for weekly deliveries, we celebrate local suppliers, along with organic, Fairtrade and gluten free items.

DETAILS:
Duncan Hider
01482 561137

Wiltshire Road, Kingston upon Hull, HU4 6PA, East Yorkshire

E: duncan@hiderfoods.co.uk
W: www.hiderfoods.co.uk

Regalex Fresh Foods

Wholesaler/distributor situated in central Hull. Supplying fresh fruit and vegetables into various markets, including Hull CC schools (approx 70 sites). Sourcing mainly from Hull wholesale market.

DETAILS:
Dean Rennison
01482 221472

Regal House, 2 - 3 Ferries Street, Hedon Road, Hull, HU9 1RL, East Yorkshire

E: info@regalex.karoo.co.uk

StaintonWard Ltd

A family owned distributor of espresso and equipment. We supply quality products to cafés and restaurants including the renowned 'London Tea' range and our own 'Wilberforce Freedom' Fairtrade coffee.

DETAILS:
Andy Lawrence
01482 442121

Unit 5 Acorn Industrial Estate, Bontoft Avenue, Hull, HU5 4HF, East Yorkshire

E: info@staintonward.co.uk
W: www.staintonward.co.uk

All across the county, pride of tradition combines with entrepreneurial spirit in award-winning producers who are constantly looking for new ways to enhance nature's gifts

South Yorkshire

The gateway to Britain's first ever National Park – the inspirational Peak District – South Yorkshire is made for exploring. Traditional rural villages and market towns thrive alongside vibrant cities, busy shopping centres and towns brimming with heritage. Enjoy the area's rich food culture in an array of locally-produced cakes, confectionery and beers and, if there's time, take in the Yorkshire Wildlife Park – home to animals from all over the world.

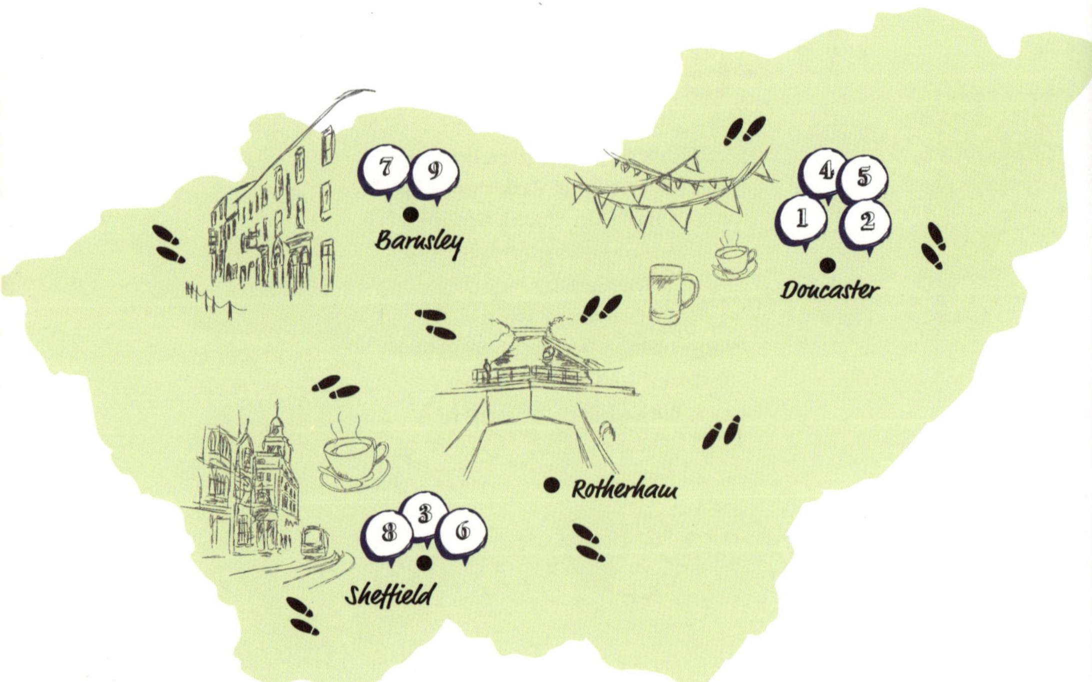
7
9
Barnsley
4
5
1
2
Doncaster
Rotherham
3
8
6
Sheffield

Food highlights

Bakers & Confectioners

A. L. Simpkin & Co Ltd

Pioneers of high grade glucose confectionery since 1921. Produced by traditional methods and recipes and incorporating only natural colours and flavours. Brands - Simpkins Travel Tins, Nipits Candy.

DETAILS:
Adrian Simpkin
0114 2348736
Hunter Road, Sheffield, S6 4LD, South Yorkshire

E: sales@alsimpkin.com
W: www.alsimpkin.com

Bakers & Confectioners

Bites of Fancy Ltd

Hand-baked continental biscuit specialities and cupcakes for all occasions. Individual service including parties, corporate entertainment and weddings.

DETAILS:
Petra Haselier
01709 864407
2 Saxon Row, Conisbrough, Doncaster, DN12 2HT, South Yorkshire

E: petra@bites-of-fancy.co.uk
W: www.bites-of-fancy.co.uk

Bakers & Confectioners

Cornscape Ltd

Exclusive distributor of POPZ products in the UK, we offer a complete range of ready-to-eat and microwave popcorn. High quality toffee, cinema style, flavoured and gourmet recipe popcorn.

DETAILS:
Steve Seddon
01226 709332
Unit 14 Albion Road, Carlton Industrial Estate, Barnsley, S71 3HW

E: info@cornscape.co.uk
W: www.cornscape.co.uk

Bedazzled

All of our cupcakes are made using only the finest ingredients and are perfect for any occasion or simply to be enjoyed as a treat.

DETAILS:
Jayne Gordon
0845 4591723
25 Rosedale Way, Sunnyside, Rotherham, S66 3LE, South Yorkshire

E: info@bedazzledcupcakes.co.uk
W: www.bedazzledcupcakes.co.uk

Cooplands (Doncaster) Ltd

One of Yorkshire's leading family bakers with over 76 shops throughout the region. BRC accredited. Supply proven high quality bakery products to wholesale market.

DETAILS:
Robert McIlroy
01302 361333
Victoria Mill Business Park, Wharf Road, Wheatley, Doncaster, DN1 2SX

E: info@cooplands.co.uk
W: www.cooplands.co.uk

Delicious Alchemy Ltd

Suppliers of the highest quality wheat/gluten and lactose free food to hotels restaurants and cafes. The range includes loaves, rolls, pizza bases, burger buns, cakes and muesli.

DETAILS:
Emma Killilea
0114 2587796
202 Meersbrook Works, Valley Road, Sheffield, S8 9FT, South Yorkshire

E: ekillilea@deliciousalchemy.com
W: www.deliciousalchemy.co.uk

Bakers & Confectioners

Fosters Bakery Ltd

Based in South Yorkshire, Fosters are ideally placed to serve local and national retailers and caterers with premium quality bread, morning goods and confectionery.

DETAILS:
John Foster
01226 382877
Towngate, Mapplewell, Barnsley, S75 6AS, South Yorkshire

E: sales@bake-it.com
W: www.fostersbakery.co.uk

Bakers & Confectioners

Maxons Ltd

Manufacturers of old fashioned hard boiled sweets including Yorkshire Mixture and Fruit Rock. Extensive product range, packaged in large weigh-out jars, small tins, pre-pack bags or bulk bags.

DETAILS:
Chris Pitchfork
0114 2554216
Bradbury Street, Sheffield, S8 9QQ, South Yorkshire

E: sales@maxons.co.uk
W: www.maxons.co.uk

Bakers & Confectioners

Opera Desserts

Italian influenced producer of fine quality desserts and ice cream. Desserts are made using locally sourced and produced ingredients, with sugar and fat free products available. Suppliers to restaurants, hotels and smaller retail.

DETAILS:
Angela Lombardo
01302 769699
42/43 Waterdale, Doncaster, DN1 3EY, South Yorkshire

E: info@operadesserts.co.uk
W: www.operadesserts.co.uk

The JuSu Pantry

Founded at the beginning of 2009, we specialise in making fresh home baked gluten and wheat free products including cakes, fruit pies, quiches, meat pies and other savouries.

DETAILS:
Julie Whitham
0114 2471024
28 Farm View Drive, Sheffield, S12 4JE, South Yorkshire

E: julie@thejusupantry.co.uk
W: www.thejusupantry.co.uk

Melanie's Celebration Cakes & Chocolatiers

Celebration cakes of the highest quality baked to order using only the finest ingredients. Traditional, themed or novelty, each wedding cake is individual and unique. Also continental chocolates made especially for you.

DETAILS:
Melanie Leonard
01226 710221
316 Barnsley Road, Cudworth, Barnsley, S72 8TD, South Yorkshire

E: cakesbymelanie@hotmail.co.uk
W: www.cakesbymelanie.co.uk

Potts Bakers Ltd

Barnsley's oldest bakers, established in 1891 and currently run by fourth and fifth generation. With four shops in the Barnsley area, we supply wholesale to local retailers and sandwich shops.

DETAILS:
Roger Potts
01226 249175
Stanley Road, Stairfoot, Barnsley, S70 3PG, South Yorkshire

E: roger@pottsbakers.co.uk
W: www.pottsbakers.co.uk

Bakers & Confectioners

Roses The Bakers

Sheffield based bakers operating since 1947. 60 years of experience ensures perfectly created bread, cakes, savouries, and other confectionery products. Also specialising in celebration cakes hand-made to your exact requirements.

DETAILS:
Seuranie Rose
0114 2434160
Atlas Way, Atlas North, Brightside Lane, Sheffield, S4 7QQ, South Yorkshire

E: seuranie@roses-the-bakers.co.uk
W: www.roses-the-bakers.co.uk

White's Bakers

A third generation, family owned business producing baked goods for its eight shops in Barnsley, and other retail chains.

DETAILS:
David White
01226 203457
The Bakery, Charles Street, Worsbrough Bridge, Barnsley, S70 5AF, South Yorkshire

E: david@whitesbakery.co.uk

Beverages (Alcoholic & Non)

Acorn Brewery of Barnsley

Meticulously crafted award-winning ales, including the supremely popular Barnsley Bitter. Distinctive beers brewed with only the finest malts and hops and the same yeast strains as the original 1850's Barnsley Brewery.

DETAILS:
David Hughes
01226 270734
Aldham Industrial Estate, Unit 3, Wombwell, Barnsley, S73 8HA, South Yorkshire

E: dave@acorn-brewery.co.uk
W: www.acorn-brewery.co.uk

Brittains Raspberry Vodka

Brittains Raspberry Vodka, created using a blend of the finest fresh Yorkshire raspberries, is infused with premium vodka (37.5%) to produce a soft delicious drink with a fruity aroma and exceptional flavour.

DETAILS:
John Raper
01302 855010
Treetops, Park Drive, Sprotbrough, Doncaster, DN5 7LN, South Yorkshire

E: john@brittainsraspberryvodka.com
W: www.brittainsraspberryvodka.com

Beverages (Alcoholic & Non)

Cafeology Ltd

CAFE OLOGY.com
Great Coffee. Great Cause.

An independently owned, exclusively Fairtrade, beverage company based in South Yorkshire. We specialise in the supply of the finest Fairtrade coffee, tea, hot chocolate and iced coffee, supplying both foodservice and retail markets.

DETAILS:
Bryan Unkles
08700 119441
7 Meersbrook Enterprise Centre, Valley Road, Sheffield, S8 9FT, South Yorkshire

E: info@cafeology.com
W: www.cafeology.com

Dairy & Eggs

Amos Kaye and Son

Amos Kaye & Son is a family business producing quality eggs from our own farm. Deliver to many areas. Suppliers to restaurants, cafes, public houses, nursing homes, etc. Competitive prices and quality guaranteed.

DETAILS:
William Kaye
01226 763134
Townhead Farm, Dunford Bridge, Sheffield, S36 4TG, South Yorkshire

E: anneandamos@hotmail.com

Dairy & Eggs

Yee Kwan Limited

Family run business producing luxury handcrafted ice cream and sorbets, specialising in oriental flavours. Available to buy in catering size packs and retail size tubs. Inspire your senses.

DETAILS:
Yee Kwan Chan
07971 492671
Unit 2 Devonshire Business Park, 90 Wellington Street, Sheffield, S1 4HX

E: yee@yeekwan.com
W: www.yeekwan.com

Fresh Ingredients

E.Park and Sons Ltd

Established in 1924 this family owned and run company supplies a wide range of wholesalers and supermarkets with a variety of potatoes.

DETAILS:
Heather Burns
01724 711222
West End Road, Epworth, Doncaster, DN9 1LB, South Yorkshire

E: heatherburns@epark.co.uk
W: www.epark.co.uk

Our Cow Molly Dairy Ice Cream

Visit the Our Cow Molly Dairy Farm and enjoy our national award-winning ice creams, see our farm animals, experience our fantastic farm shop and parlour. Open from 11am-6pm (Wed, Fri, Sat, Sun).

DETAILS:
Eddie Andrew
0114 2332683
Cliffe House Farm, Hill Top Road, Dungworth, Sheffield, S6 6GW

E: ed@ourcowmolly.co.uk
W: www.ourcowmolly.co.uk

Fish (Fresh & Smoked)

Bingham's Food Ltd

Manufacture and sell a fresh range of meat and fish spreads to the retail and foodservice sectors. Ideal on sandwiches, bread rolls, toast or crackers. Van sales including cooked meats and sandwich fillers.

DETAILS:
Peter Moon
0114 2661676
148-154 Western Road, Sheffield, S10 1LD, South Yorkshire

E: peter.moon@binghamsfood.co.uk
W: www.binghamsfood.co.uk

G W Price Ltd

Prepared fruit and vegetable specialists, GW Price Ltd produces and distributes prepared fruit and vegetables as well as dairy and organic produce.

DETAILS:
Debra Willoughby
01246 432818
13 High Street, Eckington, Sheffield, S21 4DH, South Yorkshire

E: john@gwprice.co.uk
W: www.gwprice.co.uk

Fresh Ingredients

Netherthorpe Fresh Produce Ltd

Wholesale suppliers of top quality, fresh fruit, vegetables, salads and dairy products to the catering trade.

DETAILS:
Nigel Jacobs
0114 2878789
York House, Ulley Lane, Aston, Sheffield, S26 2DR

E: nigel@simplyonions.co.uk
W: www.netherthorpe-fresh-produce.co.uk

Meat, Poultry & Game

LSA Meats Ltd

Quality suppliers of meat, poultry and game to the catering trade. Locally sourced products that have been carefully selected are delivered to customers giving a consistent quality product with provenance.

DETAILS:
Lee Allsop
07920 107311
Unit 28, Woodbourn Road, Sheffield, S9 3JL

E: leeallsop@lsameats.co.uk
W: www.lsameats.co.uk

Meat, Poultry & Game

Moss Valley Fine Meats

Award winning pork, sausages (20+ varieties), dry cured bacon and ham are hand-produced from our own pigs, born and reared on our family farm. Careful breeding enhances succulence and flavour.

DETAILS:
Karen Thompson
0114 2396904
Povey Farm, Lightwood Lane, Norton, Sheffield, S8 8BG, South Yorkshire

E: srt@poveyfarm.freeserve.co.uk
W: www.mossvalleyfinemeats.co.uk

Northern Catering Butchers Limited

Specialising in supplying high quality, fresh meat products to the catering industry, we have an extensive product range which also takes into account seasonality and changing trends.

DETAILS:
01709 789135
Unit 3 Ashley Industrial Estate, Rawmarsh Road, Rotherham, S60 1RU

E: sales@northern-catering.co.uk
W: www.northern-catering.com

Meat, Poultry & Game

Round Green Venison Company

Now in our 31st year of deer farming from our own EU approved plant, we supply the public and trade with a range of venison. From young farmed stock, you can be sure your venison is succulent and tender. Choose from joints, pies and pates along with other specialist products.

DETAILS:
Richard Elmhirst
0845 6120502
Round Green Farm, Worsbrough, Barnsley, S75 3DR, South Yorkshire

E: info@roundgreenfarm.co.uk
W: www.roundgreenfarm.co.uk

Pies

The Curry Pasty Company

Our vegetarian pasties use traditional herbs and spices, giving a deliciously unique and tantalizing taste of high quality handmade products that capture the appetite.

DETAILS:
Wendy Wilson
07904 094231
141 Sheffield Road, Warmsworth, Doncaster, DN4 9QX, South Yorkshire

E: info@thecurrypastycompany.co.uk
W: www.thecurrypastycompany.co.uk

Topping Pie Company

Manufacturers of speciality gold award-winning pork pies and quiches, a total of 21 gold awards have been received by The Topping Pie Company during the last eight years.

DETAILS:
Lynda Povey
01302 738333
Unit 2 Chappell Drive, Waterside Industrial Estate, Doncaster, DN1 2RF

E: mail@toppingspies.co.uk
W: www.toppingspies.co.uk

Prepared Food

King Asia Foods Ltd

Leading manufacturers of frozen oriental food, our 50,000 sq ft factory produces over 15 million meals a year. We pride ourselves on providing the highest quality oriental food solutions.

DETAILS:
Dan Suh
01302 760070
Middle Bank, Doncaster, DN4 5JJ, South Yorkshire

E: sofong@kingasia.co.uk
W: www.king-asia.co.uk

The Real Yorkshire Pudding Co Ltd

Producing fresh and frozen pre-baked Yorkshire puddings using only the finest fresh ingredients to satisfied customers.

DETAILS:
David Kimmins
01405 815523
Coulman Road Industrial Estate, Thorne, Doncaster, DN8 5JS, South Yorkshire

E: dkimmins@realyorks.co.uk
W: www.realyorks.co.uk

Prepared Food

Yorkshire Crisp Company

Convivial
YORKSHIRE CRISPS
www.yorkshirecrisps.co.uk

Your local handmade crisp producer. Made with local produce and 100% natural flavourings presented in unique and attractive packaging. Available in 100g barrels, 40g and 150g bags and 500g catering bags.

DETAILS:
Tim Wheatley
01909 774411
2A Waleswood Industrial Estate, Wales Bar, Sheffield, S26 5PY, South Yorkshire

E: timwheatley@yorkshirecrisps.co.uk
W: www.yorkshirecrisps.co.uk

Preserves/Honey/Condiments/Spices

Africana Chilli

Operating from a home kitchen in Sheffield, this company uses traditional African recipes and produce to create a hot chilli cooking sauce.

DETAILS:

Francis Gasana
0114 2416733
1 Smelterwood Place, Sheffield, S13 8RN, South Yorkshire

E: frolico@yahoo.com

Catherine's Choice

Producers of bespoke award winning jams, fruit curds, vinegars, dressings, chutneys, mustards and sweet and savoury sauces. All additive and gluten free. Products are available to both retail and catering outlets.

DETAILS:

Catherine Trickett
0114 2670576
59 Westbourne Road, Broomhill, Sheffield, S10 2QT, South Yorkshire

E: sales@catherines-choice.com
W: www.catherines-choice.com

Cafés & Tearooms

Walker's Garden Coffee Room

Our oak beamed coffee room creates the perfect setting to sample freshly prepared, locally sourced food, sustainably sourced fish, fine Fairtrade coffee and irresistible homemade cakes. Enjoy top quality food whilst enjoying the picturesque views of the pool and summer gardens.

DETAILS:

Lee Grant
01302 770564
Mosham Road, Blaxton, Doncaster, DN9 3BA, South Yorkshire

E: hello@walkersnurseries.tv
W: www.walkersnurseries.tv

Cafés & Tearooms

Yorkshire Wildlife Park Limited

After exciting encounters with the residents of Yorkshire Wildlife Park, enjoy a trip to The Wild Café, which offers a diverse menu with traditional Yorkshire favourites including Wilkinson's sausages and traditional Yorkshire cakes!

DETAILS:

Cheryl Williams
07788 907706
Brockholes Lane, Branton, Doncaster, DN3 3NH, South Yorkshire

E: info@yorkshirewildlifepark.com
W: www.yorkshirewildlifepark.co.uk

Hotels & Restaurants

Aston Hall (Tomahawk Group)

ASTON HALL TOMAHAWK®

A stunning luxury country house hotel set in 55 acres of gardens and meadowland. Situated one mile from the MI and therefore a perfect focal point for meeting friends and relatives for celebrations or a superb dinner. The restaurant excels in creating interesting menus featuring various fresh local Yorkshire produce.

DETAILS:
Claire Sutherland and Raquel Silva
01142 872309

Worksop Road, Aston, Sheffield, S26 2EE, South Yorkshire

E: reservations@astonhallhotel.co.uk
W: www.tomahawkhotels.co.uk

Hotels & Restaurants

Best Western Elton Hotel

Open for the quick lunch or special dinner. Freshly cooked food made with local produce served by friendly staff. Special offers on the website.

DETAILS:
Peter Keary
01709 545681

Main Street, Bramley, Rotherham, S66 2SF, South Yorkshire

E: res@eltonhotel.eclipse.co.uk
W: www.bw-eltonhotel.co.uk

Best Western Pastures Hotel

Ideally located, we offer excellent accommodation at exceptional value. Reeds Restaurant has a reputation for superb food and service, using only the finest locally sourced produce and suppliers.

DETAILS:
Janet Scott
01709 577707

Pastures Road, Rotherham, S64 0JJ, South Yorkshire

E: info@pastureshotel.co.uk
W: www.pastureshotel.co.uk

Hotels & Restaurants

Brooklands Hotel

Home of the famous Barnsley chop, and proud to promote fantastic local produce throughout the menu. Brooklands invites you to enjoy superb service, gracious surroundings and absolute comfort.

DETAILS:
Francis Hindle
01226 299571

Holiday Inn Barnsley, Barnsley Road, Dodworth, Barnsley, S75 3JT

E: enquiriesathibarnsley.com
W: www.hibarnsley.com

Visit our farm shops – an opportunity to enjoy the scenery, breathe fresh air and sample some of the produce: the original 'gate to plate' experience

Hotels & Restaurants

The Cadeby Inn

Stylish 18th century country pub serving modern British classics featuring cosy dining rooms, real cask ales, superb wines and delicious food. The Cadeby Inn is a true celebration of all things food and drink in the Yorkshire region.

DETAILS:
Greg Braithwaite
01709 864009
Main Street, Cadeby, Doncaster, DN5 7SW, South Yorkshire

E: info@cadebyinn.co.uk
W: www.cadebyinn.co.uk

Hotels & Restaurants

The Crown Hotel (Bawtry)

A rustic yet contemporary retreat, offering some of the best accommodation in South Yorkshire, serving locally sourced food and our famous Yorkshire Tapas menu.

DETAILS:
Craig Dowie
01302 710341
Market Place, Bawtry, Doncaster, DN10 6JW, South Yorkshire

E: sales@rutlandhotel-sheffield.com
W: www.crownhotel-bawtry.com

Wortley Arms

Our menu changes regularly to take advantage of the freshest regional and seasonal produce available. A warm, welcoming historic coach house. Master chef of Great Britain Andy Gabbitas uses recipes collected from around the world.

DETAILS:
Andrew Gabbitas
0114 2888749
Halifax Road, Sheffield, S35 7DB, South Yorkshire

E: thewortleyarms@aol.com
W: www.wortley-arms.co.uk

Hotels & Restaurants

Mount Pleasant Hotel

Best Western PREMIER Mount Pleasant Hotel

Doncaster's only four star hotel, set in 100 acres of wooded parkland. Food and drink lovers can dine out in our award winning AA Rosette Garden Restaurant or relax and entertain in one of the three stylish bars the hotel offers.

DETAILS:
David Rowley
01302 868696
Great North Road, Nr Rossington, Doncaster, DN11 0HW, South Yorkshire

E: reception@mountpleasant.co.uk
W: www.mountpleasant.co.uk

Deli & Independent Grocers

Wilkinson Butchers Ltd

With shops in Doncaster and Bawtry and online ordering available you have no excuse not to sample this traditional family butcher's award winning sausages, bacon and other locally sourced meats.

DETAILS:
Trevor Wilkinson
01302 365834
25 Market Hall, Doncaster, DN1 1NG, South Yorkshire
E: enquiries@wilkinson-butchers.co.uk

Yorkshire has made it to the top of the food charts with the most Michelin-starred restaurants – six – in the country

Farm Shops

Billy's Hill Farm Shop

Billy's Hill FARM SHOP

We're a friendly, family-run farm shop selling only the very best of locally sourced produce with our on-site reared, slowly matured beef and exquisite range of award winning home baked pies and cakes being our speciality.

DETAILS:
Oliver Wright
01226 754744
Hemingfield Road, Hemingfield, Barnsley, S73 0PZ, South Yorkshire
E: oewright@hotmail.co.uk
W: www.billyshillfarmshop.com

Farm Shops

Cannon Hall Farm Shop

Offering the best of Yorkshire produce, we offer a spectacular selection of homemade pies and freshly baked bread daily. We market food produced with principles and integrity.

DETAILS:
Robert Nicholson
01226 790427
Cannon Hall Farm, Bark House Lane, Cawthorne, Barnsley, S75 4AT
E: cannonhallfarm@btconnect.com
W: www.cannonhallfarm.co.uk

Marr Grange Farm Shop

Family run business specialising in home dry cured bacon and gammon. We produce and sell many meats as well as a wide range of homemade pies and cakes.

DETAILS:
Ian Randall
01302 783930
Marr Farm, Doncaster, DN5 7AS, South Yorkshire
E: enquiries@marrgrangefarmshop.co.uk
W: www.marrgrangefarmshop.co.uk

Farm Shops

McCallum's Bank End Farm Shop

An ideal place to shop for specialist and everyday produce including fruit from our farm and local meat, alongside 70 other local suppliers- we're well worth a visit!

DETAILS:
David McCallum
01302 770224
Bank End, Bankend Road, Finningley, Doncaster, DN9 3NT, South Yorkshire

E: davidmccallum@btconnect.com
W: www.mccallumsfarm.co.uk

Farm Shops

Whirlow Hall Farm Trust

Enjoy high welfare meat and eggs exclusively from our farm and snack bar, as well as a wide range of homegrown vegetables and PYO fruit in summer.

DETAILS:
Rob Waitt
0114 2620986
Whirlow Lane, Sheffield, S11 9QF, South Yorkshire

E: robw@whirlowhallfarm.org
W: www.whirlowhallfarm.co.uk

Distributors

AJ Webb & Son

This Sheffield based company focuses on providing catering establishments with fresh produce. With years of experience they are one of the most extensive providers of fresh produce in the UK.

DETAILS:
Jason Smedley
0114 2417500
Unit 1, Fresh Produce & Flower Centre, Parkway Drive, Sheffield, S9 4WN

E: salesajw@aol.com
W: www.ajwebb.co.uk

Rob Royd Farm Shop

With an in-house butchery, bakery and delicatessen, we support local suppliers by selling top quality home and locally grown vegetables - it really is fine foods fresh from the farm.

DETAILS:
Robert White
01226 248662
Genn Lane, Worsborough, Barnsley, S70 6NW, South Yorkshire

E: rob30@btconnect.com
W: www.robroydfarmshop.co.uk

Yorkshire and Humber is home to some of the world's best known food companies and the highest concentration of small, passionate enterprises

Country Fresh Foods

Yorkshire's finest distributor of quality, fresh and in-house prepared fruit and vegetables, fine foods and deli products to the hotel and restaurant trade - with a new fleet of vehicles.

DETAILS:
Adam Dowker
0114 2481188
Units A&B, Enterprise Way, Sheffield, S20 3GH, South Yorkshire

E: adam@countryfreshfoods.co.uk
W: www.countryfreshfoods.co.uk

West Yorkshire

There's something for everyone in West Yorkshire, from cosmopolitan shopping and fine dining to rewarding doses of culture at museums, galleries and theatres. Head for Leeds for a designer shopping spree in the elegantly restored Victoria Quarter, followed by a dramatic night out at the splendid Alhambra Theatre in the curry capital of Bradford. And be inspired by the breathtaking beauty of the Pennine landscape. The local menu is equally diverse and exciting at boutique hotels, rural cafes, city centre delis and gourmet restaurants.

BOOKS
Vinyl
Venables & Bainbridg
tirrup
RESTAURANT

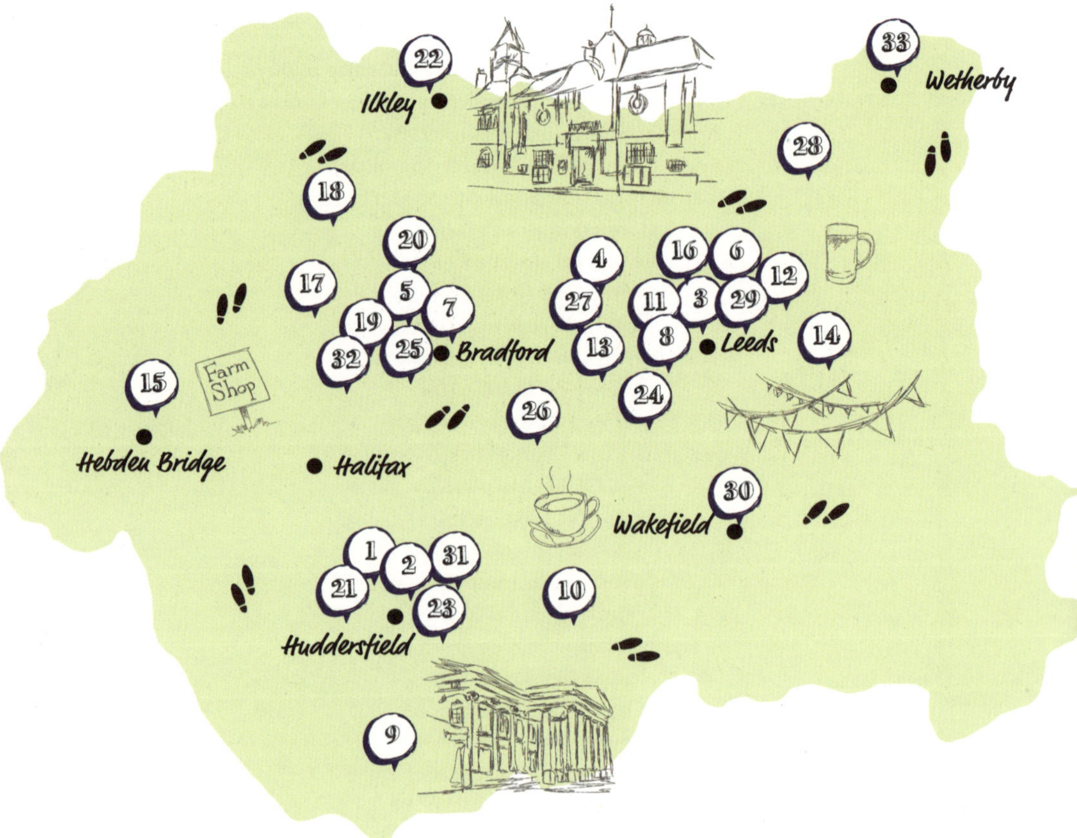
22
Ilkley
33
Wetherby
28
18
20
4
16
6
12
17
5
7
27
11
3
29
19
Bradford
13
8
Leeds
14
32
25
Farm Shop
15
26
24
Hebden Bridge
Halifax
30
Wakefield
1
2
31
21
23
10
Huddersfield
9

Food highlights

Bakers & Confectioners

Back to the Past Confectionery

Fudge company using the finest ingredients including local, innovative and traditional flavours such as rhubarb and ginger. All products sold at local markets and shows around the country.

DETAILS:
Rosalind Wrigley
0113 2866024
7 Cherwell Croft, Garforth, Leeds, LS25 2BE, West Yorkshire

E: rozfudge4u@aol.com

Bakers & Confectioners

Bloc Chocolate

Dark chocolate specialist. Single origin and plantation chocolate available. Watch the chocolatiers at work in this little gem of a shop. Tastings, demonstrations, tuition and bespoke logo chocolate.

DETAILS:
Julia Cameron
01422 330458
65 The Piece Hall, Halifax, HX1 1RE, West Yorkshire

E: julia@bloc-chocolate.co.uk
W: www.bloc-chocolate.co.uk

Bakers & Confectioners

Cookielicious

Bradford family run business, we specialise in bespoke cookies hand-iced using only the best locally sourced ingredients. Our unique designs all come beautifully packaged and make ideal gifts.

DETAILS:
Jean Boyle
07850 446005
44 Winscar Avenue, Clayton Heights, Bradford, BD6 3WX, West Yorkshire

E: yummy@cookie-licious.co.uk
W: www.cookie-licious.co.uk

Bagel Nash Ltd

One of the fastest growing dedicated bagel businesses in Europe. Our bakery produces gourmet bagels, muffins and brownies, made to original recipes using the finest natural ingredients.

DETAILS:
Karen Mizrahi
0113 2930393
Buslingthorpe Green, Meanwood, Leeds, LS7 2HG, West Yorkshire

E: sales@bagelnash.com
W: www.bagelnash.com

Bysel Ltd

Manufacture and produce traditional sugar and chocolate confectionery under the Beehive, Simply Delicious and Derbyshires brands. Purpose built factory uses skills passed down the generations. Private label enquiries welcomed.

DETAILS:
Joanne Holdsworth
01924 403857
Selby House, Batley Road, Heckmondwike, WF16 9ND, West Yorkshire

E: sales@byselcandy.com
W: www.byselcandy.com

Have you heard?

We like our food in God's Own County – with such a fantastic supply of local produce it would be a sin not to

Bakers & Confectioners

Craggs Cakes

Producer of handmade cakes, flapjacks, brownies and biscuits. Excellent natural, locally sourced ingredients, crafted with passion, into distinctive recipes. Quality not compromise. The taste is our signature.

DETAILS:
Josie Pemberton-Clarke
07788 600810

Unit 10c, Topland Country Business Park, Hebden Bridge, HX7 5RW, West Yorkshire

E: craggscakes@3-c.coop
W: www.craggscakes.co.uk

Bakers & Confectioners

Deli Delicious Gifts

We produce deliciously different food gifts. Our range includes cookie, muffin and gingerbread baking mixes, beautifully presented in a Kilner jar with spoon, the perfect gift for any occasion!

DETAILS:
Catherine Priestley
07584 046772

3A Church Street, Gildersome, Leeds, LS27 7AE, West Yorkshire

E: catherine@delideliciousgifts.co.uk
W: www.delideliciousgifts.co.uk

Ella Riley's Toffee & Traditional Sweet Shop

With shops at Holmfirth and Wakefield, Ella Riley's is home to Riley's Toffee Rolls. For a trip down memory lane why not visit us to try them for yourself?

DETAILS:
Freya Sykes
07507 731255

220 Bridge Road, Horbury Bridge, Wakefield, WF4 5PP, West Yorkshire

E: info@yorkshiretoffee.com
W: www.yorkshiretoffee.com

Bakers & Confectioners

Exquisite Handmade Cakes

We put irresistible into all of our cakes. A family owned bakery, producing a range of cakes and traybakes to supply foodservice distributors throughout the UK. We are proud to announce the rebranding of our wrapped bakery range which provides the perfect solution for the 'food-to-go' market.

DETAILS:
Viv Parry
0113 2890283

Unit C, Cardigan Works, Lennox Road, Leeds, LS4 2BL, West Yorkshire

E: amanda@exquisitehandmadecakes.co.uk
W: www.exquisitehandmadecakes.co.uk

Bakers & Confectioners

Freys Patisserie

Homemade, handcrafted bespoke baking of cupcakes, cakes, tarts, pastries, mousse cakes for all occasions. Traditional baking with a twist!

DETAILS:

Joe Walker
01274 563771

The Basement, 15 Park Road, Bingley, BD16 4NH, West Yorkshire

E: info@freyspatisserie.com
W: www.freyspatisserie.com

There's no county in the country where you'll find as great a variety of nature's abundance as in Yorkshire

Bakers & Confectioners

Gascoignes of Haworth - Home of The Bronte Kiln

Friendly family run business where our delicious homemade products are sold in our deli and fine tea room. We are also home of the Brontekiln a traditional Victorian smokehouse selling the most outstanding smoked produce.

DETAILS:

Andrew Gascoigne
01535 646059

98a Main Street, Haworth, BD22 8DP, West Yorkshire

E: gascoignea@tiscali.co.uk
W: www.brontekiln.co.uk

Bakers & Confectioners

Grandma Wilds Biscuits

Grandma Wilds award-winning biscuits baked on trays, ensuring wholesome, crunchy biscuits baked without compromise in the traditional way. Today's business holds true to the traditional family values and commitment of its founder Grandma Annie Wild all those years ago.

DETAILS:

Patrick Lynch
01535 650500

The Bakery, Millenium Business Park, Station Road, Steeton, Keighley, BD20 6RB, West Yorkshire

E: sales@grandma-wilds.co.uk
W: www.grandma-wilds.co.uk

Bakers & Confectioners

Haighs (Guiseley) Ltd

Master bakers established 1950. Family owned craft bakery supplying a comprehensive range of good quality, value, healthy eating foods. Many schools and independent retailers enjoy our products and dedicated service.

DETAILS:
Adam Haigh
01943 878766
28a Otley Road, Guiseley, Leeds, LS20 8AH, West Yorkshire

E: haighs-bakeries@btconnect.com

The Handmade Bakery

Community supported artisan bakery making slow fermented breads from ethical ingredients.

DETAILS:
Dan McTiernan
07894 036742
14 Carr Lane, Slaithwaite, HD7 5AN, West Yorkshire

E: info@thehandmadebakery.coop
W: www.thehandmadebakery.coop

Bakers & Confectioners

Isabels Naturally Free From

Benefit from this growing market with these unique and delicious products. Naturally gluten and wheat free, Isabel's growing range of home-baking mixes are the natural choice. The dough requires no rising time and can be prepared in advance to freeze and bake from frozen.

DETAILS:
Isabel Gordon
0871 2313399
Commerce Court, Challenge Way, Cutler Heights Lane, Bradford, BD4 8NW, West Yorkshire

E: bel@brazilianflavours.net
W: www.brazilianflavours.net

Bakers & Confectioners

Johnson's Toffees

With over 70 years experience, this family run company uses only the finest ingredients in their creamy caramel toffees, fudges and truffles.

DETAILS:
Tony Johnson
01977 515 961
Carrwood Road, Glasshoughton, Castleford, WF10 4SB, West Yorkshire

E: johnsonstoffee@aol.com

Joseph Dobsons and Sons

The home of the famous Yorkshire Mixture, Joseph Dobson's is a story of a family owned business which has become one of the largest privately owned confectionery manufacturers in Yorkshire.

DETAILS:
Stephen Walshaw
01422 372165
26 Northgate, Elland, HX5 0RU, West Yorkshire

E: stephen@dobsons.co.uk
W: www.dobsons.co.uk

Bakers & Confectioners

Just Desserts

Just Desserts
Award Winning Bakers and Pâtissiers

Award-winning baker and pâtissier, established for 25 years, supplying the food service industry with a range of handmade desserts and quiches.

DETAILS:
James O'Dwyer
01274 590698

Unit 1, Station Road, Shipley, BD18 2JL, West Yorkshire

E: just-desserts@dsl.pipex.com
W: www.just-desserts.co.uk

Bakers & Confectioners

Lauden Chocolate

Award-winning chocolatier supplying fine hand-made chocolates to retail, hotels, restaurants, trade and wholesalers. We also supply corporate clients with their logos and designs onto our chocolates.

DETAILS:
Sun Trigg
0113 2440289

63 Brussels Street, Leeds, LS9 8AB, West Yorkshire

E: stephen.trigg@laudenchocolate.com
W: www.laudenchocolate.com

Lippylicious Cakes Ltd

Family run, home bakery with a passion for producing delicious cupcakes, iced cakes and gateaux for all occasions. Favourites with customers include orange double chocolate chip and forest fruits.

DETAILS:
Helen Moles
07950 835252

10 Catherines Crescent, Elland, HX5 0JA, West Yorkshire

E: info@lippyliciouscakes.co.uk
W: www.lippyliciouscakes.co.uk

Bakers & Confectioners

The Loaf Tin Ltd

Delicious homemade loaf cakes using only fresh and seasonal ingredients to individuals and businesses in the surrounding areas of Bingley, West Yorkshire.

DETAILS:
Jo Bond
01274 564233

25 Odile Mews, Bingley, BD16 3QL, West Yorkshire

E: jo@theloaftin.co.uk
W: www.theloaftin.co.uk

ProperMaid

Best Bakery Product - deliciouslyyorkshire awards 2009-10.
Award-winning company, famous for creating cakes with a twist. An innovative range including; beetroot and chocolate and dandelion and burdock.

deliciouslyorkshire winner awards 2009-2010

DETAILS:
Allison Whitmarsh
01484 429285

43 Carr Street, Marsh, Huddersfield, HD3 4AU, West Yorkshire

E: allison@propermaid.co.uk

Bakers & Confectioners

Thomas's Bakery

A wholesale, craft family bakery specialising in producing and delivering teacakes, bread and confectionery. Recently launched is Lottie Shaws Seriously Good Yorkshire Parkin which is now available around the region.

DETAILS:
Ian Shaw
01422 372335
84 Southgate, Elland, HX5 0EP, West Yorkshire

E: info@yorkshirebakery.co.uk
W: www.yorkshirebakery.co.uk

Tillys Chocolate House

Based in Holmfirth, West Yorkshire we specialise in handmade chocolates. From stiletto shoes to footballs and individual truffles, we have a chocolate gift to suit every occasion.

DETAILS:
Jane Leonard
01484 684447
1A Hollowgate, Holmfirth, HD9 2DG, West Yorkshire

E: sales@tillyschocolatehouse.co.uk
W: www.tillyschocolatehouse.co.uk

Beverages (Alcoholic & Non)

Bolling Coffee

Based in Huddersfield, we specialise in sourcing, blending and roasting high quality coffees from around the world, despatched under the brand name of 'Grumpy Mule Distinctive Coffees'.

DETAILS:
Ian Balmforth
01484 852601
The Roastery, Bent Ley Industrial Estate, Meltham, Huddersfield, HD9 4EP

E: ian@bollingcoffee.co.uk
W: www.bollingcoffee.co.uk

Yorkshire and Humber is home to some of the world's best known food companies and the highest concentration of small, passionate enterprises

Beverages (Alcoholic & Non)

Coopers Coffee Ltd

cooper's
EXTRAORDINARY COFFEE PEOPLE

One of the leading coffee distributors in the UK, we specialise in award-winning coffee blends, and the latest innovative espresso machines. We also like to pass on our wealth of knowledge and train our customers in the art of coffee-making.

DETAILS:
Jason Bruce
01484 431450
Calder Trading Estate, Cooper Bridge, Leeds Road, Huddersfield, HD5 0RX, West Yorkshire

E: jasonbruce@cooperscoffee.co.uk
W: www.cooperscoffee.co.uk

Beverages (Alcoholic & Non)

Holmfirth Tea

For years we've blended and served our wonderfully refreshing teas from our family business in the heart of rural Holmfirth, supplying rare and fine teas to specialist shops and supermarkets.

DETAILS:
Onita Harrison
01484 688811
11 Huddersfield Road, Holmfirth, HD9 2JR, West Yorkshire

E: info@holmfirthtea.co.uk
W: www.holmfirthtea.co.uk

Little Valley Brewery

Best Drink Product - deliciouslyyorkshire awards 2009-10. One of Yorkshire's only organic breweries where the beers are produced using environmentally friendly techniques - all products are suitable for vegans too.

deliciouslyyorkshire winner awards 2009-2010

DETAILS:
Sue Cooper
01422 883888
Turkey Lodge, New Road, Cragg Vale, Hebden Bridge, HX7 5TT
E: info@littlevalleybrewery.co.uk
W: www.littlevalleybrewery.co.uk

Beverages (Alcoholic & Non)

The Ilkley Brewery Company

Opened in May 2009 and fast gaining a reputation for producing exceptional hand crafted beers and ales, Ilkley Brewery's multi award-winning beers are available in both cask and bottle. Full of flavour and character, why not try some for yourself?

DETAILS:
Chris Ives
01943 604604
Unit 4 The Lencia Estate, 52 East Parade, Ilkley, LS29 8JP, West Yorkshire

E: info@ilkleybrewery.co.uk
W: www.ilkleybrewery.co.uk

Beverages (Alcoholic & Non)

The Punch Brew Company

Yorkshire Punch - a non alcoholic drink made from 14 different herbs to relax and cheer. Superb new and improved fruity taste. Serve hot to relax or cold to refresh.

DETAILS:
Greg Fildes
01744 600981
49 Queensway, Moss Bank, St Helens, Altrincham, WA11 7BY

E: enquiries@punchbrew.com
W: www.punchbrew.com

Dairy & Eggs

Calderdale Cheese Company

Calderdale Cheese was the first cheese to be made in the Calderdale area in over a 100 years.

DETAILS:
Robyn Heap
01422 831123
Crow Hill End Farm, Hubberton, Sowerby Bridge, HX6 3HA

E: calderdalecheese@googlemail.com
W: www.calderdalecheese.co.uk

Dairy & Eggs

Charlottes Jersey Ice Cream Ltd

Visit our ice cream parlour to taste our 30 flavours of artisan ice cream. Whilst here, you can also enjoy our crazy golf course, train, and farm animals.

DETAILS:
Audrey Wraithmell
01924 494491
The Meadows, Lane Top Farm, Whitley, Dewsbury, WF12 0NQ, West Yorkshire

E: info@charlottesjerseyicecream.co.uk
W: www.charlottesjerseyicecream.co.uk

Dairy & Eggs

Indie Ices

Innovative Indian ice cream (Kulfi) producer – winner of the Gold Star from the Guild of Fine Food and Yorkshire Post Readers Award in 2009.

DETAILS:
Mike Tattersall
0113 2888127
30 Ayresome Avenue, Roundhay, Leeds, LS8 1BE, West Yorkshire

E: tattersallmike@yahoo.co.uk
W: www.indie-ices.co.uk

Dairy & Eggs

Longley Farm

Quality and goodness come naturally for us and are the hallmarks of an independent dairy built on firm traditional values - something for which Yorkshire is famous.

DETAILS:
Konrad Schwoch
01484 684151
Longley, Holmfirth, HD9 2JD, West Yorkshire

E: technical@longleyfarm.com
W: www.longleyfarm.com

Cryer & Stott Cheesemongers Ltd

With three deli shops, we aim to be the region's premier cheesemonger. Included in The Independent's top 15 cheese merchants, we supply award-winning rhubarb cheese, Ruby Gold.

DETAILS:
Richard Holmes
01977 510638
20-24 Station Road, Allerton Bywater, Castleford, WF10 2BP, West Yorkshire

E: info@cryerandstott.co.uk
W: www.cryerandstott.co.uk

Just Jenny's Farmhouse Ice Cream

Just Jenny's are passionate about making icecream. Jenny makes it on the family farm using milk and cream from her lovely cows. All ingredients are natural, fresh and locally sourced.

DETAILS:
Jenny Clarkson
01422 823268
Hazel Slack Farm, Barkisland, Halifax, HX4 0DU, West Yorkshire

E: jenny@justjennys.co.uk
W: www.justjennys.co.uk

Have you heard?

"Yorkshire produce gets better and better as every year goes by. Just like rhubarb, Yorkshire products will soon be known as the best in the world"

Brian Turner

Dairy & Eggs

Yummy Yorkshire Ice Cream Company

Best Dairy Product - deliciouslyyorkshire awards 2009-10.
Enjoy award-winning ice cream in a rustic ice cream parlour and coffee shop. Made with the farm's own milk and cream, Yummy Yorkshire's ice cream is completely pure, fresh and unadulterated. Fifty traditional, seasonal and contemporary flavours. Open from 11am weekdays/10.30am weekends

DETAILS:
Jeremy Holmes
01226 762551

Delph House Farm, High Flatts, Denby, Huddersfield, HD8 8XY, West Yorkshire

E: sales@yorkshiremilk.co.uk
W: www.yummyyorkshire.co.uk

Fish (Fresh & Smoked)

Pick Fisk Ltd

With a sterling reputation for supplying seafood products to any customer's exacting requirements, Pick Fisk Ltd works in most species of salmon and whitefish with an extensive network of suppliers.

DETAILS:
Chris Pick
0113 2638972
537 Tong Road, Leeds, LS15 5AT, West Yorkshire

E: chris.pick@pickfisk.co.uk
W: www.pickfisk.com

Fresh Ingredients

D. Westwood & Son

Our specialist rhubarb crop is grown at the heart of the Yorkshire Rhubarb Triangle. We provide a wide range of loose or pre-packed fresh crops for distribution.

DETAILS:
David Westwood
01924 822314
Thorpe Lane Farm, Thorpe, Wakefield, WF3 3BZ, West Yorkshire

E: dwsthorpefarms@btconnect.com
W: www.dwsyorkshireboxes.co.uk

Fresh Ingredients

E. Oldroyd & Sons Ltd

Producer and packer of high quality fruit, vegetables and rhubarb to supermarkets, packers, processors, wholesalers and retail outlets. A long established award-winning company, including Rick Stein Food Hero, Assured Produce and LEAF accredited.

DETAILS:
Janet Oldroyd
0113 2822245

Hopefield Farm, The Shutts Leadwell Lane, Rothwell, Leeds, LS26 0ST, West Yorkshire

E: janet@eoldroyd.co.uk
W: www.yorkshirerhubarb.co.uk

Fresh Ingredients

Farnley Estates

Managing over 1500 acres of farmland and over 500 acres of woodland in and around the village of Farnley Tyas allows us to grow excellent quality fruit, vegetables and crops.

DETAILS:
Paul Sykes
01484 667744
Farnley House, Manor Road, Farnley Tyas, Huddersfield, HD4 6UL

E: paulsykes@shawspetroleum.co.uk
W: www.farnleyestates.co.uk

Fresh Ingredients

Troy Foods

Leeds based manufacturer focusing on the production of fresh vegetables and dressed salads.

DETAILS:
Andrew Murphy
0113 2721433
Troy House, 1a George Mann Way, Hunslet, Leeds, LS10 1DR, West Yorkshire

E: andrew@troyfoods.co.uk
W: www.troyfoods.co.uk

Ingredient Suppliers

Gordon Rhodes & Son

The Dalesman® Group

Manufacturing specialists of seasoning mixes and blends for meat, bakery and ready meal processors throughout the UK.

DETAILS:
Jayne Robinson
01274 758000
Dalesman House, Chaseway, Bradford, BD5 8HW, West Yorkshire

E: taste@thedalesmangroup.co.uk
W: www.thedalesmangroup.co.uk

Greenfield Produce

Yorkshire grown produce, packed and prepared for major retailers. We supply most types of fruit and vegetables, however we can source other lines if your choice is out of season.

DETAILS:
Simon Dobson
0113 2826921
Cemetery Lane, Carlton, Wakefield, WF3 3QT, West Yorkshire

E: carl@greenfieldproduce.co.uk
W: www.greenfieldproduce.co.uk

W S Bentley (Growers) Ltd

Best Fresh Product - deliciouslyyorkshire awards 2009-10. Established family business growing pesticide-free salad cress and award-winning sprouting seeds, beans and peas. Supplying retail, food service and convenience sectors.

deliciouslyyorkshire winner awards 2009-2010

DETAILS:
Jan Bentley
01274 851214
Cliffe Hill Nurseries, Gomersal, Cleckheaton, BD19 4SX, West Yorkshire
E: jan@wsbentley.co.uk
W: www.wsbentley.co.uk

Ingredient Suppliers

Pennine Food Ingredients Ltd

Suppliers and manufacturers of dried food ingredients, meat cures, brines, glazes, instant soups, sauces and herb blends for meat products. Suppliers to schools, councils, food processors and manufacturers.

DETAILS:
Steve Duffitt
01422 371920
Units 5-8, The Old Mill, Wellington Business Centre, Elland, HX5 9AS

E: steve@penninefoods.co.uk
W: www.penninefoods.co.uk

Meat, Poultry & Game

Coddy's Farm

Award-winning Coddy's Farm was established in 2007. Voted local food producer 2009-2010, we retail home-reared Aberdeen Angus beef, pork, lamb, rose veal, and free range chicken.

DETAILS:
Lisa Colwill
01484 688076
Lower Whitegate Farm, Whitegate Road, Holmbridge, Holmfirth, HD9 2TH

E: alcolwill@btinternet.com
W: www.coddysfarmshop.co.uk

Meat, Poultry & Game

Far Isle Farm Ltd

Specialising in naturally reared meats for over 30 years, our family run farm shop offers a full range of handmade sausages and meats. Mail order service is also available.

DETAILS:
Chris Argent
01422 244859
259 Shay Lane, Holmfield, Halifax, HX2 9AG, West Yorkshire

E: info@farislefarm.co.uk
W: www.farislefarm.co.uk

Ulrick & Short

Suppliers of clean label functional food ingredients which are completely free from chemical, enzymic or genetic modification. We specialise in ingredients for bakery, processed meats, sauces and coatings.

DETAILS:
Andrew Ulrick
01977 620011
Walton Wood Farm, Thorpe Audlin, Pontefract, WF8 3HQ, West Yorkshire

E: us@ulrickandshort.com
W: www.ulrickandshort.com

D & C Ellis

Based in Liversedge, this farm supplies rare breed pork products with a quality of meat that is second to none.

DETAILS:
Duncan & Claire Ellis
01924 401585
Low Farm, Norristhorpe, Liversedge, WF15 7PQ, West Yorkshire

E: duncanandclaire@btinternet.com

Paul Flintoft Traditional Family Butchers

Providing customers with friendly service and good quality food, Paul Flintoft stocks 17 different types of sausage, some of which came highly commended at Yorkshire Confederation of Butchers 2005 awards.

DETAILS:
Paul Flintoft
0113 2872482
12 High Street, Kippax, LS25 7AB, North Yorkshire

E: p_flintoft@yahoo.co.uk

Meat, Poultry & Game

Hostingley Farm Free Range

Specially selected breeds of fresh free range bronze and white turkeys and geese, traditionally reared and prepared on the farm producing birds with exceptional flavour and texture. Also produce goose fat.

DETAILS:
Tim and Lynne Lindley
01924 272570

Hostingley Farm, Hostingley Lane, Thornhill, Dewsbury, WF12 0QJ, West Yorkshire

E: tim@hffr.co.uk
W: www.hostingleyfarmfreerange.co.uk

Meat, Poultry & Game

Nova Scotia Farm Produce

Fantastic suppliers of purpose bred, naturally produced beef. Fully matured from the company's excellent Limousin sired herd.

DETAILS:
Mark Darley
0113 2893890

Bramham Road, Thorner, Leeds, LS14 3ET, West Yorkshire

E: mbeef@tiscali.co.uk
W: www.dishestodinefor.co.uk

Pies

Denby Dale Pie Company

Based in Denby Dale where the world's largest pie was baked, we provide high quality frozen meat pies using traditional methods, handmade using the best quality ingredients.

DETAILS:
Janet Purcell
01484 862585

Unit 12, Denby Dale Business Park, Wakefield Road, Denby Dale, Huddersfield, HD8 8QH

E: janet@thedenbydalepiecoltd.fsnet.co.uk
W: www.denbydalepiecompany.co.uk

Pies

Andrew Jones (Pies) Ltd

Produce a range of quality pies using locally sourced ingredients, delivering baked and unbaked pies across the North. Winner of the deliciouslyorkshire Supreme Product of the Year 2008-09 with its Figit Pie.

DETAILS:
Andrew Jones
01484 548137

Units 2, 3 & 4 Queens Mill Industrial Estate, Lockwood, Huddersfield, HD1 3RR

E: info@piesnpasties.co.uk
W: www.piesnpasties.co.uk

John Lord & Sons (Take & Bake)

Traditional pork pies of all shapes and sizes, plus alternative fillings and bespoke pies made to order. New retail outlet at Huddersfield open and now available in Booths and Tesco supermarkets.

DETAILS:
John Lord
01274 544826

6 Thorn Avenue, Heaton, Bradford, BD9 6LS, West Yorkshire

E: mail@jlordandson.co.uk
W: www.jlordandson.co.uk

Prepared Food

AreOlives

Traditional Greek olives in a variety of delicious marinades and olive oil, sun-dried tomatoes and delicious deli products. Grown in Greece, made in Yorkshire.
BRC standard production unit near Wetherby.

DETAILS:
Paul Jenner
01937 844600
4 Ash Way, Thorp Arch Trading Estate, Wetherby, LS23 7FA, West Yorkshire

E: nick@areolives.com
W: www.areolives.com

Prepared Food

Foodamentalists

Do you dream of moist chocolatey muffins or soft fresh bread? At the Foodamentalists we do, which is why we've created our range of home-baked treats all of which are gluten free.

DETAILS:
Stevan Taylor
07884 064130
9 Britannia Works, Skinner Lane, Pontefract, WF8 1NA, West Yorkshire

E: stevan@foodamentalists.co.uk
W: www.foodamentalists.co.uk

Prepared Food

The Good Soup Company

With love from our kitchen to yours. Local not global. Making fresh produce, additive and wheat-free soups using regionally sourced ingredients. Available in retail and catering sizes and online.

DETAILS:
Mike Wood, 01924 451400
Unit 211 Bretton Street Enterprise Centre, Saviletown, Dewsbury, WF12 9DB

E: goodsoupco@btconnect.com
W: www.thegoodsoup.co.uk

The Crusty Pie Company

Homemade traditional and speciality pies, pasties and sausage rolls, sold with our own range of delicious chutney.

DETAILS:
Diane Congreve
01274 673664
Lion Gate House Bakery, Stanage Lane, Shelf, Halifax, HX3 7PR

E: diane@crustypie.co.uk
W: www.crustypie.co.uk

The Foodie Farmer Fresh Soup Co

Fresh soups made from own grown and local ingredients.

DETAILS:
Richard Morphett
01422 845952
Cowside Farm, Blackshawhead, Hebden Bridge, HX7 7JU, West Yorkshire

E: rb.morphett@virgin.net

Mumtaz Ventures Ltd

The world famous Mumtaz is recognised around the world for fine food and excellent products, creating ranges of restaurant quality food using authentic spices in frozen, chilled and ambient formats.

DETAILS:
Bill Kimberling
0871 7867860
Units 1-3 Orchard Business Park, Scout Road, Mytholmroyd, Halifax, HX7 5HZ
E: bill@mumtaz.com
W: www.mumtaz.com

Prepared Food

Seabrook Crisps Ltd

Seabrook are the North's best-loved crisps - known for their full flavour, crunch and pure ingredients. Now all 18 flavours are free from nasties like MSG.

DETAILS:

Phil Devine
01274 546405
Seabrook House, Duncombe Street, Ingleby Road, Bradford, BD8 9AJ

E: gordonc@seabrookcrisps.com
W: www.seabrookcrisps.com

Tiffin Foods

Convenience foods for the retail, public health, travel, forecourt, and education sectors. We put emphasis on our customers, food safety, product development and the environment with our biodegradable packaged sandwiches.

DETAILS:

John Varey
01274 494939
Prospect Works, Allerton Road, Allerton, Bradford, BD15 7AA, West Yorkshire

E: john@tiffinsandwiches.co.uk
W: www.tiffinsandwiches.co.uk

Prepared Food

Toffs Catering

Established in 1980 near Huddersfield area, we are cater for all events including weddings, funerals, birthdays, parties and business/corporate events. Menus can be altered to suit any taste.

DETAILS:

Ann Pearson
01484 608158
Carr Villa, 57 Jagger Lane, Emley Moor, Huddersfield, HD8 9TF, West Yorkshire

E: info@toffscatering.co.uk
W: www.toffscatering.co.uk

Zeina Foods Ltd

An established family business specialising in nuts, dried fruit and chocolate products. True to our passion for tasty, healthy and nutritious food, we offer high quality, award-winning brands.

DETAILS:

Martin Savage
01924 280180
Milner Way, Ossett, Wakefield, WF5 9JE, West Yorkshire

E: sales@zeinafoods.com
W: www.zeinafoods.com

Preserves/Honey/Condiments/Spices

The Chilli Jam Man

All my chilli jam is lovingly hand crafted in Yorkshire by myself after years of experimenting to get the taste and texture 'just right'. A delicious range of speciality handmade chilli jams produced from fresh ingredients. Absolutely no gelling agents, preservatives or other additives used. Welcoming trade enquiries.

DETAILS:

Simon Barrett
07876 768253
7 Ederoyd Cresent, Pudsey, Leeds, LS28 7QU, West Yorkshire

E: simon@thechillijamman.com
W: www.thechillijamman.co.uk

Preserves/Honey/Condiments/Spices

Barjees Pepped Up Ketchup

Using only the finest traditional Indian spices this is tomato ketchup with a twist - use Barjees Pepped Up Ketchup as a dressing, relish, dipping sauce or straight out of the bottle!

DETAILS:
Barjees Dawood
07852 193116
14 Enfield Walk, Bradford, BD6 3HY, West Yorkshire

E: barjees@hotmail.co.uk

Preserves/Honey/Condiments/Spices

Daisy Bank

We grow, produce and sell locally ensuring our products are nutrient-dense, full of medicinal qualities. Our range includes pesto, green, red curry pastes, and honey and mustard dressing.

DETAILS:
Susan Connor
01484 714214
31 Halifax Road, Brighouse, Huddersfield, HD6 2AA, West Yorkshire

E: daisybankfood@btinternet.com
W: www.daisybank.net

Preserves/Honey/Condiments/Spices

Fancy That From Wharfedale

High quality, handmade speciality preserves from Wharfedale, using locally grown or sourced ingredients whereever possible to create delicious pickles, fruit vinegars, fruit butters, chutneys and other seasonal delicacies.

DETAILS:
Amanda Miller
07979 847602
39 Grangefield Avenue, Burley-in-Wharfedale, Ilkley, LS29 7HA

E: info@fancythatfromwharfedale.com
W: www.fancythatfromwharfedale.com

Curry Cuisine Ltd

A range of award-winning pickles, spice blends and chutneys using local produce with an eastern twist. Also providing Indian cookery lessons to both private and corporate parties.

DETAILS:
Paresh Tejura
07952 112810
Unit 207 Bretton Street Enterprise Centre, Bretfield Court, Dewsbury, WF12 9DB

E: enquiries@currycuisine.co.uk
W: www.currycuisine.co.uk

Denholme Gate Apiary

Produce the finest quality, pure Yorkshire honey, specialise in spring blossom, summer flower and heather honey, all harvested from the varied flora of the Yorkshire countryside.

DETAILS:
Liz Joyce
01274 835490
The Gatehouse, Brighouse Road, Denholme Gate, Bradford, BD13 4EP

E: liz@denholmegatehoney.co.uk
W: www.denholmegatehoney.co.uk

Maharaja Indian Curry Sauces

Maharaja's curry sauces are made using traditional ingredients and cooking methods passed down over family generations, enabling you to create a truly authentic Indian taste in your own kitchen.

DETAILS:
Kunwar Bansil
07843 320060
294 Leeds Road, Bradford, BD3 9QX, West Yorkshire

E: k_bansil@hotmail.com
W: www.homelandfoods.co.uk

Preserves/Honey/Condiments/Spices

Shaws of Huddersfield Ltd

An independent family business manufacturing quality chutney, relish, salsa and sauces to both retail and catering customers. With over 60 to choose from, which will be your favourite?

DETAILS:
Daniel Shaw
01484 539999
Shaw Park Office Centre, Silver Street, Huddersfield, HD5 9AF, West Yorkshire

E: daniel.shaw@shaws1889.com
W: www.shaws1889.com

deliciouslyorkshire – championing and celebrating delicious locally-sourced, lovingly-made food that is the authentic, pukka product with full traceability

Preserves/Honey/Condiments/Spices

Wharfe Valley Farms

Wharfe Valley Extra Virgin Cold Pressed Rapeseed Oil is grown, pressed and bottled on the farm. With half the saturated fat of olive oil and ten times more omega 3, it's the healthy alternative. Try our new flavoured oils including oak smoked, red chilli and rosemary and garlic.

DETAILS:
Geoff Kilby
01937 572084
Lilac Farm, Jewitt Lane, Collingham, LS22 5BA, West Yorkshire

E: info@wharfevalleyfarms.co.uk
W: www.wharfevalleyfarms.co.uk

Preserves/Honey/Condiments/Spices

Womersley Fruit and Herb Vinegars Ltd

Steeped in tradition since 1975, the Parson's family recipes have recently been re-launched to create your favourite fruit and herb vinegars and jellies in stunning new designs. Catering packs available.

DETAILS:
Wendy Preston
01924 895856
Womersley House, Albert Street, Normanton, WF6 2HU, West Yorkshire

E: wendy@womersleyfoods.co.uk
W: www.womersleyfoods.co.uk

Yorkshire Pub Foods

Supplier of top quality preserves, chutneys and smoked meats, as well as seasonal goodies such as Christmas puddings all produced using fresh ingredients. Now with the option to buy online!

DETAILS:
Anita Walker
01535 633855
Colne Road, Malsis, Sutton in Craven, Keighley, BD20 8DS, West Yorkshire

E: dogandguninn@btopenworld.com
W: www.yorkshire-pub-foods.co.uk

Cafés & Tearooms

Café 1842 - Armitage's Pennine Garden Centre

Café 1842

With beautiful views of the Pennine countryside, Café 1842 offers delicious homemade dishes, daily specials, light meals and tempting cakes and pastries. Our menu boasts local ingredients including bacon and sausage served with our hearty breakfasts, available Mon to Sat from 9.30am-11.00am and Sunday from 10.30am until 12 noon.

DETAILS:

Sue Smith
01484 607248

Shelley, Huddersfield HD8 8LG, West Yorkshire

E: cafe1842@armitages.com
W: www.armitages.com

Cafés & Tearooms

The Cooking School at Dean Clough

A unique setting in which to learn new cooking skills. Catering for the leisure customer, corporate market and offers professional development courses for educationalists and health professionals.

DETAILS:

Laura Cooper
01422 383192

D Mill, Dean Clough, Halifax, HX6 5AX, West Yorkshire

E: info@thecookingschool.co.uk
W: www.thecookingschool.co.uk

Eureka! The National Children's Museum

A family focussed café within the children's museum. Wherever possible using healthy ingredients and products that are organically farmed, locally sourced and ethically produced.

DETAILS:

Liz Paton
01422 330069

Discovery Road, Halifax, HX1 2NE, West Yorkshire

E: chloe.oldman@eureka.org.uk
W: www.eureka.org.uk

Cafés & Tearooms

The Old Shop Cafe - Armitage's Birchencliffe Garden Centre

The Old Shop Cafe

Offering delicious homemade dishes, daily specials and light meals, plus tempting homemade cakes and pastries, whilst boasting regional ingredients including bacon and sausage in our hearty breakfasts.

DETAILS:

Richard Kendrick
01484 536010

Birchencliffe Hill Road, Birchencliffe, Huddersfield, HD3 3NJ, West Yorkshire

E: r.kendrick@armitages.com
W: www.armitages.com

Cafés & Tearooms

Whiteleys Garden Centre

Offering first class service, enjoy hot and cold meals, snacks and drinks in beautiful surroundings. Our chefs create mouth-watering homemade food fresh on the premises using the finest ingredients.

DETAILS:
Alex Plumridge
01924 495944
Leeds Road (A62), Mirfield, WF4 0DQ, West Yorkshire

E: info@whiteleys-gc.co.uk
W: www.whiteleys-gc.co.uk

Yorkshire Deli

A café, shop and online store selling only Yorkshire produce. Our café menu is packed with ingredients sourced from deliciouslyorkshire members. Also available to buy in our shop or online.

DETAILS:
Ian Taylor
01943 817387
27 The Grove Promenade, Ilkley, LS29 8AF, West Yorkshire

E: mail@yorkshiredeli.co.uk
W: www.yorkshiredeli.co.uk

Hotels & Restaurants

Anthony's Restaurant Limited

Anthony's Restaurant

Since opening in 2004, family run restaurant Anthony's has embarked on an ambitious expansion plan to ensure the best possible dining experiences, appealing to all food lovers.

DETAILS:
Anthony Flinn
0113 2470995
The Corn Exchange, Call Lane, Leeds, LS1 7BR, West Yorkshire

E: anthonys@anthonysrestaurant.co.uk
W: www.anthonysrestaurant.co.uk

Have you heard?

"It's no secret that I think Yorkshire is the garden of England. It has a massive range of quality produce: fantastic meat, poultry and veg, and then all the way to the coast at Brid, Scarborough and Whitby for the best tasting seafood. There's so much going on and every part of Yorkshire has something to offer"

James Martin

Hotels & Restaurants

The Black Olive Delicatessen

Known as a food lovers paradise, providing beautifully presented produce with personal and friendly service. We pride ourselves on featuring many regionally sourced items.

DETAILS:

Mike Adams
01924 275984

11 Queen Street, Horbury, Wakefield, WF4 6LP, West Yorkshire

E: michaeladams007@btinternet.com

Hotels & Restaurants

The Butchers Arms

THE BUTCHERS ARMS HEPWORTH

Aiming to bring simple, stylish food to the heart of Yorkshire, wherever possible using local, free-range foods. We support local suppliers, and offer guests a truly regional inspired menu.

DETAILS:

Tim Bilton
01484 682361

38 Towngate, Hepworth, HD9 1TE, West Yorkshire

E: thebutchersarmsathepworth@btconnect.com
W: www.thebutchersarmshepworth.co.uk

Hotels & Restaurants

Chevin Country Park Hotel & Spa

CHEVIN COUNTRY PARK HOTEL & SPA OTLEY

Lakeside Restaurant

The Lakeside Restaurant at Chevin Park Hotel & Spa offers a truly special dining experience, with high quality food and wine and stunning views we are sure your visit will be a memorable experience. There are superb private dining rooms offering the perfect location for every occasion.

DETAILS:

Enda Rylands
01943 467818

Yorkgate, Otley, LS21 3NU, West Yorkshire

E: gm.chevin@crerarhotels.com
W: www.crerarhotels.com/ourhotels/chevin_hotel

Have you heard?

"Yorkshire has plenty of coastline and great fish to be found swimming off it, so try to support our fishing folk"

Nigel Barden

Hotels & Restaurants

The City Inn

Dine in the sophisticated surroundings of City Café restaurant or alfresco on our canal side terrace. Looking to eat with a view? Our Skylounge offers breath-taking views of the city.

DETAILS:
Javier De La Hormaza
0113 2411000
Granary Wharf, 2 Leeds Approach, Leeds, LS1 4BR, West Yorkshire

E: info@fancythatfromwharfedale.com
W: www.fancythatfromwharfedale.com

The Cross Keys

A cosy city pub, boasting a wooden beamed ceiling, roaring fires and a fine outdoor courtyard. Ales from local independent breweries and a traditional locally sourced British menu.

DETAILS:
Amie Giardino
0113 2433711
107 Water Lane, Holbeck Urban Village, Leeds, LS11 5WD, West Yorkshire

E: info@the-crosskeys.com
W: www.the-crosskeys.com

Hotels & Restaurants

Dog & Gun Inn

Finalist in the White Rose Pub of the year awards in '09, this family run pub serves quality food. You can always be sure of a traditional Yorkshire welcome!

DETAILS:
Anita Walker
01535 633855
Colne Road, Malsis, Sutton In Craven, Keighley, BD20 8DS, West Yorkshire

E: anita@yorkshire-pub-foods.co.uk
W: www.dog-and-gun-inn.co.uk

Fennel

Fennel café and restaurant offers dishes that celebrate the best of local produce. With plenty to please the traditional diner we also tempt the culinary explorer to try something new.

DETAILS:
Lionel Strub
01937 588522
Victoria Court, Victoria Street, Wetherby, LS22 7YP, West Yorkshire

E: kate@justfennel.co.uk
W: www.justfennel.co.uk

Hotels & Restaurants

Great Victoria (Tomahawk Group)

GREAT VICTORIA TOMAHAWK

Housed in a landmark Victorian building in the centre of Bradford, the Great Victoria has been sympathetically restored to its former glory, while incorporating contemporary touches. The hotel includes the best bedrooms and penthouses in Bradford. The menu served in the impressive oak panelled restaurant features excellent fresh Yorkshire produce.

DETAILS:
Simon Grybas
01274 728706
Bridge Street, Bradford, BD1 1JX, West Yorkshire

E: reservations@victoriabradford.co.uk
W: www.tomahawkhotels.co.uk

Hotels & Restaurants

Harewood House

HAREWOOD

Executive chef Darren Collinson sets Harewood apart with his culinary expertise in devising clever seasonal menus using local ingredients. 'Locally sourced' takes on an entirely new meaning here with many ingredients grown in Harewood's very own walled garden and glass houses. Great for corporate and private events.

DETAILS:
Jo Cooke
0113 2181000

Harewood House Trust, Harewood, Leeds, LS17 9LG, West Yorkshire

E: info@harewood.org
W: www.harewood.org

Hotels & Restaurants

Malmaison

The bar and brasserie are at the heart of the hotel. We work with local producers to offer a home-grown menu where all dishes include fresh, organic ingredients.

DETAILS:
Zara Goodwin
0113 3981000

1 Swinegate, Leeds, LS1 4AG, West Yorkshire

E: zgoodwin@malmaison.com
W: www.malmaison-leeds.com

The Malt

Whether it's chilled champagne with homemade canapés, relaxed buffets or just drinks with friends, we aim to provide the highest level of service no matter what the occasion.

DETAILS:
Karen Wright
01943 862207

32 Main Street, Burley-in-Wharfdale, LS29 7DN, West Yorkshire

E: info@the-malt.co.uk
W: www.the-malt.co.uk

Hotels & Restaurants

Midland Hotel

MIDLAND HOTEL
Bradford

Bradford's premier city centre hotel by reputation, blending contemporary facilities with an era of opulence. Head chef Simon Thomas from the Grill Room provides a superb menu of contemporary British cuisine served with flair and imagination. Enjoy a wonderful meal of freshly prepared food and a relaxed atmosphere.

DETAILS:
Gary Peacock
01274 735735

Forster Square, Bradford, BD1 4HU, West Yorkshire

E: info@midland-hotel-bradford.com
W: www.peelhotels.co.uk

Hotels & Restaurants

Moyles Hotel & Restaurant

This family run hotel in Hebden Bridge is rapidly gaining a reputation for very good food, and has been awarded an AA Rosette. All ingredients where possible are sourced locally.

DETAILS:
Apo Ozdamar
01422 845272
6-10 New Road, Hebden Bridge, HX7 8AD, West Yorkshire

E: enquire@moyles.com
W: www.moyles.com

Have you heard?

"Yorkshire is teeming with the very best produce served up by hard-working, ingenious folk, passionate about what they do"
Alan Titchmarsh

Hotels & Restaurants

The Old Farmhouse Restaurant

THE OLD FARMHOUSE
RESTAURANT

Nestled next to Hinchliffe's Farm Shop, we pride ourselves on serving top quality, freshly prepared meals to order, using our own farm produce and locally sourced ingredients, wherever possible.

DETAILS:
Simon Hirst
01484 668949
Hinchliffes Farm, Netherton Moor Road, Netherton, Huddersfield, HD4 7LE, West Yorkshire

E: oldfarmhouse@hinchliffes.com
W: www.oldfarmhouserestaurant.com

Hotels & Restaurants

Oulton Hall Hotel

OULTON HALL
YORKSHIRE

We are passionate about the quality of dishes and the origin of the ingredients used. Sourcing locally is at the forefront of everything we do. The two AA rosettes awarded Calverley Grill offers a fine dining experience whilst the relaxed atmosphere of the Claret Jug offers hearty wholesome dishes.

DETAILS:
Dean Rogers
0113 2821000
Rothwell Lane, Oulton, Leeds, LS26 8HN, West Yorkshire

E: keith.butler@devere-hotels.com
W: www.devere-hotels.com

Hotels & Restaurants

Royal Armouries (International) plc

An unforgettable corporate occasion – The Royal Armouries is the perfect place to entertain your guests, letting them enjoy our range of deliciouslyorkshire foods, fine wines and world-class entertainment.

DETAILS:
Janna Woods
0113 2201906
Armouries Drive, Hunslet, Leeds, LS10 1LT, West Yorkshire

E: enquiries@armouries.org.uk
W: www.royalarmouries.org/visit-us/leeds

Thorpe Park Hotel & Spa

Contemporary surroundings teamed perfectly with a strong emphasis on quality, locally sourced ingredients. Choose our stylish restaurant, the stunning internal limestone courtyard or dine al fresco on the terrace.

DETAILS:
Gordon Jackson
0113 2641000
1150 Century Way, Thorpe Park, Leeds, LS15 8ZB, West Yorkshire

E: thorpepark@shirehotels.com
W: www.thorpeparkhotel.com

Hotels & Restaurants

Weetwood Hall

WEETWOOD HALL LEEDS

Built around a 17th Century Manor House, Weetwood Hall offers extensive four star hotel services and facilities. Offering three dining options, Woodlands Restaurant, the Brasserie and The Stables Pub, you will be sure to find something to suit you.

DETAILS:
Jon Coxon
0113 2306000
Otley Road, Far Headingley, Leeds, LS16 5PS, West Yorkshire

E: sales@weetwood.co.uk
W: www.weetwood.co.uk

Hotels & Restaurants

Wentbridge House Hotel

Beautiful four star hotel with a choice of restaurants depending on your mood. Choose between the elegant Fleur de Lys Restaurant, that holds two AA Rosettes, or the Wentbridge Brasserie.

DETAILS:
James Page
01977 620444
The Great North Road, Wentbridge, Pontefract, WF8 3JJ, West Yorkshire

E: info@wentbridgehouse.co.uk
W: www.wentbridgehouse.co.uk

West Yorkshire Playhouse

One of the largest producing theatres in the UK, the Playhouse's restaurant is perfect for pre-theatre meals, and the bar is perfect for escaping the bustle of the city.

DETAILS:
Helen Wilson
0113 2137265
Playhouse Square, Quarry Hill, Leeds, LS2 7UP, West Yorkshire

E: david.williams@wyp.org.uk
W: www.wyp.org.uk

Hotels & Restaurants

Wood Hall Hotel & Spa

WOOD HALL
HOTEL & SPA
WETHERBY, WEST YORKSHIRE

The Georgian Restaurant at the relaxing Wood Hall Hotel and Spa creates truly mouth-watering dishes, using mainly local and seasonal ingredients. Located in magnificent countryside with stunning views over the River Wharfe, it seems only right that this is used as the inspiration for the menus.

DETAILS:
Charles Merchie
01937 587271
Trip Lane, Linton, Leeds, LS22 4JA, West Yorkshire

E: woodhall@handpicked.co.uk
W: www.handpickedhotels.co.uk

Hotels & Restaurants

Woodlands Hotel (Tomahawk Group)

WOODLANDS
TOMAHAWK®

On the outskirts of Leeds, this luxury 23 bedroom hotel, set in landscaped gardens is home to a stylish restaurant that serves fresh, locally sourced produce. Choose from their indulgent a la carte dinners, quintessentially British afternoon teas and al fresco dining on the terrace.

DETAILS:
Sue France
0113 2381488
Gelderd Road, Gildersome, Leeds, LS27 7LY, West Yorkshire

E: enquiries@woodlandsleeds.co.uk
W: www.woodlandsleeds.co.uk

Hotels & Restaurants

Yorkshire Sculpture Park

Our contemporary, family friendly restaurant has panoramic views of the historic landscape and Henry Moore's monumental sculptures. We use only the finest local produce, including prize-winning Yorkshire Highlander beef, Whitby crab and Wakefield rhubarb.

DETAILS:
Joe Penney
01924 832500
Y.S.P. Trading Ltd, Bretton Hall, West Bretton, Wakefield, WF4 4LG
E: info@ysp.co.uk
W: www.ysp.co.uk

Outside Caterers

Leeds United Football Club

Sourcing goods locally is an important part of our food policy. All fresh produce, meats, poultry and seafood are sourced locally and ethically wherever possible.

DETAILS:
Norbert Pichler
0113 3676026
Elland Road, Leeds, LS11 0ES, West Yorkshire

E: norbert.pichler@leedsunited.com
W: www.leedsunited.com

Outside Caterers

CGC Events

CGC Events

We are Yorkshire's premier event caterer, catering for many racecourses, county shows, as well as other private and corporate events. Our team are passionate about our products - our service is always to the highest standard using the freshest, quality ingredients, many of which are sourced locally.

DETAILS:
Keith Stewart
0113 2876387

Supreme House, Lotherton Way, Garforth, LS25 2JY, West Yorkshire

E: keith.stewart@cgcevents.co.uk
W: www.cgcevents.co.uk

Deli & Independent Grocers

Bubble & Squeak Deli Ltd

Delightful village deli with bustling cafe bar alongside a fabulous combination of outside catering and take home dishes. Serving fresh seasonal vegetables, salads, homemade quiches, cakes and freshly brewed coffee.

DETAILS:
Jan Clarke
01484 300 449

97 Lidget Street, Lindley, Huddersfield, HD3 3JR

E: insideoutside@bubbleandsqueakdeli.co.uk
W: www.bubbleandsqueakdeli.co.uk

Deli Central

A family run deli business with two outlets in Wakefield, we are proud to supply local and Yorkshire produce. We also provide catering for any scale events.

DETAILS:
Tony Sykes
01924 385935

20 Northgate, Wakefield, WF1 1PQ, West Yorkshire

E: info@deli-central.co.uk
W: www.deli-central.co.uk

Deli & Independent Grocers

George Middlemiss & Son

Traditional, award-winning butchers shop established in 1881, located in the heart of the thriving market town of Otley specialising in locally sourced beef, lamb and pork.

DETAILS:
Tony, Peter & Martin Middlemiss
01943 462611

3 Market Street, Otley, LS21 3AF, West Yorkshire

E: a.middlemiss@btinternet.com
W: www.dalesnet.co.uk

There's so much wonderful food in Yorkshire – the hardest bit will be making a decision but then no-one said it was going to be easy!

Deli & Independent Grocers

Haley & Clifford Delicatessen

Haley & Clifford
DELICATESSEN

Our comprehensive range of Yorkshire produce includes local cheeses, artisan baked bread, condiments, oils, delicious cakes and award winning smoked fish. We make fresh soups and salads in our kitchen daily as well as handmade sandwiches and meals to takeaway.

DETAILS:
Val Berry
0113 2370334

43 Street Lane, Roundhay, Leeds, LS8 1AP, West Yorkshire

E: val@haleyandclifford.co.uk
W: www.haleyandclifford.co.uk

Deli & Independent Grocers

Harvey Nichols Fourth Floor Café Bar & Foodmarket

Hosting their foodmarket and Yo Sushi! Harvey Nichols Leeds Fourth Floor facilitates all day dining in their café and bar, with light treats available in the Espresso Bar.

DETAILS:
Richard Allen
0113 2048000
107-11 Briggate, Leeds, LS1 6AZ, West Yorkshire

E: contactleeds@harveynichols.com
W: www.harveynichols.com

Merus Deli

Enjoy award-winning coffee, freshly prepared sandwiches and homemade cake in our relaxed deli-cafe. You'll find a range of local cheese, artisan baked bread, preserves, olives, sauces, cooked meats and more.

DETAILS:
Sonia Hough
0113 2707970
Unit 1 Realtex House, Leeds Road, Rawdon, LS19 6AX, West Yorkshire

E: soniahough@merusdeli.co.uk
W: www.merusdeli.co.uk

Deli & Independent Grocers

Simpson's of Leeds

Local city centre grocer, offering convenience, quality and value. Locally sourced produce from fresh coffee, delicious homemade cakes, fresh bread and pastries, homemade soups and salads prepared daily and fantastic deli sandwiches.

DETAILS:
Steve Hodson
0113 2431123
28 Dock Street, Leeds, LS10 1JF, West Yorkshire

E: steven.hodson@nisa-todays.com
W: www.simpsonsofleeds.co.uk

Farm Shops

Birkhill Farm Shop

A family run farm shop selling home reared free range chickens and turkey. We also specialise in rare breed pork and sell a selection of home-grown vegetables, chutneys and pickles.

DETAILS:
Stuart & Lindsay Lazenby
0113 2852412
Birkhill Crescent, Birkenshaw, Bradford, BD11 2LJ, West Yorkshire

E: lazenbys_05@hotmail.com

Farm Shops

Blacker Hall Farm Shop

More than fifty awards for homemade products. Q Guild Butchery selling all local meats, craft bakery, delicatessen and wine loft. Coffee shop and children's play area opening August 2010.

DETAILS:
Edward Garthwaite
01924 267202
Branch Road, Calder Grove, Wakefield, WF4 3DN, West Yorkshire

E: info@blackerhall.com
W: www.blackerhall.com

Farm Shops

Bolster Moor Farmshop

Modern farm shop, butchery and bakery boasting championship status on a national level for many of its products. Fresh bread, cakes, puddings and confectionery made daily.

DETAILS:
Andrew Whitwam
01484 647311
1a Bolster Moor Road, Golcar, Huddersfield, HD7 4JU, West Yorkshire

E: bolstermoorfarmshop@sky.com
W: www.bolstermoorfarmshop@sky.com

Castle Hill Nurseries (Yorkshire Farm Shop)

A new breed of farm shop. Stock has a regional connection. More exotic items are supplied by locally based co-operative SUMA.

DETAILS:
Howard Jennings
01484 604857
291 Wakefield Road, Lepton, Huddersfield, HD8 0EL, West Yorkshire

E: howardjennings@hotmail.co.uk

Farm Shops

Far Barsey Farm Shop

Listed in The Independent's Top 50 Farm Shops, Far Barsey Farm Shop specialises in wines, beers, dairy products, preserves, cakes, quiches, sausages and more.

DETAILS:
John Dean
01422 372348
Barkisland, Halifax, HX4 0BG, West Yorkshire

E: info@farbarseyfarmshop.co.uk
W: www.farbarseyfarmshop.co.uk

Yorkshire's bountiful supply of fresh local ingredients is as a magnet to the finest chefs the UK has to offer

Farm Shops

Hinchliffes Farm Shop

HINCHLIFFE'S
FARM SHOP

Established 1929. Selling home reared meats, fruit, vegetables, beers, wines, spirits, cheeses, preserves, freshly laid eggs and baked bread. We source much of our produce from suppliers local to the area and throughout Yorkshire. Visit our superb restaurant and open farm on your visit.

DETAILS:
Simon Hirst
01484 661231

Netherton Moor Road, Netherton, Huddersfield, HD4 7LE, West Yorkshire

E: info@hinchliffes.com
W: www.hinchliffes.com

Farm Shops

Ingfield Farm Shop

Suppliers of top quality farm fresh and local produce including home reared meats, sausages, cheeses, homemade bread, pork pies, ice cream, yoghurts, fruit and vegetables.

DETAILS:
Margaret Bamford
01422 330333

Law Farm, Law Lane, Southowram, Halifax, HX3 9UG, West Yorkshire

E: enquiries@ingfieldfarmshop.co.uk
W: www.ingfieldfarmshop.co.uk

Have you heard?

“I'm always proud to shout about our great Yorkshire produce and our brilliant array of suppliers”

James Mackenzie

Farm Shops

Keelham Hall Farm Shop

KEELHAM HALL
FARM SHOP

Products are sold at prices that represent true value for money right across the board - often cheaper than the supermarkets. We also support over 150 local producers in the award-winning butchery department, fresh fruit and vegetable selection, wines and beers, deli, chef's larder and garden centre.

DETAILS:
Victoria Robertshaw
01274 833472

Brighouse Denholme Road, Thornton, Bradford, BD13 3SS, West Yorkshire

E: enquiries@thefarmshop.net
W: www.keelhamhallfarmshop.co.uk

Farm Shops

Langlands Garden Centre (Leeds)

All our cakes are baked on-site, which is why people travel from all over to eat in our coffee shop - something that makes our team of cooks so proud!

DETAILS:

Robert Ducker
01430 873426
York Road, Whinmoor, Leeds, LS15 4NF

E: robert.ducker@langlands-nurseries.co.uk
W: www.langlandsgardencentre.co.uk

Farm Shops

Tomlinson's Farm Shop

Farm shop near Pudsey offering a wide selection of fresh food and locally sourced produce, healthy food and organic food.

DETAILS:

Heidi Tomlinson
0113 2552625
89 Roker Lane, Pudsey, Leeds, LS28 9NB, West Yorkshire

E: heidi@ukhot.com

Farm Shops

David Price Food Services Ltd

We offer our customers a full logistical solution in storage and distribution of chilled and frozen products to all destinations throughout the UK.

DETAILS:

Shab Malik
01977 653990
Langthwaite Grange Ind. Estate, Langthwaite Road, South Kirby, WF9 3AB

E: davidprice@davidpricefoods.co.uk
W: www.davidpricefoods.co.uk

Robinson's Farm Shop

Farm shop with butchery counter selling locally sourced food at a reasonable price. Wide range of fruit, vegetables and organic produce. Plus dairy, fresh bread and confectionery, jams, honey and ice cream.

DETAILS:

Rachael Robinson
01422 201065
Wall Close Farm, Score Hill, Northowram, Halifax, HX3 7SH, West Yorkshire

E: shop@robinsonsfarmshop.co.uk
W: www.robinsonfarmshop.co.uk

Villa Farm Shop

Family run farm shop selling a range of quality local produce from butchery and delicatessen counters including our fresh milk, eggs, homemade cakes, game, venison and much more!

DETAILS:

Sam Gill
01484 421782
Bradley Bar Roundabout, Bradford Road, Huddersfield, HD2 2JY

E: villa.farm@btconnect.com
W: www.villafarmshop.co.uk

Yorkshire has made it to the top of the food charts with the most Michelin-starred restaurants – six – in the country

Delifresh Ltd

delifresh

We are a specialist supplier of fresh produce and delicatessen products to the catering industry throughout the North of England. We are passionate about the continued development of our product ranges, which include many of the regions finest ingredients.

DETAILS:
Robert Ramsden
01274 743737

59-62 James Market, Essex Street, Bradford, BD4 7PQ, West Yorkshire

E: info@delifreshltd.co.uk
W: www.delifreshltd.co.uk

Sykes House Farm

SYKES HOUSE FARM
The Chef's Butcher

You don't have to be a Michelin starred restaurant to buy top quality meat, poultry and game. Our new shop is for those who don't want to dine out, but want access to the same quality and unrivalled choice. Free delivery for orders over £50, please call for details.

DETAILS:
Robert Smith
01937 545249

Thorp Arch, Walton Road, Wetherby, LS23 7DR, West Yorkshire

E: enquiries@sykeshousefarm.co.uk
W: www.sykeshousefarm.co.uk

Have you heard?

"You can't beat Yorkshire produce. I love it because it's local, seasonal and very, very tasty. Be inspired and try it for yourself with this great guide to Yorkshire food and drink"

Brian Turner

North and North East Lincolnshire

Take a trip to North and North East Lincolnshire to take in its beautiful coastline, fascinating towns and heritage countryside. There's all the fun of the seaside at family-friendly Cleethorpes, while inland there's Scunthorpe and its thriving market, just a stone's throw from idyllic, tranquil Twigmoor and Broughton Woods.

Don't forget to take in the Wolds – an area of outstanding natural beauty featuring medieval villages, canals and nature reserves – and enjoy the region's delicious local fare including award-winning Lincolnshire sausages and pies.

Food highlights

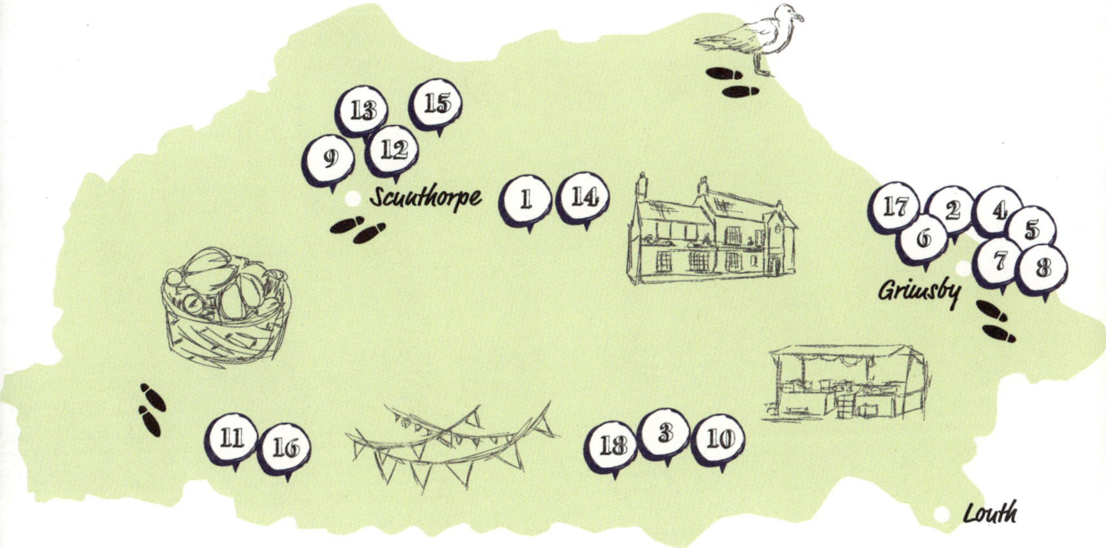

Bakers & Confectioners

Sciolti Botanical Chocolates

Beautiful, hand-crafted chocolates made by Fiona using natural botanical flavours; real fruits, teas, herbs, local cream and honey. Bespoke flavours also available for corporate, hospitality, retail and wholesale.

DETAILS:
Fiona Sciolti
07927 028734
PO Box 88, Brigg,
DN20 8WT,
North Lincolnshire

E: fiona@scioltichocolates.com
W: www.scioltichocolates.com

Dairy & Eggs

Cote Hill Cheese

The Davenport family have been farming and milking cows for 30 years. They started making cheese in October 2005 using the milk produced by their pedigree Holstein and Friesian cows.

DETAILS:
Michael Davenport
01673 828481
Osgodby, Market Rasen,
LN8 3PD, Lincolnshire

E: mdavenport@btconnect.com
W: www.cotehill.com

Fish (Fresh & Smoked)

Chapman's Finest Fishcakes

Fishcakes available in six delicious flavours. Check our website for details of your nearest stockist or farmers market.

DETAILS:
Kevin Chapman
01472 269871
c/o Riverside Food Services Ltd, Seacatch Building, Estate Road 7, South Humberside Industrial Estate, Grimsby, DN31 2TP

E: riversidefs@btconnect.com
W: www.chapmansfishcakes.co.uk

Beverages (Alcoholic & Non)

Highwood Brewery Ltd

Surrounded by land providing the finest quality malting barley for use in the brewing of their beers, Highwood Brewery produces a range of six core brands plus monthly specials.

DETAILS:
Nicola Wood
01472 255500
Birchin Way, Grimsby,
DN31 2SG, North East
Lincolnshire

E: sales@tom-wood.com
W: www.tom-wood.com

Fish (Fresh & Smoked)

Alfred Enderby Ltd

100 years old traditional fish smoking factory in the heart of Grimsby's famous fish docks. We smoke haddock, salmon and herring (kippers) slowly overnight in the proper traditional way.

DETAILS:
Richard Enderby
01472 342984
Maclure Street, Fish Docks,
Grimsby, DN31 3NE, North
East Lincolnshire

E: smoked@alfredenderby.co.uk
W: www.alfredenderby.co.uk

Fish (Fresh & Smoked)

JCS Fish Ltd

As salmon specialists, our aim is to supply high quality, fresh and frozen salmon at competitive prices, which we are able to achieve through our flexible hands-on approach.

DETAILS:
John Grey
07764 157046
Murray Street, Fish Docks, Grimsby, DN31 3RD, North East Lincolnshire

E: johngrey@jcsfish.co.uk
W: www.jcsfish.co.uk

Fish (Fresh & Smoked)

Special Foods Ltd

Innovation led company in Grimsby producing high end innovative premium fish products, including smoked haddock wellington, crunchy topped fish, cod tail with spicy tomato crunch and fish rarebit.

DETAILS:
Bob Landrey
01472 885550
Aylesby Lane, Healing, Grimsby, DN41 7QP, North East Lincolnshire

E: boblandrey@virgin.net

Meat, Poultry & Game

Farm Fresh Duck

Farm Fresh Ducks are reared on Freedom Food approved farms to strict RSPCA welfare standards. The product range consists of fresh whole ducks, duck breasts, half ducks and duck legs.

DETAILS:
Rachael Bennett
01472 371271
Rothwell, Market Rasen, LN7 6BJ, Lincolnshire

E: customer.services@cherryvalley.co.uk
W: www.farmfreshduck.co.uk

Seacatch (UK) Ltd

Frozen fish suppliers from fish fillets to goujons and glazed fish. BRC accredited.

DETAILS:
Paul Chapman
01472 360370
Estate Road 7, South Humberside Industrial Estate, Grimsby, DN31 2TP

E: paul@seacatch.co.uk
W: www.seacatch.co.uk

Ingredient Suppliers

Mr Huda's Surma Secret Spices Ltd

With ranges of products for both consumers and trade, Suma Secrets allow you to bring the taste of India to any kitchen.

DETAILS:
Mafazul Huda
01724 335492
161 Frodingham Road, Scunthorpe, North Lincolnshire, DN15 7NH

E: info@mrhudas.co.uk
W: www.mrhudas.co.uk

Meat, Poultry & Game

Redhill Farm Free Range Pork

REDHILL FARM FREE RANGE PORK

Real farmers, producing everything by hand on their farm - Redhill Farm is the real thing! Once tasted, customers are converted - our pork is slowly reared, succulent and full of flavour. We are popularly known at farmers markets as the stall with the queue!

DETAILS:
Jane Tomlinson
01427 628270

Redhill Farm, Blyton Carr, Gainsborough, DN21 3DT, North Lincolnshire

E: jane@redhillfarm.com
W: www.redhillfarm.com

Prepared Food

Axgro Foods Ltd

Axgro Foods manufactures beetroot and potato products as well as a wide range of salads, sandwich fillings, dips, sauces and meal solutions for retailers, wholesalers and caterers nationwide.

DETAILS:
Sam Shone
01724 783214

Red House Farm, West Butterwick, nr Scunthorpe, DN17 3JZ, North Lincolnshire.

E: sam.shone@axgro-foods.co.uk
W: www.axgro-foods.co.uk

TSC Foods Ltd

Specialists in delivering innovative chilled and frozen solutions. Originally producing chilled soups and sauces, today our portfolio has expanded to uniquely created risottos, prepared cooked vegetables, dips, and marinades.

DETAILS:
Jonathan Skofic
01724 272900

3-4 Arkwright Way, Queensway Industrial Estate, Scunthorpe, DN16 1AL

E: jonathan.skofic@tscfoods.com
W: www.tscfoods.com

Prepared Food

Pipers Crisps

PIPERS MADE BY FARMERS CRISPS

Since 2007 Pipers Crisps have won 10 Gold Great Taste Awards; more than any other crisp manufacturer in the country. The distinctive flavours are sourced from passionate regional producers that are detailed on the packs.

DETAILS:
Alex Albone
01652 686960

Wellington House, Wellington Way, Elsham Wood Industrial Estate, Brigg, DN20 0SP, North Lincolnshire

E: steveb@piperscrisps.com
W: www.piperscrisps.com

Farm Shops

The Pink Pig Farm

FARMA Farm Shop Of The Year 2006 selling home-grown free range pork, delicious homemade goods and loads of local foods. Licensed 90 seater restaurant and coffee shop plus Family Adventure Farm Trail.

DETAILS:
Sally Jackson
01724 844466
Holme Hall, Holme, Scunthorpe, DN16 3RE, Lincolnshire

E: sally@pinkpigfarm.co.uk
W: www.pinkpigfarm.co.uk

Uncle Henry's Farm Shop

Uncle Henry's award-winning farm shop and cafe offers fresh, local, seasonal food. The heart of good food offers a perfect location to relax with friends and source high quality local produce.

DETAILS:
Meryl Ward
01652 640308
Grayingham Grange Farm, Grayingham, Gainsborough, DN21 4JD

E: info@unclehenrys.co.uk
W: www.unclehenrys.co.uk

Distributors

Dairy Lincs Ltd

Wholesaler of quality fresh dairy and bakery products, we supply local retailers, wholesalers, residential care homes and blue chip companies regionally.

DETAILS:
Deesh Bhullar
01472 873212
Unit K2, Grimsby West, Birchin Way Industrial Estate, Grimsby, DN31 2SG, North East Lincolnshire

E: dairylincs@yahoo.co.uk

Ideal Lincs Ltd

Wholesaler of the finest fresh and ambient produce from the region. Currently supplying value added produce to multiple retailers through a regional food hub for Asda and the Lincolnshire Co-operative.

DETAILS:
Paul Davey
0870 3835280
Grange Offices Girsby Lane, Burgh on Bain, Market Rasen, LN8 6LA

E: paul@ideal-lincs.co.uk
W: www.ideal-lincs.co.uk

Yorkshire and Humber is home to some of the world's best known food companies and the highest concentration of small, passionate enterprises

deliciouslyorkshire
Committed to using Local Produce

deliciouslyorkshire menu club

The deliciouslyorkshire menu club showcases where you are guaranteed to be served the freshest, tastiest food by members who are committed to using local produce. The club covers all menus at a range of establishments, from tearooms and cafes to the homeliest B&Bs. Members' details are highlighted at www.deliciouslyorkshire.co.uk and www.yorkshire.com

All Seasons Guest House

We pride ourselves on quality produce, sourced locally, to give you the best possible start to your day. Choose from Masham specialty sausages and Doreen's award winning Black Pudding.

DETAILS:
Lesley Burr
01723 515321

**All Seasons Guest House,
11 Rutland Street, Filey
YO14 9JA**

E: lesley@allseasonsfiley.co.uk
W: www.allseasonsfiley.co.uk

Nethergill Farm

NETHERGILL FARM

deliciouslyorkshire Breakfast Member of the Year - deliciouslyorkshire awards 2009-10.
Enjoy home-baked bread, home cured bacon, freshly laid eggs from Nethergill very free-ranging chickens. Enjoy homemade lemon curd and a selection of locally sourced foods, (organic where possible). Vegetarian options and gluten free diets also on the menu.

deliciouslyorkshire winner awards 2009-2010

DETAILS:
Fiona Clark
01756 761126

**Nethergill Farm,
Oughtershaw, Buckden,
Skipton BD23 5JS**

E: fiona.clark@nethergill.co.uk
W: www.nethergill.co.uk

Whites at Broom House

Broom House
Broom House and White's Restaurant

A restaurant with four star accommodation, a golden 'gem' in the North Yorkshire Moors National Park. Surrounded by wonderful farmland and close to Whitby it will be no surprise that we choose high quality local suppliers to provide the freshest ingredients for all of our dishes.

DETAILS:
David White
01947 895279

**Whites at Broom House,
Broom Lane, Egton Bridge,
Whitby YO21 1XD**

E: mw@broom-house.co.uk
W: www.egton-bridge.co.uk

North Yorkshire

All Seasons Guest House
www.allseasonsfiley.co.uk
Lesley Burr, 11 Rutland Street, Filey, North Yorkshire YO14 9JA. T: 01723 515321. lesley@allseasonsfiley.co.uk

Alvera Court Hotel
www.alvera.co.uk
Colin Grant, 76 Kings Road, Harrogate, North Yorkshire, HG1 5JX. T: 01423 505735 admin@alvera.co.uk

Nethergill Farm
www.nethergill.co.uk
Fiona Clark, Oughtershaw, Buckden, Skipton, North Yorkshire BD23 5JS. T: 01756 761126. fiona.clark@nethergill.co.uk

Whites at Broom House
www.egton-bridge.co.uk
David White, Broom House Lane, Egton Bridge, Whitby, North Yorkshire YO21 1XD. T: 01947 895 279. mw@broom-house.co.uk

The Kings Head Hotel and Restaurant
www.kingsheadhotel.co.uk
Michael Dickinson, The Green, Newton-under-Roseberry, Great Ayton, Middlesbrough, North Yorkshire TS9 6QR. T: 01642 722 318. F: 01642 724750. info@kingsheadhotel.co.uk

Marine View Guest House
www.marineview.co.uk
Ian Rees, 34 Blenheim Terrace, Scarborough, East Yorkshire YO12 7HD. T: 01723 361864. info@marineview.co.uk

Reedness Hall Cottage
www.reednesshall.co.uk
Kate Andrews, Reedness, Nr Goole, East Yorkshire DN14 8ER. T: 01405 704555. F: 01405 704555. enquiries@reednesshall.co.uk

The Waverley
www.whitbywaverley.com
Julie & Stephen Ward, 17 Crescent Avenue, Whitby, East Yorkshire YO21 3ED. T: 01947 604389. F: 08700 633129. julie@whitbywaverley.com

Alexander Hotel
www.alexanderhotelscarborough.co.uk
Alex Testo, 33 Burniston Road, Scarborough, East Yorkshire YO12 6PG. T: 01723 363178. enquiries@alexanderhotelscarborough.co.uk

The Forge Guest House
www.theforgefiley.com
Sue Pearce, 23 Rutland Street, Filey, East Yorkshire YO14 9JA. T: 01723 512379. theforge2@bitinternet.com

The Toulson Court
www.toulsoncourtscarborough.co.uk
Jackie Power, 100 Columbus Revine, Scarborough, East Yorkshire YO12 7QZ. T: 01723 503218. info@toulsoncourtscarborough.co.uk

The Wold Cottage
www.woldcottage.com
Katrina Gray, Wold Newton, Driffield, East Yorkshire YO25 3HL. T: 01262 470696. F: 01262 470696. katrina@woldcottage.com

17 Burgate
www.17burgate.co.uk
Pat Oxley, 17 Burgate, Pickering, North Yorkshire YO18 7AU. T: 01751 473 463. info@17burgate.co.uk

Alexa House
www.alexa-house.co.uk
David Doherty, 26 Ripon Road, Harrogate, North Yorkshire HG1 2JJ. T: 01423 501988. F: 01423 504086. enquiries@alexa-house.co.uk

Angel Inn House
www.angelinnhouse.co.uk
Richard Hainsworth, York Road, Tollerton, York, North Yorkshire YO61 1QZ. T: 01347 833019. enquiries@angelinnhouse.co.uk

Ascot Lodge Guest House
www.ascotlodge.com
Sandra Hudson, 112 Acomb Road, York, York, North Yorkshire YO24 4EY. T: 01904 798 234. F: 01904 786 742. info@ascotlodge.com

Ashberry Hotel
www.ashberryhotel.co.uk
Kevin Lyon, 103 The Mount, York, North Yorkshire YO24 1AX. T: 01904 647 339. F: 01904 733 698. kevlyon@ashberryhotel.co.uk

Ashbourne House
www.ashbournehouseyork.co.uk
Paul Adams, 139 Fulford Road, York, North Yorkshire YO10 4HG. T: 01904 639912. F: 01904 631332.

Ashley Guest House
www.ashleyguesthouse.co.uk
Philip Taylor, 76 Scott Street, York, North Yorkshire YO23 1NS. T: 01904 647520. stay@ashleyguesthouse.co.uk

Atlanta Hotel
www.atlanta-hotel.co.uk
Eddie Blakeley, 60-62 Columbus Ravine, Scarborough, North Yorkshire YO12 7QU. T: 01723 360996. info@atlanta-hotel.co.uk

Bank Villa Guest House
www.bankvilla.com
Elizabeth Howard-Barker, The Ave, Masham, Ripon, North Yorkshire HG4 4DB. T: 01765 689 605. stay@bankvilla.com

Barker Stakes Farm
www.barkerstakesfarm.com
Steven Goodfellow, Lendales Lane, Pickering, North Yorkshire YO18 8EE. T: 01751 476 759. steve@barkerstakesfarm.com

Bay Tree House
www.baytreeharrogate.co.uk
Simon & Amanda Piction, 98 Franklin Road, Harrogate, North Yorkshire HG1 5EN. T: 01423 564493. info@baytreeharrogate.co.uk

Best Western Ox Pasture Hall
www.bw-oxpasturehall.co.uk
Nicolas Nasser, Lady Edith Drive, Throxenby, Scarborough, North Yorkshire YO12 5TD. T: 01723 365295. oxpasturehall@hotmail.co.uk

Black Swan Hotel
www.blackswan-helmsley.co.uk
Chris Falcus, Market Place, Helmsley, North Yorkshire YO62 5DJ. T: 01439 770466. chrisf@blackswan-helmsley.co.uk

Bootham Gardens Guesthouse
www.bootham-gardens-guesthouse.co.uk
Ian Barnard, 47 Bootham Crescent, York, North Yorkshire YO30 7AJ. T: 01904 625911. guesthouse@hotmail.co.uk

Bowmans Guest House
www.bowmansguest.co.uk
Debra Bowman, 33 Grosvenor Terrace, York, North Yorkshire YO30 7AG. T: 01904 622204. info@bowmansguesthouse.co.uk

Broad Croft House
www.broadcroft.co.uk
Cynthia Teal, Horton-in-Ribblesdale, Settle, North Yorkshire BD24 0EX. T: 01729 860302. cynthia@broadcroft.co.uk

Cedar Court Hotel Harrogate
www.cedarcourthotels.co.uk/Harrogate.aspx
Michael Weaver, Park Parade, Harrogate, North Yorkshire HG1 5AH. T: 01423 858 585. info@cedarcourthotels.co.uk

Crakehall Watermill B & B
www.crakehallwatermill.co.uk
Lionel Barnes, Watermill House, Little Crakehall, Bedale, North Yorkshire DL8 1HU. T: 01677 423240. stay@crakehallwatermill.co.uk

Crown Spa Hotel
www.crownsspahotel.co.uk
David Frank, Esplanade, Scarborough, North Yorkshire YO11 2AG. T: 01723 357400. davidfrank@crownspahotel.com

Derwent House Guest House
www.derwenthousehotel.co.uk
Keith Pratt, 6 Rutland Terrace, Queens Parade, Scarborough, North Yorkshire YO12 7JB. T: 01723 373880. info@derwenthousehotel.co.uk

Devonshire Arms (Bolton Abbey) Ltd
www.thedevonshirearms.co.uk
Brian van Oosten, Bolton Abbey, Skipton, North Yorkshire BD23 6AJ. T: 01756 718155. events@devonshirehotels.co.uk

Dunsley Hall Country House Hotel
www.dunsleyhall.com
Bill Ward, Dunsley, Whitby, North Yorkshire YO21 3TL. T: 01947 893 437. reception@dunsleyhall.com

Eleven Westgate
www.elevenwestgate.co.uk
Andrew & Mike Hawtin, Eden House, 11 Westgate, Pickering, North Yorkshire YO18 8BA. T: 01751 475111. info@elevenwestgate.co.uk

Elmfield House
www.elmfieldhouse.co.uk
Astra Towning, Arrathorne, Bedale, North Yorkshire DL8 1NE. T: 01677 450 558. stay@elmfieldhouse.co.uk

Flamborough Rigg Cottage
www.flamboroughriggcottage.co.uk
Philip Jackson, Middlemead Road, Stape, Pickering, North Yorkshire YO18 8HR. T: 01751 475263. F: 01751 475263. enquiries@flamboroughriggcottage.co.uk

Foulskye Farm House Bed & Breakfast
www.foulsykefarmhouse.co.uk
Jayne Pickup, Barmoor Lane, Scalby, Scarborough, North Yorkshire YO13 0PG. T: 01723 507423. jaynepickup@btinternet.com

Gallon House Ltd
www.gallon-house.co.uk
Sue Hodgson, 47 Kirkgate, Knaresborough, North Yorkshire HG5 8BZ. T: 01423 862 102. gallon-house@ntlworld.com

George & Dragon Inn
www.georgeanddragonaysgarth.co.uk
Mr & Mrs Wormwell, Aysgarth, Leyburn, North Yorkshire DL8 3AD. T: 01969 663 358. F: 01969 663773. ganddinn@hotmail.com

Gregory's Guest House
www.gregorysofyork.co.uk
Beverly & Martin Gregory, 160 Bishopthorpe Road, York, North Yorkshire YO23 1LF. T: 01904 627521. gregorys.york@virgin.net

Grimston House
www.grimstonhouse.com/about.html
Pat Wright, Deighton, York, North Yorkshire YO19 6HB. T: 01904 728 328. pat_wright@btinternet.com

Gisborough Hall Hotel
www.macdonaldhotels.co.uk/gisborough
Julie Diggles, Whitby Lane, Guisborough, North Yorkshire TS14 6PT. T: 0844 879 9149. julie.diggles@macdonald-hotels.co.uk

Harmony House Cookery School
www.harmonyhousecookeryschool.co.uk
Hilary Finney, The Green, Stillingfleet, York, North Yorkshire YO19 6SH. T: 01904 720933. hilary@harmonyhousecookeryschool.co.uk

Herriots Hotel
www.herriotsforleisure.co.uk
Susan Wilkinson, Broughton Road, Skipton, North Yorkshire BD23 1RT. T: 01756 792781. info@herriotsforleisure.co.uk

High Catton Grange
www.highcattongrange.co.uk
Sheila Foster, Stamford Bridge, York, North Yorkshire YO41 1EP. T: 01759 371 374. F: 01759 371374. enquire@highcattongrange.co.uk

Inglenook Guest House
www.Inglenookguesthouse.com
Carolyn Smith, 20 Main Street, Ingleton, North Yorkshire LA6 3HJ. T: 01524 241 270. inglenook20@hotmail.com

Jadellas Guest House
www.jadellashotelscarborough.co.uk
Jill Howe, 72 Columbus Ravine, Scarborough, North Yorkshire YO12 7QU. T: 01723 378811. F: 01723 378811. john@johnhowe.wanadoo.co.uk

Launceston Villa
www.launcestonvillawhitby.co.uk
Martin Prescott, 24 Prospect Hill, Whitby, North Yorkshire YO21 1QD. T: 01947 821213. launcestonvilla@btinternet.com

Lewis & Cooper Ltd
www.lewisandcooper.co.uk
Linda Walters, Unit 3, Moxon Court, Thurston Road, Northallerton, North Yorkshire DL6 2NG. T: 01609 772880. F: 01609 777820. linda.walters@lewisandcooper.co.uk

Linton Laithe Bed & Breakfast
www.lintonlaithe.co.uk
Shirley Metcalfe, Linton -in-Craven, Skipton, North Yorkshire BD23 5HH. T: 01756 753209. stay@lintonlaithe.co.uk

Lockwoods
www.lockwoodsrestaurant.co.uk
Matthew Lockwood, 83 North Street, Ripon, North Yorkshire HG4 1DP. T: 01765 607555. F: 01765 607555. info@lockwoodsrestaurant.co.uk

Lovesome Hill Farm
www.lovesomehillfarm.co.uk
Mary Pearson, Lovesome Hill Farm, Lovesome Hill, Northallerton, North Yorkshire DL6 2PB. T: 01609 772 311. lovesomehillfarm@btinternet.com

Low Penhowe Bed & Breakfast
www.bedandbreakfastyorkshire.co.uk
Christopher & Philippa Turner, Low Penhowe, Burythorpe, Malton, North Yorkshire YO17 9LU. T: 01653 658 336. F: 01653 658 619. lowpenhowe@btinternet.com

Lowther House
www.lowtherhouse.com
Phil Palmer, Newbridge, Pickering, North Yorkshire YO18 8JL. T: 01751 467157. phil@lowtherhouse.com

Lyndale Guest House
www.lyndaleguesthouse.com
Lynne Gibbon, King Street, Pateley Bridge, Harrogate, North Yorkshire HG3 5AT. T: 01423 712657. lyndale.guesthouse@talktalk.net

Mallard Grange
www.mallardgrange.co.uk
Maggie Johnson, Aldfield, Nr Fountains Abbey, Ripon, North Yorkshire HG4 3BE. T: 01765 620242. maggie@mallardgrange.co.uk

Moorlands Country House
www.moorlandslevisham.co.uk
Gill Leonard, Levisham, Pickering, North Yorkshire YO18 7NL. T: 01751 460229. ronaldoleonardo@aol.com

Netherby House
www.netherby-house.co.uk
Barry Truman, 90 Coach Road, Sleights, Whitby, North Yorkshire YO22 5EQ. T: 01947 810211. info@netherby-house.co.uk

Peasholm Park Hotel
www.peasholmpark.co.uk
Jeanette Frank, 21-23 Victoria Park, Scarborough, North Yorkshire YO12 7TS. T: 01723 500 954. peasholmparkhotel@btconnect.com

Phoenix Court
www.hotel-phoenix.co.uk
Alison Edwards, 8/9 Rutland Terrace, Queens Parade, Scarborough, North Yorkshire YO12 7JB. T: 01723 501 150. info@hotel-phoenix.co.uk

Plumpton Court
www.plumptoncourt.com
Chris Braithwaite, High Street, Nawton, Helmsley, North Yorkshire YO62 7TT. T: 01439 771223. mail@plumptoncourt.com

Rawcliffe House Farm
www.rawcliffehousefarm.co.uk
Jan Allsopp, Stape, Pickering, North Yorkshire YO18 8JA. T: 01751 473 292. stay@rawcliffehousefarm.co.uk

Red Lea Hotel (Allen Hotels)
www.redleahotel.co.uk
Nick Allen, Prince of Wales Terrace, Scarborough, North Yorkshire YO11 2AJ. T: 01723 362431. F: 01723 374230. info@redleahotel.co.uk

River House
www.riverhousehotel.co.uk
Ann Roe, Malham, Yorkshire Dales, Skipton, North Yorkshire BD23 4DA. T: 01729 830315. info@riverhousehotel co.uk

Roots Farmshop & Cafe
www.rootsfarmshop.co.uk
Katherine Hutchinson, Home Farm, East Rounton, Northallerton, North Yorkshire DL6 2LE. T: 01609 882480. info@rootsfarmshop.co.uk

Smugglers Rock Country House
www.smugglersrock.co.uk
S. Gregson, Staintondale Road, Ravenscar, Scarborough, North Yorkshire YO13 0ER. T: 01723 870 044. info@smugglersrock.co.uk

Southlands Guest House
www.southalnds-guesthouse.co.uk
Karen Greenwood, 69 Nunmill Street, York, North Yorkshire YO23 1NT. T: 01904 675966. southlandsguesthouse@yahoo.co.uk

Stoney End
www.stoneyend.co.uk
Pamela Hague, Stoney End, Worton, Leyburn, North Yorkshire DL8 3ET. T: 01969 650 652. pmh@stoneyend.co.uk

The Bentley Guest House
www.bentleyofyork.com
Margaret Bradley, 25 Grosvenor Terrace, York, North Yorkshire YO3 7AG. T: 01904 644313. enquiries@bentleyofyork.com

The Boars Head Hotel
www.ripleycastle.co.uk/hotel.html
Steve Chesnutt, Ripley, Harrogate, North Yorkshire HG3 3AY. T: 01423 771 888. reservations@boarsheadripley.co.uk

The Bridge Hotel
www.thebridgewetherby.co.uk
Patrice Lipatti-Mesme, Walshford, Wetherby, North Yorkshire LS22 5HS. T: 01937 580115reception@bridgewetherby.co.uk

The Carlton Lodge (The Stirrings Ltd)
www.carlton-lodge.com
Chris Parkin, Bondgate, Helmsley, York, North Yorkshire YO62 5EY. T: 01439 770 557. F: 01439 772378. chris@carlton-lodge.com

The Corner Café Ltd
www.thecornerfiley.co.uk
Paul Carline, 16 Bellvue Crescent, Filey, North Yorkshire YO14 9AD. T: 01723 512261. thecornercafeltd@googlemail.com

The Croft
www.crofthotel.co.uk
Gerald Wilcock, 87 North Marine Road, Scarborough, North Yorkshire YO12 7HT. T: 01723 373904. information@crofthotel co.uk

The Crown Inn
www.tchh.co.uk
Darrel Wade, Market Place, Helmsley, North Yorkshire YO62 5BJ. T: 01439 770297. info@tchh.co.uk

The Dales Haven
www.daleshaven.co.uk
Martin Crowson, Market Place, Leyburn, North Yorkshire DL8 5BJ. T: 01969 623814. info@daleshaven.co.uk

The Devonshire Fell Hotel & Restaurant
www.devonshirefell.co.uk
Stephane Leyreloup, Burnsall, Skipton, North Yorkshire BD23 6BT. T: 01756 729 000. manager@devonshirefell.co.uk

The Ellenby
www.theellenby.co.uk
Mr John & Mrs Elza Fail, 95-97 Queen Parade, Scarborough, North Yorkshire YO12 7HY. T: 01723 372916. johngail@aol.com

The Farthings
www.farthingsyork.co.uk
Helen Milner, 5 Nunthorpe Avenue, York, North Yokshire YO23 1PF. T: 01904 653545. F: 01904 628355. stay@farthingsyork.co.uk

The Full English Guest House
www.thefullenglishwhitby.com
Gary Walker, 9 John Street, West Cliff, Whitby, North Yorkshire YO21 3ET. T: 01947 604021. garybevang@aol.com

The Gallery B & B
www.gallerybedandbreakfast.co.uk
Kathryn Collington, 18 Kirkgate, Thirsk, North Yorkshire YO7 1PQ. T: 01845 523 767. kathryn@gallerybedandbreakfast.co.uk

The Golden Fleece Hotel
www.goldenfleecehotel.com
Jo Grewcock, Market Place, Thirsk, North Yorkshire YO7 1LL. T: 01845 523 108. reservations@goldenfleecehotel.com

The Grange Hotel
www.grangehotel.co.uk
Adrienne Dyson1 Clifton, York, North Yorkshire YO30 6AA. T: 01904 644744. F: 01904 612453. info@grangehotel.co.uk

The Hawthornes Bed and Breakfast
www.thehawthornes.co.uk
Paula ApplebyHigh Back Side, Middleton, Pickering, North Yorkshire YO18 8PB. T: 01751 474755. paulaappleby@btinternet.com

The Kimberley Hotel
www.thekimberley.co.uk
Mark Harrison, 11-19 Kings Road, Harrogate, North Yorkshire HG1 5JY. T: 01423 505613. info@thekimberley.co.uk

The Leeway
www.theleeway.co.uk
Karen Walker, 1 Havelock Place, Whitby, North Yorkshire YO21 3ER.. T: 01947 602604. enquiries@theleeway.co.uk

The Lodge at Leeming Bar
www.leemingbar.com
Suzanne Bailes, The Great North Road, Bedale, North Yorkshire DL8 1DT. T: 01677 422122. thelodgeatleemingbar@btinternet.com

The Lyness Guest House
www.thelyness.co.uk
David Hewitt, 145 Columbus Ravine, Scarborough, North Yorkshire YO12 7QZ. T: 01723 375952. info@thelyness.co.uk

The Mallyan Spout Hotel
www.mallyanspout.co.uk
Kay Bell, The Common, Goathland, North Yorkshire YO22 5AN. T: 01947 896486. F: 01947 896327. info@mallyanspout.co.uk

The Poplars Rooms & Cottages
www.thepoplarsthirsk.com
Amanda Richards, Carlton Miniott, Thirsk, North Yorkshire YO7 4LX. T: 01845 522 712. amanda@thepoplarsthirsk.com

The Traddock
www.thetraddock.co.uk
Paul Reynolds, Austwick, Settle, North Yorkshire LA2 8BY. T: 01524 251 224. F: 01524 251 796. paul@thetraddock.co.uk

The Wharncliffe
www.thewharncliffescarborough.co.uk
Ann Trigg, 26 Blenheim Terrace, Scarborough, North Yorkshire YO12 7HD. T: 01723 374635. info@thewharncliffescarborough.co.uk

The White Swan Inn
www.white-swan.co.uk
Lisa Fraser, Market Place, Pickering, North Yorkshire YO18 7AA. T: 01751 472 288. F: 01751 475554. lisa@white-swan.co.uk

Well House
www.wellhouse-newbywiske.co.uk
Judith Smith, Newby Wiske, Northallerton, North Yorkshire DL7 9EX. T: 01609 772 253. info@wellhouse-newbywiske.co.uk

Westfields Farm
www.westfieldsfarmbandb.co.uk
Chris Chilton, Moor Road, Bellerby, Leyburn, North Yorkshire DL8 5QX. T: 01969 622047. stay@westfieldsfarmbandb.co.uk

Wynnstay House
www.wynnstayhouse.com
Tracey & Andy Davis, 60 Franklin Road, Harrogate, North Yorkshire HG1 5EE. T: 01423 560 476. wynnstayhouse@tiscali.co.uk

York Conferences
www.yorkconferences.com
York Conferences Team, Grimston House, University of York, Heslington, York, North Yorkshire YO10 5DD. T: 01904 328431. F: 01904 328426. bedandbreakfast@york.ac.uk

South Yorkshire

Barnfield House Luxury Guest Accommodation
www.barnfieldhouse.com
Helen Rogers, Loxley Road, Sheffield, South Yorkshire S6 6RW. T: 0114 233 6365. helen@barnfieldhouse.com

Best Western Elton Hotel
www.bw-eltonhotel.co.uk
Peter Keary, Main Street, Bramley, Rotherham, South Yorkshire S66 2SF. T: 01709 545681. F: 01709 549100. res@eltonhotel.eclipse.co.uk

Best Western Pastures Hotel
www.pastureshotel.co.uk
Janet Scott, Pastures Road, Rotherham, South Yorkshire S64 0JJ. T: 01709 577795. F: 01709 577795. info@pastureshotel.co.uk

The Best Western Cutlers Hotel
www.cutlershotel.co.uk
James Hague, George Street, Sheffield, South Yorkshire S1 2PF. T: 0114 2739939. F: 0114 2768332. james@cutlershotel.co.uk

The Crown Hotel (Bawtry)
www.crownhotel-bawtry.com
Craig Dowie, Market Place, Bawtry, Doncaster, South Yorkshire DN10 6JW. T: 01302 710341. F: 01302 711 798. sales@rutlandhotel-sheffield.com

The Rutland Hotel
www.rutlandhotel-sheffield.com
Andy Taylor, 452 Glossop Road, Sheffield, South Yorkshire S10 2PY. T: 0114 266 4411. F: 0114 2670348. sales@rutlandhotel-sheffield.com

Throapham House Ltd
www.throapham-house.co.uk
Ann Holland, Olcotes Road, Throapham, Sheffield, South Yorkshire S25 2QS. T: 01909 562208. enquiries@throapham-house.co.uk

West Yorkshire

42 The Calls
www.42thecalls.co.uk
Nigel Stanley, 42 The Calls, Leeds, West Yorkshire LS2 7EW. T: 01132 440099. hbradshaw@42thecalls.co.uk

Briar Court Hotel
www.briarcourt.co.uk
Joanne Reynolds, Halifax Road, Birchencliffe, Huddersfield, West Yorkshire HD3 3NT. T: 01484 519902. info@briarcourthotel.co.uk

Castle View Guest House
www.castleviewyorkshire.co.uk
Andy Whiteley, 148 Ashes Lane, Castle Hill, Huddersfield, West Yorkshire HD4 6TE. T: 01484 307460. info@castleviewyorkshire.co.uk

Cedar Court Hotel Bradford
www.cedarcourthotels.co.uk/Leeds-Bradford.aspx
Nick Testa, Mayo Avenue, Off Rooley Lane, Bradford, West Yorkshire BD5 8HZ. T: 01274 406 606. sales@cedarcourtbradford.co.uk

Cedar Court Hotel Huddersfield
www.cedarcourthotels.co.uk/Huddersfield-Halifax.aspx
Helen Stewart, Ainley Top, Huddersfield, West Yorkshire HD3 3RH. T: 01422 375 431. helenstewart@cedar-court-huddersfield.co.uk

Cedar Court Hotel Wakefield
www.cedarcourthotels.co.uk/Wakefield.aspx
Michael Weaver, Calder Grove, Denby Dale Road, Wakefield, West Yorkshire WF4 3QZ. T: 01924 276 310. info@cedarcourthotels.co.uk

Croft Mill
www.croftmill.com
Josephine Anderson, Croft Mill Yard, Hebden Bridge, West Yorkshire HX7 8AB. T: 01422 846836. F: 01422 846836. josephine@croftmill.com

Doublejay Hotels Ltd
www.centrallodge.com
Liz Wood, 11-15 Beast Market, Huddersfield, West Yorkshire HD1 1QF. T: 01484 515 551. F: 01484 432349. joe@centrallodge.com

Five Rise Locks Hotel & Restaurant
www.five-rise-locks.co.uk
Richard Stoyle, Beck Lane, Bingley, West Yorkshire BD16 4DD. T: 01274 565296. F: 01274 565296. info@five-rise-locks.co.uk

Holme House
www.holmehousehebdenbridge.co.uk
Sallie Henry, New Road, Hebden Bridge, West Yorkshire HX7 8AD. T: 01422 847 588. mail@holmehousehebdenbridge.co.uk

Mama Mia's Cafe Bar
Andrew Mooney, Chew Magna Ltd, 29 Horton Street, Halifax, West Yorkshire HX1 1QE. T: 01422 351 209. andrewcmooney@tiscali.co.uk

Manor Guest House
www.cullingworthmanor.co.uk
Michelle Cotter, The Manor, Sutton Drive, Cullingworth, Bradford, West Yorkshire BD13 5BQ. T: 01535 274 374. info@cullingworthmanor.co.uk

Milford Hotel
www.bw-milfordhotel.co.uk
Shaun Sleath, Great North Rd, Peckfield, Leeds, West Yorkshire LS25 5LQ. T: 01977 681 800shaun@mlh.co.uk

Radisson SAS
www.radissonsas.com
Tom Gibson, No.1 The Light, The Headrow, Leeds, West Yorkshire LS1 8TL. T: 01132 366 000. F: 01132 236 6100. tom.gibson@radissonsas.com

Rombalds Hotel & Restaurant
www.rombalds.co.uk
Colin Clarkson, West View, Wells Road, Ilkley, West Yorkshire LS29 9JG. T: 01943 603201. reception@rombalds.demon.co.uk

Scaife Hall Farm
www.scaifehallfarm.co.uk
Christine Ryder, Hardisty Hill, Blubberhouses, Otley, West Yorkshire LS21 2PL. T: 01943 880354. christine.a.ryder@btinternet.com

Sunnybank
www.sunnybankguesthouse.co.uk
Peter White, 78 Upperthong Lane, Holmfirth, West Yorkshire HD9 3BQ. T: 01484 684065. peter@sunnybankguesthouse.co.uk

The Old Co-Op B & B
www.theoldco-op.com
Valda Dawson, 96 The Village, Thurstonland, Holmfirth, West Yorkshire HD4 6XF. T: 01484 663621. contact@theoldco-op.com

The Old Registry Ltd
www.theoldregistryhaworth.co.uk
Paul Widdowson, 2-4 Main Street, Haworth, West Yorkshire BD22 8DA. T: 01535 646 503. F: 01535 646 503. paul@theoldregistryhaworth.co.uk

Tower House Executive Guest House
www.towerhouseguesthouse.com
Carol Slatter, 21 Bondgate, Pontefract, West Yorkshire WF8 2JP. T: 01977 699 988. F: 01977 707111. info@towerhouseguesthouse.com

Waterfront Lodge Hotel
www.waterfrontlodge.co.uk
Fiona Walker, Huddersfield Road, Brighouse, West Yorkshire HD6 1JZ. T: 01484 715566. F: 01484 715588. info@waterfrontlodge.co.uk

Wentbridge House Hotel
www.wentbridgehouse.co.uk
James Page, The Great North Road, Wentbridge, Pontefract, West Yorkshire WF8 3JJ. T: 01977 620 444. F: 01977 620 148. Catherine@wentbridgehouse.co.uk

Whiteleys Garden Centre
www.whiteleys-gc.co.uk
Alex Plumridge, Leeds Road (A62), Mirfield, West Yorkshire WF4 0DQ. T: 01924 495944. F: 01924 489600. info@whiteleys-gc.co.uk

Woodlands Hotel (Tomahawk Group)
www.woodlandsleeds.co.uk
Sue France, Gelderd Road, Gildersome, Leeds, West Yorkshire LS27 7LY. T: 0113 2381488. F: 0113 2536773. enquiries@woodlandsleeds.co.uk

Welcome to Yorkshire

Welcome to Yorkshire

Welcome to Yorkshire is the official tourism agency working to promote Yorkshire in the UK and around the world. Our goal is to make Yorkshire one of the world's top visitor destinations.

Our award-winning website www.yorkshire.com will guide you through a multitude of heritage sites, vibrant cities, dramatic coastlines and countryside. Be inspired with a wealth of ideas to help you plan your visit to the UK's largest county. We've got ideas to excite, relax and thrill you, with stunning locations, vibrant festivals and events, delicious Yorkshire food and drink, fabulous culture and exciting outdoor adventures. And it's all wrapped up in a warm Yorkshire welcome! www.yorkshire.com/delicious

deliciouslyorkshire – we know you want it

*T*hrough its deliciouslyorkshire championing brand, the Regional Food Group is proud to support and promote food and drink producers within Yorkshire and Humber because we know they are among the nation's best.

The great thing is you recognise that too. Consumers' appetite for food of provenance is growing year on year, fuelled by a yearning for great taste and a desire to support the local economy.

So can we say a big thank you to all you foodies out there who each day venture into farm shops, independent stores and quality supermarkets and invest your 'hard-earned' in products displaying the distinctive black and green deliciouslyorkshire logo.

Together we are safeguarding our rich food heritage and putting our money, quite literally, where our mouth is on fresh, quality, local food of taste and originality.

So let's hear it for the last word in fantastic food and drink – deliciouslyorkshire.

deliciouslyorkshire
Committed to using Local Produce
deliciouslyorkshire
Committed to using Local Produce
deliciouslyorkshire
Committed to using Local Produce
Crunchy Flapjack
Fudge Flapjack
Cherry Flapjack

Farmers' Markets

Amazing artisan cheeses, meats from humanely-reared animals, flavoursome fruit and veg, melt-in-your-mouth pies, homemade jams preserves and chutneys – these are just some of the reasons why farmers' markets are enjoying a revival across Britain, and nowhere more so than in Yorkshire and Humber.

But the fantastic food and drink is just one positive aspect of an age-old tradition that is gladly spouting new life. The fact is farmers' markets are good for us on many other levels too.

Buying fresh produce direct from the farmer at local markets helps save fossil fuels by reducing food miles. It gives farming families a better return on their labours than selling through a middle man. It supports the local economy by keeping people in work and it preserves our heritage countryside for generations to come.

There's also another very good reason to grab your basket and find a farmers' market – you get to meet and talk to the very people who have put their hard graft into producing the best food and drink money can buy – and somehow the food always tastes even better for it.

North

Grassington
Village Centre
3rd Sunday
9am–3pm

Guisborough
Market Square
2nd Saturday
10am–3pm

Harrogate
Market Place
2nd Thursday
9am–4pm

Hovingham
Village Hall & Car Park
1st Saturday (except Dec & Jan)
10.30am–3pm

Kellington
Village Hall
1st Saturday
9am–12.30pm

Leyburn
Market Place
Last Saturday
(July=24th)
8am–3pm

Malton
The Market Place
2nd Sunday
9am–2pm

Northallerton
High St
Last Wednesday
8am–3pm

Pickering
The Old Post Office Yard
Every Monday
8.30am–1pm

Pinchinthorpe
Pinchinthorpe Hall, Guisborough
1st Sunday (except Jan)
9.30am–4pm

Richmond
Town Square
3rd Saturday
8am–3pm

Ripon
Town Square
3rd Sunday
9.45am–2.30pm

Selby
Outside Selby Abbey
1st Wednesday
8am–1pm

Settle
Town Square
2nd Sunday
9am–3pm

Skipton
Canal Basin
1st Sunday
From 9am

Stokesley
Town Square
1st Saturday
8am–3pm

Tadcaster
Britannia Car Park
3rd Thursday
8.30am–1pm

Thirsk
Town Square
2nd Monday
7am–3pm

York
Parliament Street
Last Friday
9am–4pm

York
York Auction Centre
1st & 3rd Saturday
From 9am

East

Bridlington
Christchurch Quay
Road)
3rd Friday
10am–3pm

Cottingham
Dunswell Road
2nd Saturday
9am–1pm

Driffield
The Showground
1st Saturday
From 9am

Holly Oaks
Cottingham
2nd Saturday
9am–1pm

Hornsea
4th Saturday
March to October at
Honeysuckle Farm
10am–2pm

Hull
Holy Trinity Square
2nd & 4th Friday of
month

Hull
City Square
Every Friday

Humber Bridge
Humber Bridge
Viewing Area
1st Sunday
9am–1pm

Market Weighton
Market Place
3rd Saturday
From 9am

South Cave
South Cave School
Playground
2nd Saturday
9am–1pm

West

Holmfirth
Holmfirth Market Hall
3rd Sunday
9am–3pm

Cleckheaton
St Johns Car Park
1st Saturday
9am–1pm

Headingley
North Lane
2nd Saturday
9am–12.30pm

Oakwood
Roundhay Road
3rd Saturday

Otley
Market Square
Last Saturday
From 9am

Huddersfield
New Street
2nd Sunday
8am–4pm

Wetherby
Market Place
2nd Sunday
(Nov=3rd Sunday)
10am–3pm

Cross Keys
The Cross Keys
Courtyard
1st Saturday
12pm–4pm

Yeadon
Market Place
2nd Tuesday
9am–1pm

Pudsey
Market Square
Last Thursday
9am–2pm

Halifax
Russell Street
3rd Saturday
8am–4pm

South

Askern
Lakeside
3rd Thursday
9am–1pm

Doncaster
Goose Hill
1st & 3rd Wednesday
10am–4pm

Penistone
2nd Saturday
9am–1pm

Rotherham
Effingham Stree
Last Wednesday
10am–3pm

Sheffield
Barkers Pool
2nd & 4th Thursday
9am–4.30pm

Thorne
Church Street
1st Sunday
9am–1pm

North & North East Lincolnshire

Brigg
Market Place
4th Saturday
9am–3pm

Gainsborough
Marshalls Yard
2nd Saturday
9–3pm

Grimsby
Bull Ring
3rd Friday
8.30am–3pm

Market Rasen
Market Place
2nd Tuesday
From 9am

deliciouslyorkshire Food Events

2010

Great Yorkshire Show (including Cookery Theatre)	**13-15 July**
Driffield Show	**21 July**
Ryedale Show	**27 July**
Thornton-Le-Dale Show	**4 August**
Bingley Show	**8 August**
Best of British Festival, York	**28-29 August**
Harrogate Autumn Flower Show	**17-19 September**
Stokesley Show	**18 September**
The World Curry Festival, Leeds	**1-3 October**
Countryside Live, Harrogate Showground	**23-24 October**
deliciouslyorkshire Awards 2010-2011, Rudding Park	**8 November**
St Nicholas Fayre, York	**25-28 November**
Knaresborough Edwardian Christmas Market	**4-5 December**

2011

Wakefield Food, Drink and Rhubarb Festival	**February/March**
York Easter Market	**April**
Harrogate Spring Flower Show	**April**
Halifax Food and Drink Festival	**June**

Index

4173